Nonconscious Social Information Processing

Nonconscious Social Information Processing

PAWEL LEWICKI

The University of Tulsa
Tulsa, Oklahoma

1986

ACADEMIC PRESS, INC.
Harcourt Brace Jovanovich, Publishers
Orlando   San Diego   New York   Austin
London   Montreal   Sydney   Tokyo   Toronto

505/93113

ACADEMIC PRESS, INC.
Orlando, Florida 32887

United Kingdom Edition published by
ACADEMIC PRESS INC. (LONDON) LTD.
24-28 Oval Road, London NW1 7DX

LIBRARY OF CONGRESS CATALOGING-IN-PUBLICATION DATA

Lewicki, Pawel.
    Nonconscious social information processing.

    Includes bibliographical references and index.
    1. Human information processing.   2. Social
perception.   3. Subconsciousness.   I. Title.
BF455-L42   1986   154   85-15618
ISBN 0-12-446120-4 (alk. paper)
ISBN 0-12-446121-2 (paperback)

PRINTED IN THE UNITED STATES OF AMERICA

86 87 88 89   9 8 7 6 5 4 3 2 1

Contents

Preface

The research program presented in this book is concerned with the processing of social information. It cannot be considered a typical social psychological research program, however, because it is not aimed at explaining any specific social psychological phenomena, nor are the cognitive processes studied specific to the processing of social information. The program explores complex or "high level" processing of information that is not mediated by conscious awareness, and social cognition seems to be an appropriate area in which to investigate this kind of processing.

Thus the book is addressed not only to personality and social psychologists, but also to cognitive psychologists concerned with information processing in general. The former may find this research relevant because most of the experiments describe some mechanisms of acquisition and utilization of social information—problems they are working on themselves. The latter may want to ignore the specific stimulus material (i.e., social information) employed in most of the experiments and focus on the general nature of the cognitive mechanisms studied. To make this task easier and to provide empirical support for the claim of generality, the program also includes replications of the major findings with nonsocial and nonsense stimulus materials of the sort that are traditionally employed by cognitive psychologists.

The research program presented in this book began with observations which suggest that nonconscious acquisition and processing of information play a major role in human development and adjustment. These observations are discussed in Chapter 1, which is devoted to the starting points of the entire program. Chapter 2 presents preliminary theoretical assumptions that clarify exactly what I had in mind when initiating this research.

The subsequent six chapters contain reports of 34 experiments on nonconscious information processing. Thus the book is mostly a long empirical report, which includes both new findings and their replications. It seems that this emphasis on presenting empirical data is well-suited to the current status (in both cognitive and social psychology) of the issues in question. In neither field is there a well-established tradition of investigating complex, nonconscious information processing nor is there a consensus regarding the ubiquity of such processes. Moreover, the theoretical implications of this program suggest modification or extension of some current general views of human information processing. Thus, the first and the major question that should arise for the reader at this point is whether in the data reported there is actually adequate empirical support for these theoretical propositions.

Most of the research reported in this book involved the close cooperation of undergraduate and graduate students from the University of Michigan and the University of Warsaw (Poland); I am very grateful to all of them. Those who contributed are listed at the beginning of each report.

Many thanks are due to those who read parts of the manuscript and provided valuable comments: Tom Hill, Steve Briggs, Joseph Danks, Don Dulany, Sam Glucksberg, David Hamilton, Alice Healy, Hunter Hoffman, Charles Judd, Larry Jacoby, Marcia Johnson, John McCloskey, Douglas Medin, Richard Nisbett, Jane Piliavin, Arthur Reber, David Schneider, Tod Sloan, Jeanne Smith, Sharon Stanners, and Robert Zajonc.

I would also like to acknowledge a grant from the American Council of Learned Societies and a grant from the National Science Foundation (BNS-8504502) that partially supported the research and the writing of this book, and the University of Michigan, the University of Warsaw (Poland), and the University of Tulsa, for providing facilities for the research and work on the manuscript.

Nonconscious Social Information Processing

CHAPTER 1

Starting Points

In this chapter I will discuss the initial reasoning that led to my belief that complex cognitive processes may occur without mediation on the part of conscious awareness and that such processes play an important role in human adjustment. This belief led eventually to starting the research program presented in this book. My initial reasoning involved two types of premises: lay observations and recent developments in cognitive psychology. They will be discussed in subsequent sections.

Lay Observations and Common Intuitions

"Automatic" Processes

It seems widely accepted among lay observers of human psychological functioning that numerous cognitive processes operate on a level not available to one's conscious awareness. This observation refers, however, mostly to "automatized" regulation of behavior. For example, everybody knows that driving a car requires no attention on the part of an experienced driver; the driver may think intensively about some topic completely unrelated to changing the gears or pushing the clutch and still drive the car smoothly.

Another type of process that seems also to be widely recognized as nonconscious is the "housekeeping" mental process that maintains and supports one's conscious activity. For example, one never knows the specific algorithm according to which memory is being scanned in search of necessary information. The only thing one does on a conscious level is to give a "command" to an unknown executor; for example, "I need the telephone number of Aunt Hazel." A moment later the desired number "jumps" into consciousness, providing, however, no information on how or where it was found. Probably most people have had that kind of intro-

1

spective observation and have wondered at the speed and reliability of this mysterious job of the executor.

Speech Production

The outcome becomes even more spectacular when the processes of accessing the meanings of words and speech production are considered. The desired words are being found in memory with such enormous speed that the delay is unnoticeable to the speaker. Moreover, there is no time for consciously giving any commands (unlike in the example of the telephone number) and the process of finding consecutive adequate words still proceeds smoothly.

This example suggests not only that the algorithms of accessing the words in memory are nonconscious but also that the processes of deciding what kind of word is currently necessary and should be accessed are also nonconscious. The appropriate consecutive commands of the type "now search for X" are being given automatically. For instance, one has no time to think "I need an adjective that would express my fascination with the speed of speech production processes, but I don't want it to be too emotional or personal like 'incredible' or 'unbelievable,' since it seems inappropriate in the context of delivering a formal speech on theory xyz. I would rather prefer a more descriptive term . . ., etc."

Obviously, it sometimes happens that words are selected consciously, but usually most of the processes involved in speech production proceed automatically. One thinks only about what one would like to say and the "executor" automatically completes the rest of the task. The completion includes choosing the specific, proper general structure of the sentence, selecting the adequate words, taking into account the goals of the speech and its social context, et cetera. People often become observers of their own speaking, as if they were not the authors and as if somebody else had completed the job of turning ideas into words.

This phenomenon can be easily demonstrated when a speaking person is unexpectedly interrupted and asked to describe the process of producing the last phrase. For example, an individual could be asked why those specific words had been selected, what other alternative words or possible ways to communicate the same message had been considered and why they were rejected, and other questions applicable to a situation in which something has been done in a certain way but could also have been done in many other ways. The almost certain result of such a probe question would be that the subject was unaware of the processes that led to putting the sentence into its final form and that he or she did not remember selecting particular words or considering any alternatives to the structure of the sentence. On the other hand, it is obvious that the alternatives were in fact considered and rejected since the subject knows other compatible ways to say the same thing, and the choice was probably not a random one. The particular choice finally made is theoretically predictable, and it could be explained by referring to the general goals of the speech, social context, priming effects of what happened just before, individual preferences and other dispositions of the subject, and so on.

The above processes can be described in terms of long sequences of fast and nonconsciously made decisions. For example, decisions like "conjunction of adjectives x and y would sound awkward, so only one of them will be used," "adjective x is better than y because y would sound too formal and sophisticated in this context," "one adjective is not enough to characterize the unusual object z, so a second one will be added," "let's look for one less formal and sophisticated than y, and then we will check on its relation to x," etc. The examples of these decisions are probably not exactly isomorphic to the actual cognitive processes (i.e., algorithms of selecting consecutive words at various levels of the speech production mechanism), but these actual cognitive processes must provide outputs that are functionally equivalent to the results of making such decisions.

Let us consider a little bit more closely the nature of the above-mentioned algorithms or rules according to which the decisions are being made. These processes or decisions are nonconscious in the sense that a subject is unaware that they are going on. Even if they were available to one's conscious awareness, they are too fast to be noticed, and there is no way (or at least we don't know the way) to stop their execution for a moment and examine them, as we can do with the execution of an interpreted computer program.

Moreover, common observations seem to indicate that the rules are nonconscious not only in the sense that the subject is unaware of their current activity but also in the sense that the subject never knows what the rules are that he or she actually follows. Most people are simply unable to formulate in any (even informal) way the grammatical, semantic, and syntactic rules of the language they use correctly and fluently. On the other hand, there is no doubt that they actually follow some general rules and do not just employ a few well-learned concrete expressions, because there is an infinite diversity of new contexts in which the rules are being used correctly by a person unaware of using them.

That state of affairs can be well illustrated by the situation in which a person unfamiliar with a language X asks a native X language speaker questions concerning the rules of X. Exempting the case in which the native X speaker is a language professional, he or she would probably be unable to answer most questions of the type "why is this correct and that incorrect'' or ''what is the general rule,'' although in most cases the native speaker would have no doubts regarding which was correct. The native X speaker simply ''feels'' that this is how it should be said. It even happens that one learns for the first time about how some general rule of his or her own mother language reads from a foreigner, although that rule has always been applied in his or her spoken language.

A good example involves languages having several declinations with changes in suffixes of nouns (e.g., Latin or Slavic languages). For instance, a vast majority of Poles do not know how many regular noun declinations exist in their mother language and would not be able to list the rules or the appropriate suffixes for even one of them (most Poles probably do not even understand the word or the concept of 'declination'). Native Polish speakers, however, apply those rules with ease and, as noted earlier, there is no doubt that what they apply are the actual rules and not simply concrete expressions learned by heart, for if you invented a new word (which does not happen in Polish), a native Polish speaker would use it effortlessly in context with appropriate suffixes, and the choice of a particular declination would probably be based on some structural similarity between the new word and some Polish word that belongs to that declination.

The question arises as to how people acquire these nonconsciously operating linguistic rules, which are complicated and numerous (there are apparently thousands of them in each language). The simplest answer would be that they had learned them explicitly at some time, then started to use them slowly and consciously, and after mastering them, the rules began to operate automatically. Thus, the ability to use the rules would last longer than the memory for how exactly they read. This is the process, for instance, by which we learn to drive a car; it cannot be applied, however, to explain the processes of acquisition of the linguistic rules. Most people never hear about the existence of any of the general rules governing their native language until after they master using them. After all, people usually master the use of these rules by the age of four—an age when they are unable to formulate or understand these rules at the level of consciousness.

This reasoning suggests strongly the existence of mechanisms of nonconscious acquisition of general rules of using language. Moreover, these rules do not seem to be acquired in a general form ready for use, as in experiments with posthypnotic suggestions that are ''implanted'' in a subject by a hypnotist. Instead, they seem to result from some processes of generalization of instances, because these rules operate fairly effectively even in young children who have encountered nothing but concrete instances as far as the language is concerned (e.g., children raised in uneducated families who definitely never speak about the grammatical rules or the language in general).

Thus, such an important aspect of human cognition as verbalization is based on an extensive set of complicated rules, which are not acquired through the mediation of consciousness, which are not operating at the level of consciousness, and which are not even consciously available.

Recognition of Faces

As far as the involvement of nonconscious processing is concerned, the processes of speech production discussed above do not seem to be very different from other cognitive processes traditionally attributed to the level of consciousness.

Let us consider an apparently simple task involving recognition of faces. Imagine that you look at an old, not very sharp, and generally poor quality photograph of a group of 6-year-old first graders, showing you and a group of your fellow pupils standing in front of your elementary school building. Despite the fact that all of these children may be "objectively" very similar to each other, for example, that all of them are white, all of them are about the same height, and so on, you are able to recognize immediately most or all of them. It requires no effort on your part, and you do not employ any conscious inferential strategy (i.e., you don't look for any particular cues, you don't compare color of hair, etc.). You simply look at the face of the first kid from the left and "that's Jimmy" immediately "jumps" into your consciousness like the telephone number of Aunt Hazel. How have you identified him? You would most likely be unable to provide an answer. You have simply taken a short look at the face of the first person and recognized him! In fact, however, what you did was employ an apparently complicated inferential strategy comparing some features of the face in the photograph (e.g., some crucial proportions or some other definition of the pattern) with the respective codes in your memory.

Again, in the above example the rules operated on a level not available to conscious awareness. It seems also that these rules, like the rules of language, were not acquired consciously in a ready-to-use form, nor were they ever formulated explicitly. Moreover, these rules seem less obvious than the previously discussed linguistic rules. It is well known to linguists what rules a given language is based on; it is only the people who speak the language who are ignorant of them. In contrast, cognitive psychologists concerned with pattern recognition mechanisms are unable to formulate the exact rules by which people are able to memorize and easily recognize faces.

One might object that what happened in the example with the photograph was not the application of any general rules but instead an apparently simple operation of memory search for the mental representation of a face that would match exactly or approximately the one that was to be recognized. Theoretically, it is possible that there are concrete "images in the head" that are ready for use in recognition tasks without the necessity of applying any general rules. There are, however, real-life examples of recognition tasks that cannot be explained by such a simple operation on the representations of concrete images and that thus must involve employing some general rules. They will be discussed in following the section.

Judgments

Let us consider the task of recognizing the age or sex of a person in a photograph when only the middle part of the face is visible and when there is no make-up, beard, or other details that would make such a judgment obvious. Hair, dress, posture, and so on, are also not available to infer from. Most people are able to recognize the sex or to estimate the age based only on the middle part of the face, even when features of the face are not salient (e.g., "dot-matrix" type of newsprint photos). The same is true with recognizing the sex of children. People make mistakes up to the age of 3 or 4, but past that age "something masculine" appears in the faces of boys and "something feminine" in the faces of girls, and there is usually no problem with figuring out who is who. What are these crucial cues that make the judgments so easy and accurate? It is, again, unclear—not only for people making the judgments but also for investigators studying pattern recognition processes. It seems that everybody possesses a set of rules or algorithms "specifying" how to estimate an age or recognize sex. These rules are not, however, available to conscious awareness and they were apparently acquired in a kind of nonconscious process of generalization of instances (i.e., they had never been learned in a ready-for-use form).

When the person making the judgment is asked to reconstruct what he or she was inferring from, the only available bases for the answer are theories or stereotypes, for example, boys have "sharp" features as opposed to girls whose features are "soft." But this is not what the judgment was actually based on; subjects cannot provide operational definitions of the "sharp" or "soft" features and cannot explain how to recognize them.[1]

It is worthwhile to underline the fact that in the examples with both linguistic rules and recognition of age or sex, the nonconsciousness is not simply a matter of difficulties with verbalization of the rules (which might be due to lack of specific, appropriate education), but it is a matter of being unaware of the very nature of the rules. People have no access to the nature of such inferential processes; they can only observe them and infer about this nature as if it were somebody else making these judgments.

Besides sex and age, an observer is able to estimate "automatically" (i.e., without employing consciously any inferential strategies) numerous other characteristics of a face he or she is exposed to, for example, whether the face is physically attractive, whether the person seems educated, whether the person seems kind, and so on. And again, the inferential rules are not available to the inference-maker. For example, when he or she is asked *why* the face on Photo A has been judged to be more attractive than the one on Photo B, or *why* the face on Photo C rather than the one on Photo D has been judged as belonging to an intellectual, the observer has a hard task providing an answer.[2] On the other hand, the initial task of making the judgment itself was trivially easy and the observer had no problems at all with making that judgment immediately. For example, the observer "recognized" immediately that the woman in Photo A was really beautiful, whereas the one in Photo B was quite nice but far less attractive than the other, and that Person C is much more likely to be a highly educated individual than Person D, although neither of them had obvious attributes of any profession.

Judges are unable to provide in any form their working "definitions" of beauty, of looking like an intellectual, or looking kind, although they employ such definitions very often in everyday life. Thus, such definitions must exist somewhere in their minds (e.g., in form of inferential algorithms). Judges probably have acquired them nonconsciously at some point in their socialization, and they work fine, in the sense of being able to provide immediate estimations of desired characteristics of people being observed (obviously their accuracy is another matter).

Asking subjects first to judge a stimulus person's attractiveness, intelligence, kindness, and so on, based on that person's face and then to substantiate their judgments provides an instructive lesson for a psychologist, since it illustrates ease and confidence with which judgments are made and total lack of the knowledge on which these judgments are actually based. People easily make the judgments, but they are unable to point out their premises.

Again, the nonconsciousness of these rules pertains to all of their aspects. They were nonconsciously acquired; moreover, they were not acquired in any ready to use form but rather in the course of some process of nonconscious abstraction or generalization of concrete instances. The rules operate on a level not available to conscious awareness, and they cannot be reported by a person who uses them because they are not available to the user. Thus, the existence of these rules cannot be checked or examined in any other way than by comparing the inputs they receive with the outputs they produce.

People cannot articulate even the most basic proportions of the human face. On the other hand, they are very sensitive to even small violations of these proportions, and in such cases they instantly have a "feeling" that something is wrong. For example, eyes divide the human head into two segments (i.e., top and bottom) according to a proportion that is strictly met in every normal human head. When photographs or schematic sketches of human faces are slightly deformed to modify this proportion by as little as 10%, all observers say that "something is unrealistic" in the faces, although they cannot specify what in particular (Lewicki, 1981). Thus, they apparently use (directly or indirectly) this particular proportion in encoding information about the faces. However, when asked directly, hardly anyone is able to correctly estimate this proportion using his or her memory alone.

Try to do it yourself: Close your eyes (don't look at people or photographs) and estimate this proportion. The correct answer is shown in the Notes section at the end of the chapter.[3]

Behavioral Dispositions

The reasoning, suggesting that people's judgments might depend directly on the cognitive algorithms they are unaware of and have no access to, may be applied to various real-life judgmental situations analogous to those previously discussed. Because the judgments obviously lead to related behaviors on the part of the judges, that reasoning could also be applied to considering the nature of various preferences people have and other behavioral dispositions they manifest.

Let us consider first a simple example, namely, the often discussed problem of what is the nature of the stimuli that make people laugh. As far as I know, nobody has been successful yet in discovering the exact definition of "being funny." On the other hand, almost everybody possesses some kind of working definition—with no access at all to its nature or to how it works. That cognitive algorithm—which says whether a stimulus is funny—is "functionally" always available in the sense that it is always ready to work. It categorizes immediately and automatically (i.e., without waiting for any starter-commands consciously generated by the observer) all available stimuli in terms of their being funny or not. Moreover, the output of this automatic cognitive algorithm, categorizing stimuli in terms of being funny, is capable of forcing the observer to an immediate, automatic (i.e., independent of the will) behavioral reaction—laughing. The nature of such an algorithm is clearly dependent on socialization and experience (it is very different in different people), so it is acquired in the course of some process of learning. It is unclear, however, how this process of learning proceeds, and what exactly is being learned.

It seems that there are various other automatic categorization processes operating analogously to the one discussed above, that is, those that automatically process all available stimuli in terms of belonging to a certain category and then force an immediate behavioral response.

Consider, for example, situations that touch people to the quick or melt them into tears. People usually cannot control this kind of reaction. Sometimes they are even surprised and wonder why they have responded this way, because they consciously classify the situation as unrealistic, naive, or melodramatic (e.g., films like *Lassie come home* or *Love story*), but they still get tears in their eyes. It is very difficult to define the specificity of such situations (e.g., there were not very many films as successful in this respect as *Love story*), and it is especially difficult to predict what would move a particular person. Most people are unable to define what exactly moves him or her, and in what contexts or circumstances he or she is moved, or even to explain what specifically has moved him or her in some material the person was exposed to.

Good exemplars of nonconsciousness are the responses people give to questions about what in particular has "moved" them in a certain film. These answers do not discriminate between the particular, actually moving situation presented in the film and many other situations that do not produce such reactions on the person's part. For example, most people who melted into tears watching *Love Story* cannot say much more than "that was so sad because they loved each other so much, and one of them had to die." However, it is obvious that such an answer is not correct since not all situations that meet that criterion produce the observer's reaction of feeling touched. Usually, the actual differences that discriminate the class of "touching situations" from others could finally be more or less accurately reconstructed by a person. It could not be done, however, by means of "looking inside one's feelings" but rather by means of making, from an "external viewpoint," systematic observations of one's own reactions to various situations (e.g., making comparisons between touching and nontouching situations), as if it were somebody else feeling touched. This seems analogous to the case in which a person unfamiliar with grammar tries to formulate a certain rule of his or her native language to explain to a foreigner *why* some expression is correct and some other is not correct. The rule is without exception fulfilled in that person's speech—analogous to the fact that the person always reacts with tears to a certain situation. But the rule is not available to the person in the sense that the person cannot say what in particular has made him or her say this that way—analogous to the fact that the person cannot say what in particular has made him or her react that way (i.e., feeling touched).

The above examples seem to demonstrate an apparent independence between the "level" on which the discussed cognitive algorithms operate and the level of consciously controlled reasoning. A person may think "it's a stupid joke" or "one is not supposed to laugh at things like this" and still cannot control his or her own reaction of laughing; or a person may think "this film is a primitive manipulation designed to melt people into tears" and continue to feel melted. Moreover, even when a person finally discovers the very "formula" of a cue producing the automatic behavioral response (e.g., "I always feel moved when I hear the national anthem in the context of sport or military parades, never when in the context of White House celebrations"), it does not change anything— automatic responses still occur.

Everyday life provides numerous examples of such situations, in which cognitive algorithms produce certain categorizations of events and generate automatic, compulsive reactions independent of will and barely correctible, for example, reactions of feeling shy, anxious, embarrassed or disconcerted. Even when a person knows that certain conditions (e.g., the situation of delivering a speech to a group of people) always produce anxious reactions in him or her, such knowledge usually does not provide any help in controlling the bad feelings. It seems that in such a case there operates some nonconscious cognitive algorithm that categorizes all incoming cues in terms of the potential threat they contain and that automatically forces immediate behavioral manifestations, related to what the algorithm has determined. Its operation is nonconscious in all possible aspects: (1) a person never knows when and exactly how he or she learned that cognitive algorithm, that is, when he or she learned to identify threatening situations in the way specified by that particular algorithm; (2) a person has no control over its operation, it operates totally outside awareness and the person faces only his or her own uncontrollable, automatic reactions to the results of that categorization process, for example, feeling anxious; (3) a person knows the crucial cues the categorization process employs only from observation of his or her own behavior, and there is no other access to the specificity of the algorithm.

Often, however, people are unable to detect what aspect of a situation or what pattern of stimuli produces their specific responses of feeling good or bad, what causes changes in their moods, what makes them situationally more optimistic or pessimistic. The respective cognitive algorithms, however, "have no such doubts" at all and give immediate, automatic "behavioral outputs" (i.e., they produce situational changes in feelings or emotions).

Concluding Remarks

When people learn some cognitive algorithm (e.g., to react in a certain way to certain stimuli) following a consciously controlled process of learning, and then repeat a number of times what they have learned, it often happens that the cognitive algorithm becomes automatic and starts to operate without mediation of conscious awareness (e.g., driving a car and other "automatized" behaviors). This point is obvious and probably few would object that this is in fact the case.

However, the lay observations discussed in the previous sections seem to suggest something more, which is apparently less obvious. Namely, they suggest that human processing of information involves at its various levels numerous such nonconscious cognitive algorithms: (1) that definitely have never been learned at the level of consciousness, (2) that operate totally beyond one's conscious control, and (3) that are available to a person who follows these algorithms in no other way than by an "outsider's viewpoint" observation of how they operate.

Moreover, these cognitive algorithms seem to be responsible for much more than performing highly specialized cognitive operations maintaining the consciously controlled processes ("housekeeping operations"), like installing new information in memory or scanning the memory in search of desired information. They seem to be ubiquitous and directly responsible for outcomes of various "high level" cognitive processes traditionally attributed to a conscious level of processing, like judgments, inferences, or evaluations. Because these "high level" cognitive operations are, in turn, responsible for triggering moods, emotions, feelings, preferences and all possible phenomena of human psychological adjustment, it follows that the importance of the previously discussed nonconscious processing can hardly be overestimated.

While the concrete, lay observations of human cognitive processes seem to be consistent with common intuitions, the general conclusions these observations seem to imply are far from obvious. For example, a necessary implication of these observations is the existence of some mechanism of learning that nonconsciously transforms concrete experiences into some form of generalization (e.g., an algorithm of how to generate a certain judgment or how to identify a certain stimulus). Moreover, the generalization produced in such a process seems to operate beyond one's conscious control and to be unavailable to any conscious modification or even examination. This inference really does not sound like a common view of human cognition.

The previous discussion indicates the need to postulate a powerful and ubiquitous process of nonconscious learning that accompanies everyday conscious cognitions and produces memory traces that are capable of regulating various crucial aspects of human information processing and behavior in general (e.g., preferences, attitudes, behavioral reactions, personality dispositions). Despite the ubiquity of this process and its power in controlling psychological activity, its operation is totally beyond conscious awareness. The nonconsciousness pertains to three important aspects of the process:

1. The acquisition of this knowledge is not mediated by conscious awareness.
2. The memory trace of this process of learning (i.e., a resulting cognitive algorithm stored in memory) cannot be consciously changed, controlled, or even examined.
3. The nature of the influence of this nonconsciously acquired cognitive algorithm on a person's feelings, judgments, or behaviors is not available to conscious awareness: One is only able to observe or experience the final outcome of this influence (e.g., preferences, feelings, emotional reactions, or changes in mood) and to reconstruct how this mechanism works, as if the outcome of the process were observed in somebody else.

One is compelled to conclude that there exists such a process since there is no other way to explain the phenomena of language acquisition, pattern recognition, or social-behavioral reactions and dispositions.

I do not intend to deny the important role of controlled cognitive processing in the regulation of human behavior. What I am arguing is that the controlled regulation of human behavior is only a small part of the total picture of cognition and that to consider this small part exclusively leaves us with an incomplete and totally inadequate image of the human cognitive system.

A presentation of hypotheses regarding the nonconscious processes of acquiring durable cognitive algorithms is made in Chapter 2. There I outline the theoretical background for the research program presented in all subsequent chapters of this book. Prior to that, in the remainder of this chapter, I discuss research relevant to the problem of nonconscious processing of information.

Research on Nonconscious Cognitive Processes

The general view that cognitive processes inaccessible to conscious experience play an important and ubiquitous role in human adjustment is consistent with the beliefs now commonly declared by cognitive psychologists:

> Most of what we do goes on unconsciously. . . . It is the exception, not the rule, when thinking is conscious; but by its very nature, conscious thought seems the only sort. It is not the only sort; it is the minority. (Lachman, Lachman, & Butterfield, 1979, p. 207)

> Even the notion of unconscious inference . . . appears to be necessary in order to account for elementary perceptual phenomena. (Kihlstrom, 1984, p. 156)

> It appears that a great deal of procedural knowledge is unconscious, in the strict sense that we have no awareness of or control over it. Procedures are instantiated by appropriate inputs, run themselves off, and deliver appropriate outputs automatically. A case in point is the knowledge by which we generate and interpret linguistic utterances (Chomsky, 1980). We have no introspective access to the rules of transformational grammar that yield surface structures from deep structures. . . . Similarly we have no access to the basic processes involved in feature detection, pattern recognition, perceptual recoding, and meaning analysis (Mandler, 1975; Neisser, 1967), or to the kinds of rules or strategies involved in perceptual inference and problem solving (Hochberg, 1978; Kaufman, 1974; Rock, 1975). We know these processes only indirectly, by inference. This principle, which seems to apply broadly to the kinds of cognitive skills involved in perception, memory processing, communication, and motor response, has recently been extended to the higher mental processes involved in thinking and judgment. . . . We have no direct introspective access to the skills by which declarative knowledge is acquired, organized, stored, retrieved, manipulated, and transformed. (Kihlstrom, 1984, p. 168)

Despite these commonly declared views on the importance of nonconscious cognitive processes, conclusive research evidence relevant to these claims is relatively scarce so far.

Research on unconsciousness was initiated by psychoanalysis and until the 1950s unconscious processes were investigated almost exclusively within the psychoanalytical realm. The evidence collected within this framework is ambiguous since the methods used do not meet formal criteria and are incompatible with available tests of conclusiveness. However, many researchers (and not only those psychoanalytically oriented, e.g., Bowers & Meichenbaum, 1984) believe, that despite the problems with methodology, psychology as a whole has benefitted from the psychoanalytic approach to the nature of unconscious processes. A number of useful clinical observations concerning processes not mediated by conscious awareness have been made by psychoanalysts, and these may inspire or even serve as heuristics for empirical research.

Despite its positive contributions, psychoanalysis seems also to have done some harm to the research on unconscious processes. Unconsciousness was for many years associated exclusively with psychoanalysis to the point of producing strong stereotypes about what investigating unconscious processes is usually about and how psychologists view it. For nonpsychologists, unconsciousness is still associated mostly with primitive sexual and aggressive impulses and irrationality. For psychologists, investigating unconscious processes was viewed with suspicion until very recently, probably until the development of the information-processing paradigm.

It is probably due to the rich psychoanalytic tradition and the lack of hard empirical evidence that has encouraged the abundant theoretical speculations about unconscious processes (see most chapters in the book recently edited by Bowers & Meichenbaum, 1984). That kind of scientific inquiry may be valuable, and on many occasions throughout the history of psychology, it proved to be fruitful. However, given the current status of research on unconscious processes and the limited quantity of relevant empirical results, the task of collecting relevant empirical data that can back up commonly formulated claims and speculations about how unconscious processes influence behavior seems especially urgent.

Therefore, the theoretical introductory sections of this book are brief. In this section I review only those data and empirical problems that are directly relevant to the major concern of the research presented in this book—the problem of nonconscious acquisition of cognitive algorithms. The theoretical model proposed in Chapter 2 focuses only on those statements that will be empirically verified in the experiments reported in the subsequent chapters.

The most basic empirical question that can be asked about nonconscious processing of information is whether stimuli may be processed at the level of semantic analysis without the mediation of conscious awareness. In other words, can meanings be processed nonconsciously? This question was first addressed in the early 1950s in research on subliminal perception or so-called "subception" (Lazarus & McCleary, 1951). The authors interpreted their results as proving that stimuli exposed so briefly that subjects cannot notice them may be still processed outside conscious awareness and that their subjects had been able to discriminate stimuli without being aware of having any relevant knowledge. This early research on subception was criticized in a number of influential articles by Eriksen and his associates (Dulany & Eriksen, 1959; Eriksen, 1956, 1960, 1962; see also Lazarus, 1956) on both methodological and theoretical grounds and their arguments discouraged further research on subliminal perception for several years.

The problem returned in a new theoretical context involving an information-processing paradigm (Atkinson & Shiffrin, 1968; Deutsch & Deutsch, 1963; Kahneman, 1973; Posner, 1978; Posner & Snyder, 1975). A number of experiments investigated the processing of the meanings of stimuli outside of conscious awareness using the method of the dichotic listening task. In the dichotic listening task, words are presented to the two ears, and subjects are instructed to attend to one ear only, to shadow (i.e., repeat loudly) what they hear in that ear, and to ignore stimuli presented to the other ear. Subjects in dichotic listening tasks are able to keep the contents of the rejected channel out of conscious awareness. Some results suggest, however, that these unattended words are still processed. Certain words, like a subject's name exposed in the rejected channel tend to "break into" consciousness. This phenomenon has been referred to as the cocktail party effect (Moray, 1959). Some results suggest that all stimuli presented to the unattended channel are processed at the level of semantic analysis since shock-associated words and even their synonyms produced automatic responses (like heightened galvanic skin responses) when presented in the ignored channel (Corteen & Dunn, 1974; Corteen & Wood, 1972[4]; von Wright, Anderson, & Stenman, 1975). In addition, words presented to the unattended channel that are semantically related to words being presented simultaneously to the attended channel can produce interference effects (increase of shadowing errors) without entering consciousness (Lewis, 1970; see also Treisman, Squire, & Green, 1974). Recently, Nielsen and Sarason (1981), and Bargh (1982) observed decreases in the controlled level of processing (shadowing) when information deemed "important" was exposed to the rejected channel (sex-relevant and self-relevant words).

The phenomenon of nonconscious processing of the meanings of stimuli was also recently demonstrated in subliminal exposure experiments with visual stimuli. Marcel (1980, see also 1983a, 1983b) presented his subjects with words exposed below the individually diagnosed detection level of stimulus onset asynchrony (SOA) and masked them immediately (i.e., the words were exposed so briefly that subjects could not determine whether a word or a blank was exposed). Despite the apparent inaccessibility of these stimuli to subjects' conscious awareness, subjects in these experiments were able to indicate at an above chance level which of two words exposed after the subliminal exposure was more closely associated semantically with the subliminal word.[5] Marcel found also that the subliminally exposed words produced semantical priming effects since they facilitated the process of making lexical decisions about subsequently exposed words. When the subliminally exposed priming word was semantically related to the subsequently exposed word, the response latency for the lexical decision about the latter word was shorter.

Marcel's results were found to be "counterintuitive" and "startling" by Fowler, Wolford, Slade, and Tassinary (1981, p. 341) because they clearly implied that "subjects have accessed the meanings of words that, due to the effects of the mask, they may be unaware even of having seen" (p. 341). Fowler et al. (1981) replicated Marcel's experiments controlling for some potential artifacts. Their results clearly demonstrated that subliminally exposed words produced specific priming effects on the processing of subsequently exposed words. This finding indicated that the subliminally exposed words were processed at the level of semantic analysis outside of subjects' conscious awareness.

The results of Fowler et al. (1981) have been replicated many times since their publication. In one of these successful replications, social stimulus material was used (Czyzewska, 1984). Subjects in this experiment were presented with a long list of adjectives exposed one at a time on a video monitor, and after the exposure of each adjective they were asked to respond as quickly as possible as to whether or not the adjective could describe people. Some of these adjectives pertained clearly to people (e.g., "kind"); some of them did not (e.g., "metallic"). During the breaks separating subsequent exposures of the adjectives, subjects were subliminally exposed to priming adjectives that were either semantically related (synonyms, antonyms) or semantically unrelated to the supraliminally exposed adjectives. The subliminally exposed words apparently were processed at the level of semantic analysis since they produced specific nonconscious priming effects: They facilitated processing of semantically related words. In other words, they decreased the response time for lexical decisions for both synonyms and antonyms, and they did not produce any effects for processing of semantically unrelated words. This study extends the generality of the Fowler et al. (1981) findings, which were collected using simple nouns, to the area of processing social information.

Social subliminal stimuli were also used in a recent study by Bargh and Pietromonaco (1982). In the learning phase of their experiment, subjects were exposed to a series of subliminal exposures of words that contained 0%, 20%, or 80% hostile words. In the testing phase, subjects were presented with a short description of a stimulus person (who was described ambiguously regarding her hostility), and they then rated this person on a number of evaluative dimensions. Subjects subliminally exposed to hostile words rated the stimulus person more negatively than other subjects. The authors proposed a number of alternative explanations for their finding: (1) increased accessibility of the category of hostility at the point of encoding information about the stimulus person, (2) increased accessibility of some general negative category ("undesirable" or "unpleasant"), (3) change in subjects' mood. Each of these interpretations, however, assumes that subliminally exposed words were processed at a level of semantic analysis and that they influenced subsequent cognitive processes.

Thus, after years of doubts regarding the existence of subliminal perception, this phenomenon now seems to have been conclusively demonstrated, and the fact of its existence is widely acknowledged among cognitive psychologists.[6]

The effects obtained in all the above experiments may be explained in terms of relatively simple phenomena (such as priming) that seem to be far less complex than the processes of nonconscious acquisition of cognitive algorithms discussed in the first section of this chapter. These studies are still very important, however, since they open the way for investigation of processes of nonconscious learning by demonstrating that conscious awareness is not a necessary condition for the perception and processing of stimuli at a level of semantic analysis. Additionally, these experiments introduced methods for providing subjects with stimuli without making the subjects aware of them. These methods are used in some of the experiments reported later in this book.

Having established that conscious awareness is not a necessary condition for the perception and semantic analysis of stimuli,[7] the next logical step is to ask whether such nonconsciously perceived and processed knowledge may be stored in long-term memory and whether it may influence future cognitive processes. This question is basic and crucial for research on nonconscious acquisition of cognitive algorithms since the argument regarding nonconscious learning presented in the first section of this chapter implies that nonconsciously acquired knowledge can continue to influence subsequent cognitive processing for some time.

Unfortunately, there is relatively little research evidence demonstrating that nonconsciously processed information can be stored in long-term memory, and some authors still perceive such a possibility as controversial. For example, some authors failed to find any long-term memory effects of words presented in the unattended channel during the dichotic listening task (Glucksberg & Cowen, 1970; Norman, 1969), although there is some evidence for the long-term storage of unattended visual information (Allport, Antonis, & Reynolds, 1972; Kellogg, 1980; Rollins & Thibadeau, 1973).[8]

Some theories postulate explicitly that information may enter long-term memory directly from the sensory buffer without the mediation of short-term memory, which is usually associated with attention and awareness (Atkinson & Shiffrin, 1968). Conversely, other theories claim that long-term storage is impossible without mediation of conscious attention (Erdelyi, 1974; Neisser, 1967; also, to some extent, Shiffrin & Schneider, 1977). Because none of the theories that preclude long-term storage without mediation of conscious awareness substantiates or even fully elaborates this position, this claim sounds more like an intuitive preference of the authors for a certain solution, rather than a necessary consequence of their models.

The influential theory of Shiffrin and Schneider (1977) is not very conservative regarding this claim. They propose that a controlled process (associated with short-term memory and attention) is a necessary condition for any long-term storage. They also propose, however, so-called "veiled" controlled processes in short-term memory, which could last so briefly that they may not involve conscious experience. It follows that attention and short-term memory (STM) processes need not always involve consciousness.[9] In a recent set of studies devoted to the problem of long-term memory (LTM) storage and controlled versus automatic processing, Schneider and his associate (Fisk & Schneider, 1984) argue again "that LTM modification and controlled processing are closely related, but automatic performance can occur with little or no LTM storage" (p. 195). In one of the studies (Experiment 2), however, they observe some LTM storage that accompanies automatic processing. The authors suggest that it might be due to subjects' having "allocated some control processing resources" (p. 195) to the automatically performed task.

The experiments by Fisk and Schneider (1984) are a good illustration of methodological difficulties in proving that something does not exist. Theoretically, a conclusive point could be made only on the basis of a positive and not on a negative result. An additional reason why this particular research cannot conclusively contribute to the problem of LTM storage without mediation of conscious awareness is the definition of automatic processing postulated in Shiffrin and Schneider's (1977) theory and operationalized in their studies and in the experiments by Fisk and Schneider (1984). Automatic processes, as defined by Shiffrin and Schneider (1977), allow fast and effortless performance of well-developed skilled behaviors that are not limited by short-term memory capacity and do not interfere with controlled processing. Thus, automatic processing of information is a very special kind of nonconscious cognitive process, and even if it does not produce LTM effects, one could not argue that other nonconscious processes do not produce LTM effects.

Probably the strongest empirical evidence that supports LTM effects of nonconscious processing of information comes from research on the so-called preattentive processing of affective information. The research was inspired by Zajonc's conception of a relative independence of cognitive and affective processing of information (Zajonc, 1980, 1984). Zajonc claimed that the processing of affect may take place outside of conscious awareness and "that it arises early in the process of registration and retrieval, albeit weakly and vaguely, and it derives from a parallel, separate, and partly independent system in the organism" (p. 154). Before a stimulus is processed on a level of cognitive analysis that allows a descriptive discrimination of stimuli (a level of "discriminanda"), it is always processed on a level of affective analysis ("preferenda"). Zajonc's claims are based on research showing that subjects preserve a preference for certain stimuli without remembering the stimuli (e.g., Wilson, 1979). In one of the experiments (Kunst–Wilson & Zajonc, 1980) subjects were subliminally exposed to a series of 10 irregular polygons each of which was presented five times. These stimuli were exposed very briefly, so subjects had no conscious access to what they were presented with. After the learning phase they were unable to discriminate between the polygons that had been exposed and other similar polygons. However, consistent with Zajonc's theory, in a preference task, it appeared that subjects picked up reliably more often those polygons that were subliminally exposed in the learning phase of the experiment. This particular prediction was based on the so-called mere exposure effect (Harrison, 1977), which consists of a relation between repeated exposures (or familiarity) and liking. Regardless of the extent to which this result is a crucial test of Zajonc's theory about independence of descriptive and affective levels of information processing (see Seamon, Brody, & Kauff, 1983a, for a recent discussion of this issue), the experiment of Kunst–Wilson and Zajonc (1980) is a clear demonstration of a LTM storage of nonconsciously processed information. The experiment has been replicated successfully a number of times (Seamon, Brody, & Kauff, 1983a, 1983b; Seamon, Marsh, & Brody, 1984), and the robustness of the effect has been additionally demonstrated by including mediating variables like cerebral laterality (Seamon, Brody, & Kauff, 1983a).

These experiments demonstrate an effect that is crucial for the reasoning concerning nonconscious acquisition of cognitive algorithms presented in the first section of this chapter. Subjects in these experiments nonconsciously acquired a tendency to prefer certain polygons and this tendency was preserved long enough afterwards to assume that there was a long-term memory effect (see Seamon, Brody, & Kauff, 1983b). Thus, subjects in these experiments nonconsciously acquired a cognitive disposition that at least to some extent was stable.

Unfortunately, the list of conclusive research studies demonstrating the

LTM storage of nonconsciously processed information is now nearly exhausted. There is, however, a long list of studies that cannot be considered as conclusive as the above experiments regarding this issue, but which are still difficult to interpret without referring to the phenomenon of LTM storage of nonconsciously acquired information. We will look at a few of them now.

Hasher and Zacks (1979, 1984; Alba, Chromiak, Hasher, & Attig, 1980) proposed a theoretical conception of automatic and effortful cognitive processes according to which LTM storage requires conscious attention. They claim, however, that certain kinds of basic information about the environment (like time, spatial location, and frequency of events) are encoded into LTM automatically and without the mediation of conscious awareness. All of their research has been devoted to automatic processing and storage of information about frequency. Their experiments have had an especially unfortunate design (from a general methodological viewpoint), since Hasher and Zacks always demonstrate that the processing of frequency data is not sensitive to various dispositional and situational factors. Thus, they consistently demonstrate a lack of effect. Nevertheless, as a whole, these numerous experiments (see, Hasher & Zacks, 1984, for a recent review) provide an impressive and intuitively convincing image of a very basic cognitive process which is independent of type of instruction, practice, motivation, and even important dispositional factors (e.g., age or depression).[10]

Directly relevant, and consistent with the general idea of the process of nonconscious acquisition of cognitive algorithms, is the research on "implicit learning" initiated by Arthur Reber (1967). In the learning phase of implicit learning experiments, subjects are exposed to a list of strings of letters generated by a set of specific rules. These rules constitute an artificial "grammar" that specifies permissible orders of letters. Subjects are asked to watch the strings but they are not instructed to search for any rules or regularities implicit in the entire list. In the testing phase, subjects are presented with some new strings of letters and are asked to judge which of them are consistent with the rules established by the material presented in the learning phase. In a series of studies, Reber and his associates found that while making judgments about whether novel items obey the rules, subjects behaved as if they were able to employ the rules implicitly contained in the stimulus material they had been previously exposed to, but they were unable to articulate the rules and were unaware of the fact that they were employing any such rules (Reber, 1967, 1976; Reber & Allen, 1978; Reber & Lewis, 1977). Moreover, Reber (1976) found that when subjects were given an explicit instruction in the learning phase to search for rules, their performance in the testing phase deteriorated, which suggests that implicit, unconscious processing of information about the rules is superior to the explicit, consciously controlled search (see also, Reber, Kassin, Lewis, & Cantor, 1980).[11] Gordon and Holyoak (1983) replicated Reber's results and additionally found that after a typical implicit learning phase, subjects showed a preference for those novel items that were structurally consistent with the rules followed by the learning phase items. This finding is consistent with the mere exposure effect (cf. the above-reported experiments employing subliminal stimuli by Kunst–Wilson & Zajonc, 1980; and Seamon and associates).

Reber concluded that while watching the stimulus material, subjects "implicitly learned" the crucial rules and that such implicit and *unconscious* learning is a natural product of attending to structured stimuli. Reber postulated "a nonconscious abstraction system" (1976, p. 88), and he proposed

> that complex structures, such as those underlying language, socialization, perception, and sophisticated games are acquired implicitly and unconsciously; that such knowledge is memorially encoded in the form of abstract representational systems; and that the acquisition process itself contains at its core an induction process whereby relations among parts of the stimulus environment are mapped in an order that corresponds roughly with the ecological salience of these relations. (Reber et al., 1980, pp. 492–493)

Reber's reasoning was extensively discussed by Brooks (1978) who also observed that his subjects behaved as if they followed certain abstract rules that they were unable to articulate. Brooks proposed, however, an alternative explanation to the one postulated by Reber, and he suggested that in his experiments subjects in fact did not abstract general rules but rather based their judgments on some integral or holistic similarity between a test item and items encountered in the learning phase. Brooks (1978) proposed a discrimination "between deliberate, verbal, analytic, control processes and implicit, intuitive, nonanalytic processes" (p. 207).

Thus, whereas Reber assumes a process of nonconscious abstraction, Brooks proposes a process that involves a nonanalytic drawing of analogies. These processes differ considerably in terms of how relevant knowledge is represented in memory and accessed while making subsequent judgments. According to Reber, the knowledge is represented in terms of abstract rules ("abstract representational systems," Reber et al., 1980); according to Brooks, it is represented in terms of exemplars and accessed through a process of drawing analogies.[12] This issue is also of relevance to the important question about the structural representation of and the mechanism for accessing tacit knowledge. We will return to this problem a number of times throughout the book. At this point, however, it is worthwhile to note that despite the basic structural differences between these two possibilities (i.e., the abstract and exemplar-based representation of tacit knowledge), both lead to a generally similar notion regarding the manner in which the nonconsciously acquired knowledge influences behavior. Brooks' (1978) final conclusions regarding the accessibility of important cognitive algorithms sound similar to those (quoted previously) formulated by Reber and his associates, and are consistent with lay observations discussed in the first section of this chapter:

> We don't have a sufficient grasp of the representation of knowledge to provide a good answer as to why so many of our complex concepts and categories, such as those in grammar and chess, are so resolutely beyond explicit formulation by experts, let alone the average practitioner. (Brooks, 1978, p. 207)

This reasoning concerning the process of implicit learning seems perfectly consistent with the argument presented in the first section of this chapter about the nonconscious acquisition of cognitive algorithms. The weak points of the research on implicit learning, however, pertain to the specific experimental paradigm used in all studies demonstrating the phenomenon in question. On the one hand, the paradigm seems to be an adequate laboratory analogue of the natural process of learning the grammatical structure of a language. On the other hand, it seems impossible to differentiate between the nonconscious process of abstracting rules or the nonconscious drawing of analogies, and consciously controlled, yet not very easy to verbalize, drawing of analogies (e.g., based on the shape of stimuli, density of strings of letters, etc.).

Recently, Dulany, Carlson, and Dewey (1984; 1985) attempted to replicate one of Reber's experiments and they concluded that Reber's claim about the nonconsciousness of the process of learning and employing knowledge is problematic. Dulany et al. found that:

> Subjects evidently acquired . . . personal sets of conscious rules, each of limited scope, and many of imperfect validity. Those rules themselves were shown to embody abstractions, consciously represented novelty that could account for abstraction embodied in judgments. The better explanation of these results, we argue, credits grammatical judgments to conscious rules within informal grammars rather than to unconscious representations of a formal grammar. (p. 541)

Reber and his associates (Reber, Allen, & Regan, 1985) found the critique of Dulany et al. (1984) totally unjustified for a number of reasons, but mainly because "the constraints of the task they use to assess subjects' knowledge base carries demand characteristics that may make implicit knowledge appear to be explicitly represented" (Reber et al., 1985, p. 17). Dulany, Carlson, and Dewey (1985), in turn, acknowledged that the questions raised by Reber et al. (1985) should be examined, but found no reason to revise their interpretation.

A considerable amount of evidence directly relevant to the hypothesis of nonconscious acquisition and operation of cognitive algorithms comes also from research that is unrelated to the information processing paradigm. In an influential paper, Nisbett and Wilson (1977a) discussed a number of person perception and attribution studies which demonstrate that subjects in these experiments had no access to inferential strategies that were in fact responsible for their final judgments or decisions. Nisbett and Wilson showed that in a number of experiments, subjects' perceptions of what they based their judgments on were only reflections of their private theories about how they reason, rather than reflections of the actual process of inference. For example, in one of the experiments (Nisbett & Wilson, 1977b), subjects watched an interview with a professor who acted kind and warm in one condition, and hostile and cold in the other (different subjects were tested in each condition). Subjects rated the warm professor more positively, but they also rated the appearance of the warm professor higher, which according to the authors, indicates a nonconscious "halo effect." Subjects consistently denied, however, that personality of the professor had any impact on their ratings of his appearance. In another study (Nisbett & Wilson, 1977a), subjects evaluated articles of clothing, and there was a very strong tendency to prefer articles located in right-hand position. When subjects were asked whether position of an article might influence their choice "virtually all subjects denied it, usually with a worried glance at the interviewer suggesting that they felt either that they had misunderstood the question or were dealing with a madman" (p. 244).

Nisbett and Wilson (1977a) made a very strong point concerning the nonconsciousness of the inferential strategies that are responsible for social judgments and decisions, and subjects' general lack of access to their own mental processes influencing their behavior.[13] Their work contributed to the growing interest in nonconscious cognitive processes.

There is numerous evidence supporting Nisbett's and Wilson's (1977a) general conclusions and consistent with the reasoning presented in the first section of this chapter. These studies suggest that human everyday information processing involves the constant use of complex and totally nonconscious cognitive algorithms. This is true not only with regard to relatively elementary processes like meaning analysis or pattern recognition (Kaufman, 1974; Rock, 1975) which require nonconscious inference and decision processes. It also applies to complex processes such as creative thinking or problem solving. For example, chess masters do not have access to the specific playing strategies (and underlying cognitive algorithms) they follow (de Groot, 1965).

A spectacular demonstration of the operation of nonconscious cognitive algorithms at work when perceiving and interpreting the motor activity of stimulus persons was provided recently by Runeson and Frykholm (1983), using a "patch-light technique." The stimulus persons wore dark tight-fitting clothes with 2 cm wide strips of retroreflective cloth-based tape wrapped around ankles, knees, wrists, and elbows and 15 cm long strips attached to hips, shoulders, and forehead. Various kinds of motor activities were filmed in a way that made all details of the entire picture totally invisible (dark) except the marked points on the stimulus persons' bodies. The subjects' task in these experiments was to answer a number of questions about the actions and intentions of the stimulus persons. It appeared that subjects, following some apparently complex and nonconscious inferential strategies, were able to determine accurately (using only the specific dynamics of the movements of the shining points on the stimulus persons' bodies), their gender and a number of motor and psychological characteristics of what they were doing. For example, subjects were able to estimate the weight of an object lifted by the stimulus persons, how far they threw an object, and whether they were actually performing these activities or trying to deceive the observers (e.g., the box they lifted was empty [4 kg], but the actors tried to make an impression that the box weighed 6.5, 11.5, or 19 kg).

There is also evidence supporting the notion that when forming impressions of people based on their appearance, subjects follow inferential strategies of which they are not aware. A recent experiment suggests the existence of culturally determined (yet not accessible to subjects' conscious awareness) strategies of judging personalities of people based on how they look. In an exploratory study, Stefanski (1984) had subjects rate on 10 dimensions the personalities of four stimulus persons based on schematic sketches of their faces. The faces were introduced as digital transformations of photographs of real persons, and the entire task was introduced to the subjects as a "test of psychological intuition." Two features were manipulated in this stimulus material: spread of the eyes and width of the nose (each face was represented in the stimulus material an equal number of times in each combination of spread of eyes and width of nose). Reliable effects were found for 4 of 10 dimensions. For example, subjects perceived stimulus persons with spread eyes as "confident, having trust in others" (as opposed to persons with closed eyes who were rated as "suspicious"); stimulus persons with a narrow nose were rated to be more introverted than persons with a wide nose, who were rated as extroverted.[14] After making their judgments, subjects were extensively interviewed regarding the perceived basis for their judgments, and the interviews were designed to minimize demand characteristics and social desirability factors. It appeared that the subjects could not articulate any of the strategies they used. This was true even when the experimenter asked directly about whether and how the two manipulated features influenced their impressions—subjects consistently denied that these two features had any influence on their judgments at all.

A process of acquisition of a cognitive algorithm that was probably not mediated by conscious awareness was recently demonstrated by Beair, Peterson, and Whitmire (1984). In the learning phase of their experiment, subjects were placed between two target areas (19 and 20 ft distance from a subject) and they were asked to throw a bean bag into one target, then to turn around and throw it into the other (this was repeated 12 times). Subjects were informed that both distances were equal and they did not discover that this was not true. After a 15 min distractor task subjects threw the bean bag again; control subjects threw the bag in the same conditions as in the learning phase, for experimental subjects, however, during the break one of the targets was moved (by 10%: from 19 to 21 ft) but the subjects were not informed about it nor did they recognize the difference. It appeared that the experimental subjects made many more "misses" than the control subjects ($p < .0001$); they also explicitly expressed surprise with their deteriorated performance (e.g., they claimed that they were "out of form" during the second phase of the experiment). This strong difference in performance between the groups occurred only with the target that was moved. The authors interpreted these results as evidence for nonconscious learning of how much force should be used when throwing the bag in each of the two directions. The process of development of this algorithm turned out to be more sensitive to the real distances between a subject and the targets than his or her consciously controlled estimation of the distances. Moreover, the algorithm was preserved in memory during the 15 minute break and was reactivated in the testing phase of the experiment.

The evidence reviewed above indicates that the concept of the nonconscious acquisition of cognitive algorithms (outlined in the section entitled "Lay Observation and Common Intuitions") is quite consistent with research on cognition and information processing. A number of experiments support directly the hypothesis that stimuli may be semantically processed outside of conscious awareness and that the results of this processing may be stored in long-term memory in the form of cognitive algorithms capable of influencing subsequent cognitive processes (e.g., processes generating preferences).

In the Chapter 2, I formulate a general model of the nonconscious

acquisition of cognitive algorithms and their influence on subsequent information processing. The model will pertain to basic properties of the
process, and it will provide a general framework for the research reported
in all subsequent chapters of the book.

Notes

1. Experiments demonstrating the inaccuracy of subjects' explanations of what they
based such judgments on are presented in a number of experiments reported later in this
book.
2. It happens that some such observations are based on obvious cues like "the face is
unattractive because there is a large, disproportional nose and the eyes are unusually close
to each other." Usually, however, there are no such salient and obvious cues helpful in
making inferences.
3. The correct answer to the question asked is "1:1" (most common answer is "1:2"
or "2:3").
4. See also Wardlaw and Kroll (1976) for a failure to replicate Corteen's and Wood's
(1972) experiment, as well as a critique of their procedure. Research evidence undermining
Corteen's and Wood's (1972) conclusions was also obtained in an unpublished study by
Dawson and Schell reported by Bargh (1984).
5. Similar results were reported earlier by Allport (1977). However, there were important flaws in his data analysis (see, Ellis & Marshall, 1978).
6. "Despite shortcomings in the early demonstrations of these effects (e.g., Eriksen,
1960, 1962), the case for them [i.e., for the effects of nonconscious processing of subliminally exposed stimuli] seems now to have been made." (Kihlstrom, 1984, p. 164).
7. See also recent research on automatic semantic processing of words (Fisk & Schneider, 1983).
8. Nonconsciousness of the visual stimuli in these experiments is questionable since
these procedures allow for less control of subjects' attention than is the case with the use of
shadowing in a standard dichotic listening task. However, some authors found these results
as a proof of a long-term storage not mediated by conscious awareness (see Kellogg, 1980).
9. Shiffrin and Schneider (1977, see also Schneider & Schiffrin, 1977) did not elaborate
their concept of veiled controlled processes any further; they defined it, however, in such a
way that it might account for the processes of long-term storage not mediated by conscious
awareness (e.g., for a long-term storage of subliminally exposed stimuli).
10. See Fisk and Schneider (1984), for a recent critique of Hasher's and Zack's (1979)
research.
11. This kind of comparison between voluntary and involuntary modes of processing
should always be treated with caution, however, since explicit instructions usually involve
additional uncontrolled factors (like stress or changes in motivation) that may nonspecifi-
cally interfere with the task. Explicit instructions may also prompt the use of inefficient
strategies. (See Anderson and Bower [1972], for an example of the experiment in which
subjects in an intentional learning condition performed poorer than subjects in an incidental
learning condition, due to employing ineffective memorization strategies.)
12. See Elio and Anderson (1981) for a discussion of this problem in the context of the
structure of semantic memory.

13.   See Smith and Miller (1978) and White (1980) for a critique of Nisbett's and Wilson's (1977a) position. See also a relevant discussion by Ericsson and Simon (1980).

14.   It is unclear to what extent the results of this study are culturally general across various types of faces (i.e., whether these two features always would produce the same biases). Although these results were consistent across the four faces used in Stefanski's (1984) study, the specific relations found may well reflect interactions between the two features and other characteristics of all four faces employed in the experiment. Even if this were the case, this represents no threat to the general conclusion about the operation of nonconscious inferential strategies in this experiment.

CHAPTER **2**

Internal Processing
Algorithms

The reasoning presented in Chapter 1 in the section entitled "Lay Observations and Common Intuitions" suggested the need to postulate a mechanism for nonconscious acquisition of cognitive algorithms. The evidence reviewed in Chapter 1 in the section entitled "Research on Nonconscious Cognitive Processes" indicated that the existence of such a mechanism has been supported in recent research on information processing. In this chapter, I propose categories by which such a process can be described and that provide a general theoretical framework for the experiments presented in subsequent chapters.

Processing Information of Covariations

The most basic category involved in processing information, such as concrete episodes and general concepts or procedures, is a notion of cooccurrence or, more generally, covariation. To encode any kind of information, a cognitive system has to process data in terms of covariations.[1] For example, there is no other way to acquire a concept of any object than to discover cooccurrences between some of its features; the only way to interpret any stimulus is to check whether features cooccur in a stimulus. Processing information about covariations is a basic aspect of any act of cognition.

Covariation is not only a basic formal structure for representing declarative knowledge, it is also a basic structure for representing procedural knowledge.[2] For example, in order to find out about an unknown property x of a given object which also has some other property y, one may use knowledge about covariation between x and y, and based on y, infer something about x. Such an inference process is a basic functional unit of interpretation about any kind of stimuli (Kaufman, 1974; Rock, 1975). Obviously, most knowledge we are concerned with is far more complex than what can be represented by simple (i.e., first order) covariations. However, systems of interrelated covariations may represent declarative knowledge or procedures involving a high degree of complexity.

Also, all the examples of nonconsciously acquired and nonconsciously operating knowledge discussed in Chapter 1 involve covariations or complex systems of covariations. In order to account for these phenomena we must assume that

1. Information about covariations can be detected, processed, and stored (i.e., acquired) without mediation of conscious awareness.
2. The nonconsciously acquired information about covariation can influence subsequent cognitive processes, again without mediation of conscious awareness.
3. Even after the information about covariation has begun to influence a person's behavior and has become a stable element of his or her cognitive system, the person has no access whatsoever to it: The person cannot control it or change it, and cannot even learn directly about it.

These statements constitute the major hypotheses that are examined in the experiments presented in subsequent chapters of this book. Before we present this research, however, it would be useful to consider these statements and their implications in greater detail.

The Concept of Internal Processing Algorithms

To discuss the processes outlined above, we need a term that will denote the result or cognitive consequences of a nonconscious acquisition of information about covariation. I propose the term *internal processing algorithm* (IPA). IPA refers to the memory representation of covariation between two or more features or events, but only if it meets the three conditions listed above: that it be acquired nonconsciously, that it nonconsciously influences behavior, and that it not be consciously controlled or directly examinable (i.e., a person may learn about the contents of his or her internal processing algorithms only by means of external observations of his or her own behavior). In what follows, I will explain the choice of this particular term.

The word *internal* emphasizes the fact that an IPA is represented in a code that is not directly accessible to examination in conscious awareness. Using a computer analogy, IPA is a compiled program, and the source code of this program either does not exist or is not accessible. This analogy is also relevant in terms of speed and flexibility. IPAs (like object code programs) are executed very rapidly, but once compiled they cannot be flexibly modified in run-time. For example, after a certain type of grammatical structure is nonconsciously acquired (in terms of the computer analogy, stored in a compiled form in memory), it executes rapidly and instantly influences process of speech production. However, it cannot easily be modified or even accessed by conscious control processes. Similarly, after learning nonconsciously to encode a certain combination of information as funny, the respective IPA will instantly detect such a combination and will trigger immediate behavioral reaction (laughter). However, neither the process that detects the covariation nor the one that triggers the reaction is accessible to conscious control; neither of them can be directly examined by the person who in fact acts on this IPA (i.e., who "detects" the information and "reacts" to it).

In contrast, an interpreted program is like the consciously controlled processing of information. Both have their source code easily accessible, and their execution can be flexibly controlled and modified. The execution, however, is considerably slower. For example, if a decision is made under the control of consciously controlled processing, the individual making the decision has access to how the final output of the process (making one's mind up) is generated. Moreover, he or she can flexibly manipulate and tailor various components of the process. It requires, however, considerably more time than processing based on IPAs.

The word algorithm reflects the fact that an IPA represents not only declarative but also procedural knowledge; it contains an algorithm concerning how to determine one thing based on another. An IPA contains information relevant to the relation between (at least) two features or events, and this represents declarative knowledge; but this knowledge is active in the sense that it shapes processes of interpreting relevant stimuli and generating reactions.

In most of the experiments presented in subsequent chapters of this book, structurally simple IPAs were studied (i.e., either simple cases of cooccurrence between two events or linear relations between two dimensions). However, I do not intend the category of IPA to be confined to such cases. It seems probable that the nonconscious processing discussed in Chapter 1 is based on nonconsciously acquired information about more complex types of relations between events or features, or that it is based on complex sets of interrelated IPAs.

Memory Representation of IPAs

The question of how internal processing algorithms are represented in memory constitutes an empirical problem, and at this point I will formulate no specific hypotheses concerning it. Two general types of representations may be taken into account: (1) abstract representations of relations between features or events and (2) more or less concrete sets of exemplars (cf. Reber's vs. Brook's interpretations of implicit learning phenomenon, discussed in Chapter 1). Although both types of representations may produce the same behavioral consequences, the actual structure of the memory representation of an IPA is of major importance for understanding the process by which an IPA is acquired and for understanding the particular mechanisms of its influence on subsequent cognitive processes.

It seems unjustified, however, to assume that IPAs are always represented by only one of these two types of structures. IPA is a theoretical category denoting in general terms the *functional* properties of certain observable phenomena; it need not be structurally homogenous. In other words, IPAs could be acquired in different ways (i.e., through structurally different mechanisms) and may, accordingly, be stored in memory in different ways. This problem is addressed in a number of the experiments presented in subsequent chapters. Yet, in none of these experiments is the problem formulated as pertaining to the structure of IPAs in general. Instead, these experiments explore the memory representations for the particular types of IPAs generated in those studies.

Nonconsciousness of IPAs

The word *nonconscious* is used throughout this book in its most widely accepted sense: It denotes cognitive contents and processes that a person cannot become aware of simply by directing his or her attention to them, even when the person is motivated to access that content or process.[3]

IPAs and Consciously Controlled Knowledge

Both everyday experience and experimental evidence indicate that people are consciously able to register and estimate consistent covariations among stimuli (Alloy & Tabachnik, 1984). However, conscious processing occurs only when the covariation is very salient. In light of the evidence discussed in Chapter 1, it seems reasonable to expect the development of IPAs to occur when covariations are not sufficiently salient to be detected and processed at the level of conscious awareness. This expectation is tested in many of the experiments presented in subsequent chapters.

The fact that the IPA is nonconscious in all aspects of its acquisition and subsequent operation constitutes its distinctive and central feature. Even without making any assumptions about the nature of nonconscious versus conscious processing of covariations, the mere fact that consciously controlled processes cannot directly influence at any stage the development or operation of IPA, makes its development and operation distinctively different from the development and operation of knowledge of which we are aware. I will now discuss some of the most important aspects of this difference.

First of all, an IPA does not have to be consistent with relevant consciously controlled knowledge, and this makes it independent of consciously controlled and accepted standards, attitudes, preferences, and the entire system of categories that a person uses to consciously interpret (understand) incoming stimuli. A good example of this independence is the fact that we feel empathic or "moved to tears" while watching a film that we consciously recognize as designed to manipulate the feelings of the audience (see Chapter 1). Another example are neurotic feelings of fear and anxiety in situations consciously interpreted by the neurotic person as perfectly safe. Neurotics cannot overcome their dysfunctional feelings just by convincing themselves that it is irrational to be anxious in a given situation. Also, one cannot help by trying carefully to explain to them that their behavior or feelings are irrational. The respective IPAs interpret certain kinds of situations as threatening, thus automatically triggering the reaction of anxiety and leaving no room for any consciously controlled intervention in the process. The person may only observe his or her own irrational reactions. In this sense the IPAs responsible for neurotic behavior function like the above discussed IPAs, triggering various "normal" uncontrollable reactions (e.g., laughter, empathy, or shame). (A number of experiments presented in subsequent chapters demonstrate the development of IPAs that are inconsistent with preexisting and consciously controlled knowledge.)

Secondly, IPAs may pertain to cues that are irrelevant to consciously controlled knowledge. In other words, IPAs may process stimuli that, from the viewpoint of consciously experienced cognition, have no interpretable, relevant meaning, and may trigger respective reactions in response to such stimuli. For example, IPAs may trigger certain consciously experienced feelings, intuitions, or preferences that a person cannot explain (i.e., he or she cannot determine what.caused them).

Moreover, it seems consistent with the postulated nature of IPAs that they may also generate preferences, choices, or decisions that are completely introspectively unrepresented. In other words, one may think that a decision or behavior was completely random, and not experience phenomenologically any sense of control or choice, when in fact the decision was directed by respective IPAs. (Again, a number of experiments presented in subsequent chapters explore such a possibility.)

Finally, IPAs do not have to use categories that are interpretable in terms of consciously controlled knowledge. For example, an IPA that estimates the age of a person based on the appearance of his or her face does not have to use categories from one's consciously articulated experience with faces nor does it have to be interpretable in terms of categories one uses in controlled processing of faces (e.g., length of nose). IPA may be formulated in categories that cannot be readily articulated or interpretated in terms of conscious equivalents. For example, they may be formulated in terms of some very complex systems of proportions. An operation of IPAs based on categories that cannot be interpreted, or at least not articulated in terms of conscious cognition, was demonstrated in research using the patch-light technique (see Chapter 1, Runeson & Frykholm, 1983). In these experiments, subjects were able to detect gender or recognize intentions of stimulus persons based exclusively on some (impossible to verbalize) characteristics of the dynamics of movements of a few points on their bodies. (This property of IPAs is also explored in one of the experiments reported in Chapter 6.)

The employment of categories that have no equivalents in controlled processing of information raises questions as to how these unique categories were developed, and what the limits are for development of IPAs in terms of number of possible categories that could be taken into account? Evidence (like experiments using the patch-light technique) that demonstrates the processing of categories which have no consciously represented equivalents, indicates that nonconscious processing of information involves developing concepts and categories independently of controlled cognition. Those nonconsciously acquired concepts and categories may play the role of IPAs and they may develop as a result of the same process. (Some research presented in subsequent chapters may help to formulate hypotheses concerning this process.)

Development of IPA

Some of the research presented in subsequent chapters investigates structural aspects of the development of IPAs. Yet, most of these experiments and the following discussion deal with development of IPAs in terms of the functional properties of this process.

In the following argument, I assume that IPAs may be "weaker" or "stronger" and that the process of development involves the strengthening of an IPA. By "strength of an IPA" I mean its relative influence on other cognitive processes or behavior as compared to other factors influencing the same processes or behavior. Thus, strength of an IPA is defined in functional terms and involves no assumptions about how it is represented structurally (i.e., how respective memory representations change when IPAs become stronger). Also, at this point, no assumptions are being made as to what extent the process of development of an IPA uses the limited processing resources of a perceiver.

The independence of IPAs from consciously accepted standards leaves open the question as to what amount of consistent evidence is necessary in order to initiate development of an IPA. A possible explanation of the higher sensitivity of nonconscious as compared to conscious processing of covariations is that the amount of consistent evidence needed to initiate the development of an IPA is lower than the respective amount of evidence required by the standards of consciously controlled processing of covariations. In other words, evidence that would be too sparse to be consciously considered as an indicator of some covariation among features or events, may be sufficient nevertheless to initiate development of the respective IPA. (This possibility is explored in a number of experiments presented in Chapters 4–7.)

IPAs play an important role in the development of cognitive representations of concepts; in many cases IPAs and concepts may result from the same process. People acquire many concepts (like grammatical structures) nonconsciously, and later, even when they are able to use these concepts in their consciously controlled processing of information, they may be unaware of certain aspects of these concepts. In other words, many concepts involve associations (i.e., some kind of IPAs) of which a person is unaware, despite the fact that the person consciously uses the concept. For example, a person may dislike people who speak loudly, may use the concept "speaking loudly" consciously, and may in fact be aware that it is the loudness he or she dislikes. Nevertheless, that person may have no access to the reasons for this dislike; he or she may have no consciously controlled knowledge as to what in particular is related to "speaking loudly," or to what IPAs are involved in the concept. Early stages of development of an IPA may involve small nonconscious changes in memory representations of the relevant concepts, which, as a result, would either increase or decrease the strength of relationship between these concepts. (These possibilities are explored in experiments presented in Chapter 4.)

It is hypothesized that nonconscious acquisition of IPAs is an ubiquitous process involved in the development of cognitive dispositions, social preferences, and other basic elements of personality. This claim is based on an assumption that the development of an IPA may be, in the long run, a self-perpetuating process. An initial tendency to follow certain covariations increases the likelihood that a subsequent stimulus would be encoded (perceived) in a way that is consistent with and would support the initial tendency, and that any ambiguities would be interpreted consistently with the IPA. The next relevant stimulus would be encoded in an even more biased way, and so forth. It seems that in small children there are especially good conditions for the operation of this self-perpetuating process, since due to their lack of experience, many aspects of incoming stimuli are ambiguous to them and, therefore, open to encoding tendencies that perpetuate IPAs.

The perception of ambiguities as consistent with relevant IPAs may be due to the fact that IPAs produce respective category accessibility effects. For example, if an IPA pertains a covariation between feature x and feature y, then perception of feature x in a given object that is ambiguous regarding y, would temporarily increase accessibility of feature y, and this, in turn, would increase the likelihood that feature y would be used and thus that the object would be perceived as y. (Some research presented in Chapters 4–7 tests this hypothesis.)

If an IPA pertains to social information, then social interaction might additionally contribute to this self-perpetuating process. For example, an IPA reflecting covariation between introversion and aggressiveness might produce a tendency to behave toward introverts in a manner consistent with the expectation that they are aggressive. This, in turn, makes it likely that their responses would be consistent with the perceiver's expectations ("a self-fulfilling prophecy"), and thus, would reinforce the initial IPA.

Another hypothesized mechanism through which the nonconscious processing of covariation may contribute to the development of stable personality dispositions is its assumed sensitivity to perceiver's permanently accessible categories. It has been suggested that such categories are nonconsciously processed to a larger degree than less accessible categories (Bargh, 1982; Logan, 1980; Nielsen & Sarason, 1981; Posner & Snyder, 1975) and, therefore, are more likely to participate in processing covariations, which eventually may solidify or even increase their status as permanently accessible categories in a perceiver's personality. For example, a child who had some social experience that temporarily increased his or her sensitivity to any information related to social insecurity or threat would not only consciously, but perhaps nonconsciously, process more information related to these categories. This sensitivity would promote processing of covariations between various cues and insecurity or threat and would produce encoding biases that would develop according to the self-perpetuating mechanisms. This person would eventually acquire a tendency to perceive many types of stimuli as related to insecurity and threat, and this might eventually increase his or her general expectation of negative social experience or anxiety level. (This reasoning is tested in a number of experiments presented in Chapters 4 & 8.)

The above reasoning suggests that once initiated, the development of an IPA may become a self-perpetuating process that does not need much supportive evidence in order to continue. Moreover, its development might continue even if there is no supportive evidence. This seems to be a viable explanation of why people develop dispositions that are not (or not clearly) related to "objective" characteristics of what they have encountered or experienced. It is reasonable to assume that after reaching a certain level of strength, an IPA may even bias cognitive processes to an extent that makes disproving the IPA difficult even in the face of consistent evidence in contradiction with the IPA.

However, in the early stages of development of an IPA (i.e., when the IPA is weak), the biasing effects of the IPA should not preclude encoding evidence inconsistent with the IPA. Therefore, it may be expected that if the amount of disproving evidence is sufficient, then the disproved IPA can be modified or rejected. As mentioned earlier, processing complex information requires complex IPAs or sets of conditional IPAs; for example, certain IPAs that would be adequate in one type of circumstance might be totally inadequate in another. The development of complex IPAs (or systems of IPAs) would occur if an IPA that at a certain point had been found consistent with incoming stimuli, but later was disproved and rejected, did not disappear completely from memory, but rather was only deactivated and replaced by a new one. This residual might speed up the eventual development of conditional IPAs; the former IPA might not be totally incorrect, rather it might be applicable to certain conditions. When these conditions occur, the former (deactivated) IPA might be reactivated and might replace the latter one. Such process would allow for the flexible development of complex systems of IPAs. (Experiments presented in Chapter 3 explore these possibilities.)

The Issue of Ecological Validity

The primary goal of the entire series of experiments presented in Chapters 3 to 8 is to demonstrate the existence of internal processing algorithms and to explore the ubiquity of these phenomena. My first experiments on nonconscious processing of covariation (see Chapter 3) used a purely cognitive type of methodology in which subjects scanned matrices of digits in search for a target (matrix scanning paradigm). These experiments demonstrated the development of IPAs and showed some basic properties of that process. I found these experiments conclusive and convincing in regards to the existence of IPAs as defined in this chapter. I realized, however, that this kind of methodology (which puts subjects in conditions that are very unlike the natural settings in which people learn about their environment) makes the research less relevant to the issue of how important and ubiquitous the role of IPAs is in the development of stable dispositions and for adjustment in general. Methodologies like the matrix scanning paradigm allow for a relatively high level of laboratory control. Yet, they can be criticized on the grounds that they mainly demonstrate some "artificial ability" that may be induced in task-oriented subjects by the specific requirements of the unnatural settings and that this ability may be irrelevant to or play a minor role in everyday cognitions in natural settings.

Therefore, in most of the experiments presented in Chapters 4 to 8, I try to use stimulus material similar to what people are exposed to in everyday life, namely, social information.

Notes

1. Only less complex categories (e.g., those involving basic and primitively perceived feelings) need not involve a formal representation in terms of covariations. For example, a primitive understanding of "pain" might be cognitively represented (unidimensionally) without involving a formal category of covariation; this understanding would assume, however, absolutely no knowledge whatsoever about what causes or is associated with pain. Assuming that there is no prenatal learning, humans and animals possess such a category of pain only in the very moment of their birth. A moment later, however, associations start to build around this feeling, and the cognitive representation of pain starts to grow based on processing covariations.

2. The terms declarative and procedural knowledge were proposed by Winograd (1975).

3. In a recently edited book on unconsciousness, Kihlstrom (1984) defined the term of unconsciousness in a similar way: "Evidently what the editors of this book, and most other psychologists as well, have in mind when they use the term [unconsciousness] are those cognitive contents and processes, existing in the cognitive system at some point in time and actively influencing ongoing cognition and action, of which the person is not aware" (p. 155), but "it seems inappropriate to label . . . as unconscious" those contents and processes that "we could bring into awareness by the simple expedient of turning our attention to them" (p. 156).

CHAPTER **3**

Processing Covariations (I): Experiments Employing The "Matrix Scanning" Paradigm

Introduction

This chapter represents my first exploratory attempts to demonstrate nonconscious detection and processing of covariations. The following experiments were based on the argument, presented in Chapter 2, that nonconscious detection of covariation produces a memory trace in the form of an internal processing algorithm (IPA). This algorithm, in turn, is capable of influencing subsequent information processing without influencing the perceiver's conscious awareness.

In the basic experimental paradigm, subjects were exposed to stimulus material containing a covariation that was not accessible to conscious awareness and were then asked to complete a task related to the covariation. It was predicted that if the covariation was in fact nonconsciously processed and stored in the form of an IPA, it would influence subjects' performance on the task despite the inaccessibility of the covariation to subjects' conscious awareness.

The first series of studies employed a search task using response latency as a dependent measure. Subjects were asked to view a succession of frames of visual distractor characters and to search for the location of a target character within each frame. The frames were matrices consisting of digits. All possible digits were represented in each matrix more than

38

once (i.e., in more than one location), but there was only one digit "6" (target) among them. The matrices were divided into quarters and a control box with four buttons matched the quarters of the matrix. The subjects' task was to detect the specific location of the target in each matrix and to respond as quickly as possible by pushing the appropriate button on a control box so that latency and accuracy of responses could be registered. The covariation that subjects were exposed to pertained to the relation between locations of the target (i.e., specific quarters) and certain incidental cues presented with each frame (e.g., subliminally exposed strings of characters, specificity of the frame, or pitch of the warning tone that preceded presentation of each frame). If the covariation was processed and stored in the form of an IPA, it was expected to influence the search for the target by providing information as to where (i.e., in which quarter) to search. Such a process would thus eventually influence the time necessary to complete the search. The time would decrease when the specific frame was consistent with the acquired IPA since it would make attempts to localize the target in a wrong quarter less likely. On the other hand, the time would increase when the specific frame was inconsistent since in such a case the IPA would always first direct the search into the wrong quarter (which would eventually produce longer total search times than a random search).

There were no separate learning and testing phases in the experimental paradigm; subjects were exposed to the crucial covariations in the course of completing the search task. Over the course of successive blocks of trials, the content of the covariation was systematically manipulated. Subjects' performance on the task was expected to undergo predicted changes as a function of the manipulated (nonconsciously acquired) covariations and the consistency or inconsistency of successive frames with the covariations.

The paradigm allowed for the test of the hypothesis that the covariation had actually been employed in such a process by comparing a subject's performance on consistent and inconsistent frames (i.e., frames that are consistent or inconsistent with the specific covariation that the subject had the opportunity to acquire). The paradigm also allowed for the flexible manipulation of a number of factors that were expected to influence subjects' processing of covariations. Especially important from the viewpoint of verifying the general reasoning presented in Chapters 1 and 2 was the question of whether, in face of sufficient evidence inconsistent with the current IPA, perceivers are able to switch from one IPA to another, and whether the "rejected" (or "disproved") IPA is preserved in LTM and can be "reactivated" if new conditions occur.

Experiment 3.1

The opening experiment of the series had a very simple design, and it was aimed at testing only whether, in the above experimental settings, subjects would be able to nonconsciously process the covariation to which they were exposed. Strings of characters were presented subliminally with each frame to provide subjects with the crucial covariation.

Method

Overview

Subjects were exposed to a succession of 120 frames. Their task was to search for a target within each frame. The presentation of each frame was preceded by a subliminal exposure of a string of characters ("A235A," "A358A," "A582A," or "A823A") that covaried with the location of the target within the respective frame (i.e., with the specific quarter of the matrix in which the target was located). In other words, each of the four strings systematically co-occured with the location of the target in one of the four quarters of the matrix.

There were two different covariations between the subliminally exposed strings of characters and locations of the target (i.e., quarters of the matrix) employed in the experiment. They will be referred to as Covariations A and B. The covariations were different in that, in each covariation, the same string implied that the target was located in a different quarter of the matrix. These different quarters (paired with the same string in the two covariations) were never adjacent but always opposite. For example, in Covariation A, string "A235A" was associated with a target located in the upper left quarter, while in Covariation B, the same string was associated with a target located in the lower right quarter of the matrix.

There were two experimental conditions, AA and AB, which differed regarding which covariation was present in which part of the series of frames. Subjects in Condition AA were exposed to stimulus material that invariably included the Covariation A throughout the entire succession of 120 frames. Subjects in Condition AB were exposed to stimulus material that included the Covariation A in its first part (60 frames) and the Covariation B in the second part (remaining 60 frames).

It was expected that if Covariation A was nonconsciously processed in the first 60 trials and stored in memory in the form of an IPA, subjects in Condition AB (as compared to Condition AA) would show a deficit in their performance in the second 60 trials, since the IPA they had acquired in the first 60 trials (i.e., Covariation A) would misguide the search in the second 60 frames.

Subjects

Forty-eight undergraduates (men and women) participated voluntarily in the study.

Stimulus Material and Procedure

Subjects participated individually. Each subject was alone in a small lab room; all instructions were presented on a CRT screen.

Only one kind of frame was shown to the subjects in this experiment: It was a matrix (6 × 6) consisting of 36 digits, divided into quarters (see Figure 3.1). All possible digits were represented in the matrix more than once except for the target digit "6," which was represented only once in each matrix, replacing one of the elements of the matrix. However, to eliminate trials that would not require subjects to move their sight, the target never appeared in the foveal area—that is, in any of the 12 locations that were closest to subjects' fixation point in the middle of the matrix. These (impossible) locations of the target are marked with the line in Figure 3.1. Throughout the succession of frames the target was randomly located in different quarters and in different locations within the quarters. Exactly the same sequence of 120 locations of the target were shown in each condition. The conditions differed, however, regarding the sequence of subliminally exposed strings that accompanied the successive frames.

All stimuli were presented on a 12 in, fast decay CRT (refreshing cycle less than 1 ms) controlled by a computer that also registered subjects' responses and response times. The location of the chair was fixed, and when a subject sat straight in the chair the center of the CRT was about 55

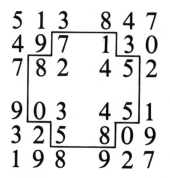

Figure 3.1   A basic frame exposed in Experiment 3.1.

cm distant from the subject's eyes. All characters were 4.5 mm high, and they appeared as black on a white background; the level of illumination of the white background was kept constant and equal to 4.0 lx. All instructions were shown on the CRT. Subjects were asked to use the index and middle fingers of their dominant hand and to respond as quickly and accurately as possible. They were also asked to focus their sight on the middle of the screen before the onset of each matrix; this was explained to be "a strategy leading to fastest responses."

Matrices were presented in the middle of the screen (i.e., the fixation point was also the middle of the matrix). Each matrix was preceded by a 100 ms warning tone. A subject's response, which consisted of pressing one of four buttons on a control box, terminated exposure of the matrix and triggered exposure of a mask that was an analogous matrix consisting of "X's" substituting for all digits of the original matrix. The mask remained on the screen for 500 ms. There were 500–1000 ms intervals between the end of the mask and onset of the next matrix, during which the display was blank. Their lengths were randomly generated, but their sequence was the same for all subjects. Approximately in the middle of each interval the crucial string of characters was subliminally exposed, and subjects could experience it as a very brief disturbance on the screen. The string was presented in the very middle of the CRT (subjects' fixation point) for 30 ms and was immediately masked by a string of five uppercase letters, "O" overprinted by uppercase "X's," that is, "⊗⊗⊗⊗⊗'s," which remained on the screen for 50 ms.

In the first 60 trials, subjects in both conditions were exposed to "covariation A." String A235A always preceded a frame in which the target was located in the upper left quarter of the matrix, String A358A always co-occurred with the target's location in the upper right quarter, String A582A with the lower right, and String A823A with the lower left quarter. On the next 60 trials, subjects in Condition AA were exposed to exactly the same covariation; subjects in Condition AB, however, were then exposed to the different covariation (Covariation B) which implied a new ("reversed") co-occurrence between the strings and locations of the target.

The entire succession of 120 trials was separated by three breaks, 10 s long each. Breaks occurred after the 30th, 60th and 90th trial. During the breaks, subjects were encouraged to take a deep breath and to relax.

Pilot Study

It seemed improbable that subjects were able to consciously recognize strings exposed for as brief as 30 ms followed by an immediate mask (Marcel, 1983a). An additional pilot study was conducted, however, to test for any potential idiosyncracies of the apparatus that could make the stimuli easier to recognize. Twenty-four subjects were informed that each "disturbance on the CRT" would be one of four strings with which they were provided, and were asked to indicate after each exposure which string it was. They were also encouraged and motivated to be accurate, and were informed that the stimuli were in fact recognizable "if one focuses all his or her attention on the task." All subjects said they were unable to recognize the stimuli and in fact none of them was accurate. Further, an additional pilot study indicated that subjects were unable to recognize whether the subliminally exposed stimulus was one of the crucial ones (i.e., "A + three digits + A"), five digits, or five letters.

Results and Discussion

Mean response latencies in the first and second 60 trials in each of two experimental conditions (AA and AB) are displayed in Figure 3.2. The means indicate a clear effect of training, since response latency decreased in both conditions. Consistent with expectations, however, this decrease was more pronounced in the AA as compared to the AB condition. A 2(Condition AA vs. Condition AB) × 2(first vs. second 60 trials) ANOVA with repeated measures on the second factor revealed a significant interaction between the two factors, $F (1,22) = 6.14$, $p < .025$.

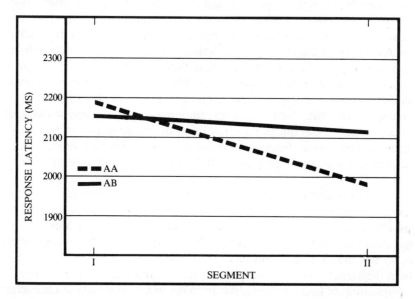

Figure 3.2 Mean response latency in two segments and two conditions (AA, AB) of Experiment 3.1.

These results suggest that during the first 60 trials subjects noncon-sciously processed Covariation A and that they stored it in the form of an IPA. In the second 60 trials, subjects in Condition AB apparently contin-ued to be guided by the IPA they had acquired during the first 60 trials, and, since it was inappropriate to the material that followed Covariation B, it produced the relative increase in response latency (i.e., lead to slower improvement in subjects' performance).

Experiment 3.2

The next experiment of the series was designed to test whether, consis-tent with the reasoning presented in Chapter 2, an IPA that has once been acquired and later rejected (disproved) is still preserved in memory in a form that makes the IPA easier for the subject to reactivate than to ac-quire a completely new IPA.

Additionally, the procedure was modified to make the entire learning situation more similar to the real-life conditions under which individuals acquire IPAs. The subliminal exposure paradigm employed in Experi-ment 3.1 has the virtue of conclusively demonstrating that the processes studied were not mediated by subjects' conscious awareness. Its major shortcoming, however, is that such stimulus material is very different from stimuli to which people are naturally exposed. The objection arises, therefore, that the paradigm represents an inadequate laboratory ana-logue of everyday situations (discussed in Chapters 1 and 2) in which perceivers, while consciously processing (serially) a stream of stimuli, are presumably not aware of the fact that they also process that stream of stimuli in terms of covariations. In real-life situations, perceivers may be perfectly aware of every detail of each consecutive item or episode of the stream. At the same time, however, they may not be aware of the "me-taknowledge" about the entire set of items or episodes (i.e., of the covari-ations among certain features of these items or episodes), nor about the fact that they are acquiring this "metaknowledge" and storing it in the form of IPAs.

In order to make experimental conditions more similar to real-life situa-tions, the covariation between type of frame (which was potentially ac-cessible to the subjects' conscious awareness) and target location was manipulated, and no subliminal stimuli were used in the following experi-ment. Instead, four different matrices (frames) were used, and in each of them the target was presented in a different quarter. In other words, the manipulation of four different, subliminally exposed strings of characters from Experiment 3.1 was substituted in this experiment with manipulation of four different frames. A number of methods, described below, were used to demonstrate that, while completing the search task, subjects do not pay attention to the features of frames nor do they make any comparisons between frames, but instead they focus entirely on the search for the target.

Method

Overview

The procedure was basically the same as in Experiment 3.1 except that the manipulation with subliminal stimuli was substituted by a manipulation with frames. The new design was developed in order to address the issue of reactivation of an IPA that had been previously acquired and then rejected. The entire succession of frames had 60 frames more than in Experiment 3.1; thus, there was a total of 180 frames, which were divided into three segments, 60 frames each. There were three experimental groups. The first group was exposed to the same covariation (Covariation A) in all three segments (Group AAA). The second group was exposed to the same covariation (A) in the first segment, but the group was exposed to a new ("opposite") covariation (B) in the second segment. In the third segment, this group was exposed again to Covariation A (Group ABA). A third group was exposed in the first segment to material that contained no covariation between the frames and locations of the target, and in the next two segments it was exposed to Covariations B and A, respectively (Group #BA).

Subjects

Seventy-two undergraduates (men and women) voluntarily participated in the study. Subjects were recruited in a way designed to minimize the probability that they knew each other, since it was important in the present experiment that subjects did not know the procedure before entering the lab room.

Stimulus Material and Procedure

The sequence of locations of the target was exactly the same in each of the three segments and in each of three conditions. The conditions differed only in the sequence of frames. Four different matrices (i.e., frames) were used in this experiment to provide the background in which subjects were to detect the target (i.e., the digit "6"). The four matrices were different with regard to the arrangement of digits. However, the four matrices (frames) were designed to be similar physically (e.g., if one contained more round digits, like 8, 9, or 0, and the other more dash digits, like 1, 4, or 7, the matrices could generate different images). Each of nine digits (except for "6," which was the target) was represented in each of the four matrices four times; thus, they differed exclusively in terms of the locations of the digits. The 12 locations constituting the foveal area were filled with exactly the same numbers in each of the four matrices (i.e., the middle of the matrix remained unchanged over the trials).

As in Experiment 3.1, the manipulated Covariations A and B, were *opposite;* that is, the same frame was associated with the location of the target in opposite (and not adjacent) quarters of the matrix in the two manipulated covariations.

The instructions, procedure, and timing of exposures were the same as in Experiment 3.1, except for more breaks, since the session was longer. As before, there was a 10-s long break after every 30 trials.

At the end of the session, subjects were comprehensively interviewed on the strategies they had employed and any possible cues in the stimulus material that they had attempted or tried to observe to facilitate their search. At the end of the interview subjects were informed that there was in fact "some systematic relation between the location of the target and some cues contained in the material," and they were encouraged to guess what it was. Forty percent of the subjects responded that they had no idea what it could be. All other subjects guessed that the relation in question involved somehow the sequence of locations of the target within the matrix. Again, 40% of these subjects had no more specific ideas. The remaining 60% (i.e., 36% of all subjects) had some more or less certain observations. These observations ranged from very simple ones, such as "Digit 6 very rarely appeared in the middle of the matrix, and it never appeared on the edge of the matrix twice in row, and always after some edge location it was located closer to the middle," to some more complicated ones, such "It seemed to me that often after three locations that followed a clockwise route (like upper left quarter, upper right, lower right), the next location was in the second of the previous three quarters (in this example, in upper right quarter)." None of the subjects mentioned the frames.

It also seemed important to ask subjects about how many different frames they saw. This question could not be included, however, in the interview, since either the above questions about "cues systematically related to locations of the target" would suggest to the subjects the correct answer to the question about number of different frames, or vice versa. Thus, this question was included in separate pilot studies.

Two pilot studies were completed prior to starting Experiment 3.2 and were designed to test whether subjects are able to pay conscious attention to and memorize specific frames while completing the search task. The first was a short, postexperimental interview with each of the participants in Experiment 3.1, completed directly after the experimental session. They were asked how many different matrices were presented in the course of the experiment (as mentioned before, there was in fact only one matrix presented in Experiment 3.1). To motivate the subjects, the question was introduced as a "test of perceptiveness." The results were quite clear. Subjects insisted that they were involved in the search task under time pressure, and that they paid no attention at all to the frames. They were then asked whether it was more likely that there was only one matrix presented in all trials, or more likely that there was a different matrix in each trial. Twenty percent of the subjects said that they were unable to discriminate these alternatives; 70% responded that it was more likely that each of the matrices was different; only 10% responded that it was more likely that there was only one.

The second pilot study (with 20 participants) involved a procedure identical to the one employed in Condition AAA of the original experiment except that after the session subjects were not interviewed on their strategies, but instead they were asked directly to state how many different matrices had been presented in the experiment. The question was again labeled "a test of perceptiveness." Again, it appeared that subjects had paid no attention to the frames and that they were unable to recall how many different ones they saw.

Results and Discussion

Mean response latencies in the three segments of the stimulus material in each of the three experimental conditions (AAA, ABA, and #BA) are displayed in Figure 3.3. The means indicate a clear effect of training since response latency decreased consistently over the segments in all conditions. However, there were also clear differences between the conditions in terms of the relative decrease of response latency as the different slopes for each segment indicate. The response latency data were analyzed by means of a 3(Condition) × 3(Segment) ANOVA with repeated measures on the second factor. There was an interaction between the factors revealed, indicating that the shapes of the curves differed reliably, $F(4, 138) = 4.00$, $p < .004$. In order to explore the nature of the interaction, a series of planned comparisons (contrasts) was performed on the

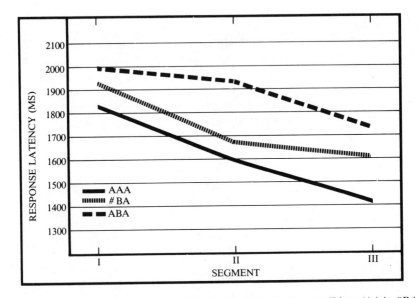

Figure 3.3 Mean response latency in three segments and three conditions (AAA, #BA, ABA) of Experiment 3.2.

data. Consistent with expectations, the decrease in response latency of Group ABA was attenuated in the second segment, as compared to Group AAA, $F(1, 69) = 7.67, p < .007$. Moreover, Group #BA, which was also exposed to Covariation B in the second segment, did not show such effect of attenuation, and this group made a reliably better improvement in response time between the first and the second segment than Group ABA, $F(1, 69) = 11.42, p < .002$.[1] Thus the attenuation effect was not produced by any specific difficulty of the material containing Covariation B as compared to A, but rather by the fact that Group ABA had already been exposed to and had acquired Covariation A in the first segment. These results are consistent with Experiment 3.1, and they indicate that subjects in this experimental paradigm nonconsciously processed the manipulated covariation between frames and locations of the target, and that, in turn, this covariation influenced subjects' behavior by guiding their search. It therefore may be concluded that the covariation was stored in form of an IPA.

A comparison of changes in subjects' performance between the second and the third segment also revealed predicted differences between the conditions. Especially important here is the comparison between Groups ABA and #BA: Both groups had to switch from Covariation B to A and differed solely in what they were able to acquire in the first segment (either Covariation A or nothing). As may be seen in Figure 3.3, the improvement of Group #BA, which was unfamiliar with Covariation A, was clearly attenuated, as compared to Group ABA, which improved much more, $F(1, 69) = 6.98, p < .009$. This attenuation was also significant as compared to Group AAA, $F(1, 69) = 3.88, p < .049$.

These results are consistent with the expectation that, even after rejecting a certain IPA because of its inconsistency with a sufficient amount of evidence and replacing it with a new one that fits reality better, the disproved algorithm is still preserved in memory in some passive form. When a sufficient amount of consistent evidence is encountered it is relatively easily reactivated. "Relatively easily" can be interpreted here as requiring less new evidence in order to be reactivated than is necessary for a completely new IPA to develop. This fact was well demonstrated in the comparison between ABA and #BA conditions: ABA subjects, who had acquired Covariation A in the first segment, later switched more easily from B to A in the third segment than #BA subjects, who in the third segment encountered (acquired) Covariation A for the first time.

The major question that arises at this point is whether subjects from Group ABA actually acquired during the second segment a working knowledge about Covariation B (i.e., IPA based on B). It might be argued that the behavior of subjects in Group ABA was a series of attempts to employ the already working IPA based on Covariation A. Such a possibility, which cannot be ruled out at this point, would undermine the hypothesis that passive knowledge about rejected IPAs is preserved in memory in at least two related ways. First, the IPA associated with Covariation A may actually never be abandoned, but it may instead be present and producing false attempts to locate the target according to Covariation A. Second, the working knowledge about Covariation B might never be acquired in this condition.

The next experiment was designed to test this possibility and to further explore the hypothesized long-term memory effects of acquired IPAs.

Experiment 3.3

The procedure employed in this experiment was basically the same as in Experiment 3.2; the design, however, was changed by increasing the number of groups and number of segments to allow for an analysis that would address the problem discussed above.

Additionally, the procedure was modified to explore the resistance of the IPAs acquired in the experiment to such distractors as subjects' involvement in some completely unrelated activity. The procedure employed in Experiment 3.2 kept the subjects almost constantly busy with the search task throughout the entire session. Thus, it might be argued

that these conditions helped in preserving in memory any IPAs related to
the current task and that any effects revealed in the experiment cannot be
interpreted in terms of long-term memory. Therefore, in the present experiment the breaks between the segments were made much longer, and
during the breaks subjects were involved in a completely new activity that
was very different from the search task.

Method

Overview and Stimulus Material

There were four segments of 60 trials each. There were also four experimental conditions. Three of these conditions were analogous to the conditions employed in Experiment 3.2, except that an additional segment was
added at the end. The segments could be defined, using the symbols
introduced in the previous two studies, as AAAA, ABAB, and #BAB.

There was also one additional condition, ACAB, which was introduced
mostly to examine the relationship between acquiring a new, and opposite, IPA and preserving in memory the disproved one. The design of this
condition must be discussed in more detail in order to present the idea of
the crucial test. This condition differed from the condition ABAB only in
the second segment, in which both of these groups encountered evidence
disproving Covariation A but at the same time consistent with some other
covariation (either B or C). Thus, subjects in these two conditions (ABAB
and ACAB) encountered the same amount and arrangement of evidence
consistent with Covariation A in the first and in the third segment and the
same amount of evidence inconsistent with that covariation in the second
segment. To ensure comparability between these two groups, Covariations B and C were related to Covariation A in exactly the same way.[2]

The crucial test for subjects' ability to switch from one IPA to another
and for their ability to reactivate in memory an IPA that had been once
acquired and then rejected was the comparison between these two groups
(ABAB and ACAB) regarding their performance in the fourth segment,
which was consistent with Covariation B. If subjects from Group ABAB
were better than those in Group ACAB, it would indicate that they had
acquired some working knowledge of Covariation B in the second segment and that they were able to reactivate that knowledge in the fourth
segment.

Subjects

Eighty-eight undergraduates participated voluntarily in the study. They
were recruited in the same way as in Experiment 3.2.

Procedure

In addition to the above difference in the number of segments, there were two other differences between the procedure of Experiments 3.2 and 3.3. The first pertained to the breaks; the second to the postexperimental interview.

In Experiment 3.3, there were breaks every 30 trials. The breaks in the middle of segments were 10-s long, as in Experiment 3.2. Every other break, however, consisted of a 10-s long break followed by a 2-min long task, which was introduced to the subjects as "a test of reflexes." A series of 20 flashes appeared either in the left or right part of the CRT; subjects were asked to react to the flashes as quickly as possible by pressing either the left or right button on a control box. These flashes served two purposes: They provided a distractor task for the present experiment, and they were also part of the procedure of a separate study that was completely unrelated to the present problem; these flashes were in fact subliminally exposed words. (The results from the "unrelated" study are presented in detail in Chapter 8 [Experiment 8.2]). At the beginning of each of these three "tests of reflexes" subjects were asked to read aloud the instructions exposed on the CRT. This procedure was designed to make the breaks longer and, additionally, to distract subjects from the search task.

At the end of the session subjects were interviewed as in Experiment 3.2. The responses were similar to those obtained in the previous study. Even the subjects in Condition AAAA did not notice the covariations. Most subjects did not attempt to employ any strategies, but rather they tried to concentrate on the search for the target. Those who thought that the locations of the target were not random, but rather followed some rule, focused exclusively on the sequence of locations.

The difference between this interview and the one from the previous study was that the subjects were also asked to recall and rate on a 6-point scale "how tired you felt" during each of the four quarters (segments) of the search task. The answer to this question was expected to reflect the difficulty subjects experienced in later segments.

Results and Discussion

Mean response latencies in the four segments of stimulus material in each of four experimental conditions (AAAA, ABAB, #BAB, and ACAB) are displayed in Figure 3.4. A 4×4(Condition $\times$ Segment) ANOVA with repeated measures on the second factor revealed an interaction between the factors, $F(9, 252) = 2.75, p < .005$, indicating that the

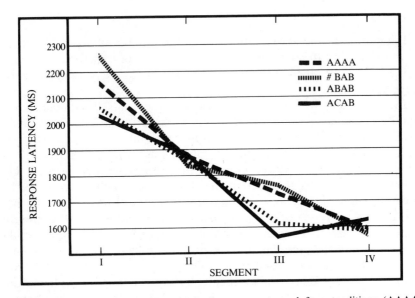

Figure 3.4 Mean response latency in four segments and four conditions (AAAA, #BAB, ABAB, ACAB) of Experiment 3.3.

groups differed in their improvements in performance over the segments. The means in the first three segments replicated the pattern revealed in Experiment 3.2, and the crucial differences between the conditions were reliable, as shown by a series of planned comparisons (contrasts). For example, the improvement between the first and the second segment was reliably attenuated in Conditions ABAB and ACAB, as compared to the remaining two groups, $F(1, 84) = 6.35$, $p < .013$, which indicates that subjects in these groups were misguided in their search during the second segment by the covariation A acquired in the first segment.

The comparison between the performance of subjects from Conditions ABAB and ACAB in the third–fourth segment was of special interest here, and it was found that, consistent with expectations, the improvement in response time of subjects in Condition ABAB was attenuated much less than in Condition ACAB, where subjects' performance even decreased. This decrease in performance may be seen in Figure 3.4. Planned comparison revealed that the performance of ACAB subjects decreased between segments three and four significantly more than the performance of ABAB subjects, $F(1, 84) = 4.24$, $p < .040$. This result seems to indicate that subjects in Condition ABAB, who in the first segment acquired an IPA consistent with Covariation A, were able to acquire some working knowledge about Covariation B in the second segment, and then, in the third segment, deactivated that knowledge and preserved it in memory until encountering some new material in the fourth segment, when they were able, in turn, to reactivate the IPA based on Covariation B and to allow it again to guide their behavior. This result provides strong support for the notion that people are able to switch flexibly from one IPA to another and preserve deactivated IPAs in long-term memory.

Subjects' ratings of how tired they felt in each quarter of the task revealed only one clear difference between groups. Subjects in Condition AAAA felt less tired in the last segment of the task than all three remaining groups, $t(86) = 2.40$, $p < .02$. This seems consistent with the manipulation, since in the last segment that group employed an IPA that was used nonstop for a longer time than the IPA employed in that segment by Groups #BAB, ABAB, or ACAB. It is probable, therefore, that while using such a well-developed (i.e., "strong," see Chapter 2) IPA, the task seemed less difficult to them, and thus they felt more relaxed.

Experiment 3.4

A final study using the same paradigm will be presented briefly. Its design was exactly the same as in Experiment 3.3: That is, there were four segments of the stimulus material and there were four experimental conditions (AAAA, #BAB, ABAB, & ACAB). There were two major differences between the two experiments, however.

First, only one frame was employed (as in the first study of the series—Experiment 3.1). Instead of manipulating four frames co-occurring with locations of the target, there were four pitch levels of the warning tone preceding presentation of each matrix. In a given covariation each of four pitch levels co-occurred consistently with the location of the target in one quarter of the matrix. The pitch levels were very close to each other (beginning with D, ending with E flat, with two intermediate tones at equally spaced pitch levels). A pilot study indicated that subjects were unable to consciously discover the crucial covariation.

A second major difference consisted of introducing one additional dependent variable. After the standard session, subjects were asked to perform a distractor task (5 min), after which they were presented with a succession of 12 frames that contained no target. The task was introduced to subjects as "a test of intuition." They were told that although it was invisible, the target was in fact "hidden" in each of the frames, and they were asked to indicate, by pushing a button on a control box, where they "intuitively suspect" the target to be located. In this case, they were not encouraged to respond quickly. Subjects were expected to follow the appropriate IPA, that is, to nonconsciously base their responses on pitch levels of the warning tone.

The results of the response latency session were consistent with Experiment 3.3, including the crucial difference between Conditions ABAB and ACAB, which indicated the long-term memory effect of the abandoned IPA. Moreover, the effects obtained seemed to be unrelated to subjects' ear for music. In a postexperimental questionnaire labeled "structure of abilities" subjects located themselves on six 4-point scales pertaining to various talents. "Ear for music" was one of them. The response latency effects obtained for subjects in the lower half of the distribution of all subjects regarding self-perceived "ear for music" ($N = 88$) were not less pronounced but were even somewhat stronger than in the remaining half.

The results of subjects' "guessing" were consistent with expectations. The means of responses consistent with Covariation A were as follows, Condition AAAA: 3.95, ABAB: 3.27, ACAB: 3.26, and #BAB: 2.35. A one-way ANOVA, performed on a number of responses consistent with Covariation A, revealed a significant main effect: $F(1, 86) = 2.78$, $p < .045$. A contrast analysis indicated that the mean accuracy in Group AAAA, which was expected to become best accustomed to employing an IPA based on Covariation A, was reliably higher than in the remaining groups, $F(1, 86) = 6.37$, $p < .013$. In addition, the mean accuracy in Group #BAB, which was expected to be less likely to acquire an IPA based on Covariation A, was reliably lower than in the remaining groups: $F(1, 86) = 4.69$, $p < .031$.

One part of the postexperimental interview was devoted to assessing the basis of subjects' "guesses" while responding to "the test of intuition." None of the subjects mentioned the pitch level of the warning tone. About half of the subjects responded that they had no specific intuitions and that they simply "guessed." The other half claimed to have some kind of "intuitions," but most of them were unable to verbalize anything more specific about the nature of their feelings. It seems possible that demand characteristics contributed to such a high percentage of subjects claiming to have "intuitions," since the test was labeled as "a test of intuition" (which was necessary to make the task meaningful to the subjects). No clear differences were found between these two groups of subjects regarding their accuracy (consistency of guesses with either Covariation A or B) or the experimental condition in which subjects had participated, although there was a tendency ($p < .12$) for subjects in Condition AAAA to claim that they had more intuitions than subjects in any other condition.

The results of the guessing task have demonstrated for the first time the influence of a nonconsciously acquired IPA on subsequent consciously controlled judgments, representing a step forward in demonstrating the important role of nonconscious processing of covariations in human cognition. It might be argued that the generalizability of the response latency effects obtained in the matrix scanning paradigm (i.e., generalizability of how an IPA influences one's performance in the search task) is confined to situations of time pressure, that is, to situations in which subjects had no time to think or make conscious decisions, and which, therefore, may facilitate the operation of nonconscious mechanisms. In the guessing task, however, subjects' judgments were not made under time pressure. Subjects were not encouraged to respond as fast as in the main search task, and, therefore, the judgment situation might be considered to some extent analogous to real-life situations in which judgments are made without relevant evidence accessible to one's conscious awareness.

Subjects' performance in the guessing task and their reports on the basis of their feelings indicated that, in some cases, when people make "random" decisions (e.g., whether to turn left or right, or which of two alternative driveways to take, etc.), these decisions may in fact not be random at all but may be determined by factors to which the decision maker has no access. Moreover, these factors may just not be incidental cues, but they may be stable dispositions (e.g., IPAs) that were acquired some time before.

Conclusions

The evidence obtained in the studies presented in this chapter indicates that, parallel[3] to consciously controlled serial processing of a stream of stimuli, people nonconsciously process these stimuli in terms of covariations between features or events. Nonconsciously processed covariation is stored in memory in a form that makes the covariation inaccessible to the perceiver's conscious awareness; he or she does not know what the covariation implies nor even whether it exists. However, the cognitive representation of the covariation is capable of influencing the perceiver's behavior by making the relevant cognitive operations (e.g., "decisions" as to where to start the search for a target) consistent with the covariation, independent of the perceiver's will. This is the type of cognitive representation of a covariation that is referred to as an IPA.

The evidence obtained also indicates that when an existing IPA proves to be inappropriate, it is abandoned and replaced by a new one based on the new evidence that has been found inconsistent with the abandoned IPA. The abandoned IPA is not forgotten completely, however. It is rather "deactivated" and preserved in long-term memory in a form that makes it neither accessible to one's conscious awareness nor capable of influencing one's behavior. If a sufficient amount of new evidence consistent with the deactivated IPA is found, the current IPA is abandoned and replaced by the formerly deactivated (but still preserved in memory) IPA. Such "reactivation" of an abandoned IPA requires less evidence than developing an entirely new IPA. This result supports the hypothesis about the mechanism by which conditional or higher order IPSs may develop.

The perceiver is not aware of the dynamics of the above processes; the perceiver does not know that he or she is switching from one IPA to another. Sometimes, however, he or she might experience some "externally observable" consequences of this dynamic, like an increase or decrease in level of performance. For example, in one of the experiments, subjects in one condition thought they were more tired than subjects in another condition.

It was also shown that such a nonconsciously acquired IPA is capable of nonconsciously influencing a perceiver's subsequent judgments generated in conditions of no time pressure. Subjects in these experiments thought that nothing concrete had determined their judgments (choices), while in fact their judgments depended on nonconsciously acquired IPAs.

The empirical question arises at this point as to the generalizability of these phenomena and their applicability to the processing of more complex information. It was hypothesized in Chapter 2 that the processes of nonconscious acquisition of IPAs contribute to the acquisition of various kinds of general knowledge, including most sophisticated meanings, concepts, and behavioral dispositions. This hypothesis is tested in Chapter 4.

Notes

1. Although subjects responded consistently to the manipulation by either increasing or attenuating their improvement, there were large individual differences among subjects in their initial response latency (i.e., baseline for any further changes). Moreover, it happened that subjects with different initial response latencies contributed unevenly to each of the experimental conditions. For example, there were 5 subjects among 72 tested whose mean response latency in the first 30 trials was higher than 2700 ms and as many as 4 of them were randomly assigned to condition ABA; the remaining one was found in Condition #BA, while none were found in Condition AAA. This uneven assignment of subjects to groups produced the overall differences between the groups, as visible in Figure 3.3. It was found, however, that there were no differences between subjects with longer and shorter initial response latency in the patterns of their reaction to the manipulation.

2. Covariations B and C were related to A in exactly the same way; that is, they were generated by exchanging the horizontal (B) or vertical (C) quarters connected with each frame in Covariation A. The relation between Covariation A and Covariations B and C is displayed in the following table. The four frames are labeled with Roman numerals and the quarters of the matrix, containing the target according to the respective covariation, are numbered clockwise starting with the upper left.

	Quarter of matrix paired with frame			
Covariations	I	II	III	IV
Covariation A	1	2	3	4
Covariation B	2	1	4	3
Covariation C	4	3	2	1

3. By stating that the process was "parallel," I do not assume that it was precisely simultaneous or synchronized with controlled processes. What I mean here is that subjects did not think that they had acquired any cognitive algorithms, while completing the task, although in fact they did acquire the respective IPA.

CHAPTER 4

Processing Covariations (II): Experiments Employing Social Stimulus Material*

Introduction

The experiments that are described in this chapter all used similar designs. First, subjects were presented with relatively complex (as compared to experiments presented in Chapter 3) stimulus material (verbal, pictorial, auditory, or some of their combinations) that included many features that potentially could be used for detecting covariations. Only very few of them, however, were correlated and these features were hidden in the stimulus material in a way designed to make conscious discovery of their co-occurrence as difficult as possible. For example, they were never located close to each other, they were never located in similar contexts, and so on.

After being exposed to such stimulus material, subjects were usually asked to complete some entirely unrelated task that was designed to interfere with any possible effects of short-term memory. After the distractor task, subjects completed dependent measures designed to test for the hypothesized effects of the covariation manipulated in the stimulus material.

The experimental design just outlined seems straightforward. Its application, however, requires several precautions. The first of these pertains to designing the specific stimulus material. The necessary condition it has to meet is that on the one hand the crucial covariation should be system-

* Portions of this chapter were adapted from Lewicki, 1982, in press.

atically present in the material, while on the other hand it should be undetectable to the subjects as far as their consciously controlled cognition is concerned. If at least some of the subjects consciously discover the systematic covariation, then its impact on a dependent measure (e.g., the use of the crucial covariation in subjects' subsequent perceptions) could be attributed to demand characteristics or some similar phenomenon. Thus, each version of the stimulus material has to pass a rigorous test of the potential detectability of its crucial aspects. Moreover, such a test should be performed not only under conditions identical to those in the experiment, but also under conditions in which subjects are encouraged and motivated to search for covariations. Even under the latter conditions, the crucial covariation should be undetectable.

Obviously, it was also important not to lead subjects in the experiment to suspect that the material constituted part of any memory or intelligence test, that it should be memorized, or that there was something "hidden" in the material that was to be "discovered." The reason is analogous to the one discussed in the context of why it is important to demonstrate the existence of nonconscious processing of convariations in the domain of social cognition (Chapter 2). Namely, if the nonconscious detection and processing of covariations actually has the hypothesized status of a basic and ubiquitous cognitive process, then it should operate even under conditions in which subjects are not asked to make any kind of inquiry into the material they are presented with (searching, comparing, etc.). Thus, it should operate even when perceivers are relaxed and have passive rather than active attitudes toward what they are exposed to.

Based on this reasoning, in almost all of the following experiments on processing covariations, considerable efforts were made to lead subjects to believe that the presentation of the (crucial) stimulus material was not the crucial part of the experiment, but instead that this was a kind of psychological training that was aimed at helping subjects to relax and to isolate them from what they were concerned with before the experiment. Different instructions were used only in the experiments designed to investigate the consequences of such analytical attitudes toward the stimulus material.

The dependent measures employed in the experiments had to be indirect because subjects were not expected to have any clear, conscious experiences concerning the manipulated covariations, and thus they could not be asked directly what they thought. Instead, subjects were put into a situation in which the hypothesized memory trace from the nonconsciously processed covariation should nonconsciously influence the subjects' performance (e.g., ratings assigned to some new stimulus material or processing times in response to certain questions).

Experiment 4.1

The stimulus material employed in this and in five subsequent studies consisted of a series of relatively long and comprehensive descriptions of persons containing mainly psychological characteristics. The descriptions permitted a manipulation of correlations between stimulus persons' characteristics in order to produce the desired patterns of interrelations. The total number of characteristics used and the arrangement of the descriptions made the crucial correlations not salient to the perceivers.

In the present experiment half of the subjects were exposed to descriptions in which the relationships between several traits disconfirmed stereotypic notions concerning these relationships (disconfirmation condition), while the other half was exposed to material that was consistent with the stereotype (confirmation condition). The results of this manipulation were assessed both from subjects' explicit estimates of trait relationships (which constituted one of the tests of the consciousness of the effects) as well as from ratings of new stimulus persons (fictitious and real).

It was hypothesized that if the new (i.e., disconfirming) information about the covariations was in fact processed, it would be capable of influencing the subjects' subsequent perceptions. It was not expected that the manipulation would entirely change the way in which the crucial traits were used by subjects in the impression formation processes. It was expected, however, that the manipulation would increase the number of "exceptions to the rules" in subjects' perception, that is, the number of instances in which an object is perceived (rated) as inconsistent with regard to the stereotypic notions concerning the relationship between the crucial traits. Such an effect would be due to modifications in the cognitive representations of concepts (traits) involved in the manipulated covariation, as hypothesized and discussed in Chapter 2. This modification would attenuate the existing IPA and would increase the likelihood of ratings that would be inconsistent with the previous contents of the representations (i.e., inconsistent with the stereotypic notions), without involving any effects on the level of subjects' consciousness.

It should be noted that this first experiment in the series was initially designed only as a kind of exploration of the method and as a means to test roughly what level of subjects' sensitivity to such "hidden" covariations could be counted on. Thus, the aspirations of this first experiment were merely to obtain *any* effect on subjects' ratings that could be produced by the structure of the co-occurrences of features in the stimulus material and that could not be mediated by conscious awareness. It was assumed that a "concentration" of disconfirmation cues in one group (disconfirmation condition) would be most likely to yield effects and that it was worthwhile to sacrifice in the first experiment the possibility to separate the effects of each of the manipulated trait relationships.

Method

Subjects and Design

All subjects who took part in pilot studies and the main study were students of introductory psychology (men and women) who participated for course credit. In addition to several pilot studies necessary for the construction of the stimulus material, there was one main pilot study with 62 subjects who participated only in the learning phase of the experiment (i.e., presentation of the stimulus material) and then had their memory for the crucial aspects of the material tested. In the main experiment 57 persons participated.

In both the main pilot study and the experiment, subjects were tested in groups of 12–15 persons, 2 in the disconfirmation condition and 2 in the confirmation condition. Assignment was random (separately by sex). There were no reliable differences on any dependent measures between session groups in the same condition at the .10 level.

Stimulus Material

The material consisted of narrative personality descriptions, each about 200 words long, of six stimulus persons. They referred to four young women and two men (more or less explicitly college students of about the same age as the subjects), all of them presented in a rather positive light.

Six trait dimensions were manipulated in the stimulus persons' descriptions: "active" or "passive," "demanding" or "not demanding," "warm" or "cold," "dependent" or "independent," "persistent" or "easily discouraged," and "having a lot of confidence in himself or herself" or "having no confidence in himself or herself." Subjects in the confirmation condition received personality descriptions in which stereotypic trait relationships appeared: All active stimulus persons were also described as demanding (and all passive persons as not demanding); warm persons were dependent (and cold persons were independent); and persistent persons had a lot of confidence in themselves (while easily discouraged had no confidence in themselves). In a pilot study it was revealed that the above-named pairs of traits were commonly assumed to be positively correlated and that their relationships were perceived as symmetric.[1]

Subjects in the disconfirmation condition received personality descriptions involving exactly the same six traits, except that the crucial trait pairs were negatively correlated across descriptions, that is, inconsistent with stereotypic relationships (e.g., all active persons were described as not demanding, warm persons were described as independent, etc.).

To mask the actual correlations between crucial traits, the location and order of those traits were systematically altered within the six stimulus persons. It was important to know what in particular in the stimulus material produced the hypothesized disconfirmation effects, and thus stimulus persons were constructed such that there were no correlations among traits across different crucial pairs. Similarly, the other characteristics of the stimulus persons were chosen as having no clear relationship to any of the crucial traits and therefore did not create additional confirmation or disconfirmation effects.

It was crucial for the present study that the only difference between the two versions of the stimulus material was the correlation across the descriptions between the manipulated trait dimensions, and not, say, realism, peculiarity, idiosyncracy, positivity, salience, or some other consciously recognizable characteristic of either a certain part or of all of the material. Therefore, the process of preparing the stimulus descriptions required an extensive pilot study involving several stages, in which subjects freely recalled each description, rated each description on several dimensions, evaluated parts or all of the material, and compared two respective versions of the same description. Subjects were also interviewed on their impressions when listening to the material. Subjects were usually able to recognize the difference when exposed to two versions of the same description, one after the other (e.g., that in the first version the person was characterized as persistent, while in the other as easily discouraged). There were, however, no systematic differences between the ratings of the general characteristics of the individuals described in the two versions when the versions were rated separately (i.e., one not following the other).

Procedure

The first part of the experiment was introduced to the subjects as a form of "psychological training or practice in forming impressions of people," that was "necessary for the second part of the experiment." The experimenter, blind to the nature of the manipulation, read the descriptions slowly. As compared to presenting text from a tape recorder, this method has the advantage of better attracting subjects' attention, and it was important for the present manipulation that not one word in the stimulus material be omitted or ignored. Subjects were asked to try to imagine the personalities of the persons described but not to relate these images to impressions of any real persons they knew. The experimenter also told subjects that they did not have to remember the descriptions because they would not be asked about anything connected with these descriptions.

Subjects then completed a 15-min distractor task designed to interfere with their short-term memory. In this task they were asked to prepare forms necessary for the next stage of the experiment. The experimenter talked to them throughout, explaining the process of preparing the forms in a particularly complicated way.

The subjects were then asked to rate six stimulus persons (defined by the experimenter) on 12 dimensions by choosing one word from a bipolar pair (e.g., active–passive). Six of these dimensions were those to which the manipulation was addressed—these ratings constituted a test of the effects of the manipulation on subsequent perception of other people. Each one of the stimulus persons was rated by the subject on a separate sheet of paper that was put into an envelope before starting the next one. This was done to prevent the ratings of one stimulus person from directly influencing subsequent ones and, therefore, to make conscious creation of consistency between ratings more difficult. The time sequence of all stages of the experiment was controlled and made identical for each session group.

The first three stimulus persons were fictitious, whereas the last three were real and known to the subject. It was hypothesized that the images of real, known stimulus persons would be more resistant to change than the images of fictitious ones.

The first two fictitious stimulus persons were presented to subjects as real persons by means of descriptions similar to those presented in the first stage of the experiment, although they were shorter (about 150 words each). These descriptions did not contain information referring directly to the dimensions that subjects had to rate. The third stimulus person was defined as "the average of your (i.e., subjects') closest social environment."

The next three stimulus persons were real and defined as follows: "A cold person I know," "Professor X from this university," and "myself" (subject).[2] It was not expected that the manipulation would modify subjects' stable images of well-known persons. It was hypothesized, however, that the manipulation may influence (presumably only temporarily) the contents of the crucial categories subjects use in their ratings, which, in turn, would affect the way in which these stable images are formulated.

After all ratings had been completed, subjects were asked (1) one "either/or" question directly about each of the manipulated three trait relationships (e.g., "People who are active are more likely to be (a) demanding, (b) not demanding") and (2) their estimation of how many times they had rated the stimulus person on two dimensions in a way that was inconsistent with the perceived relationship between traits. That is, if a subject had stated that "people who are active are more likely to be demanding," he or she was asked to estimate how many persons he or she described as both active and not demanding or passive and demanding.

An index of the inconsistency of the subject's rating with the common stereotype was computed for each of the three trait relationships and separately for each type of stimulus persons (fictitious and real) by the number of crucial trait pairs rated inconsistently with the empirically obtained stereotypic pattern.

Main Pilot Study

Presentation of the stimulus material in the main pilot study was the same as in the experiment. However, after presentation of the material, there was no distractor task, but instead subjects were told that, in the material they had just been exposed to, certain traits systematically co-occured across the six descriptions and that their task was to recall these consistent correlations.

More than half of the participants in both conditions reported that they were unable to recall any correlations, and not one person of the remaining ones (i.e., those who tried to point out some correlations) detected the crucial covariations.[3]

Results and Discussion

No differences were found between conditions with regard to the explicit statement of the crucial trait relationships. Only one subject in the disconfirmation condition and two in the confirmation condition failed to answer all three trait inference questions according to the pattern expected from the stereotypic notions. Each of those three subjects gave an atypical answer to only one question (which was different in each case). The groups were also nearly equal regarding their estimates of the consistency of their ratings and their explicit formulations of the trait relationships: Twenty-four subjects in the disconfirmation group (80%) and 22 in the confirmation group (81.4%) reported that all their ratings were completely consistent with the trait relationships they indicated. Out of the 11 who did not report total consistency, 10 subjects reported one inconsistency and only 1 subject reported two inconsistencies.[4]

However, a different picture emerges when we examine the actual trait ratings for the stimulus persons. Subjects in the disconfirmation condition made more inconsistent ratings ($M = 3.72$) than subjects in the confirmation condition ($M = 1.26$). The difference does not seem very high since the maximum possible number of inconsistent ratings was 18 (inconsistent ratings on each of three trait relationships for each of the six stimulus persons). However, the means follow the predicted pattern and are reliably different. An analysis of variance performed on the number of inconsistent ratings, treating experimental condition (confirmation vs. disconfirmation) as a between-subjects factor, and type of stimulus person (fictitious vs. real) and trait relationship (the three crucial trait pairs) as within-subjects factors, yielded a main effect for condition, $F (1,55) = 5.84$, $p < .05$. There were no reliable effects for trait dimension, $F = 1.59$, ns., type of stimulus person, $F = 2.21$, ns., or for any interaction among the factors. Planned comparisons revealed that the difference between confirmation and disconfirmation subjects in the number of inconsistencies was separately significant for both fictitious and real stimulus persons ($ps < .05$), and the difference between the number of inconsistent ratings for fictitious and real stimulus persons was far from being significant (even when the comparison was made exclusively for the disconfirmation condition).

The means indicate that in both the confirmation and disconfirmation conditions a great majority of subjects' ratings were consistent with the common stereotype of trait relationships; therefore the manipulation did not change the direction of the relationships completely, but it did increase the number of exceptions to the rules. One may suppose that the manipulation weakened the strength of those trait relationships.

The objection might arise that despite the attempt to make the two versions of the stimulus material equal regarding their reality, the descriptions of the stimulus persons for subjects from the disconfirmation group might have appeared less realistic or that it was more difficult to form impressions of those persons. This discrepancy could have weakened subjects' motivation to participate in the study and, therefore, decreased the strength of trait correlations because of more random responding. If this were the case, subjects from this group would give more random ratings for all the traits. To test this possibility, groups were compared with regard to trait relationships between those traits that were not part of the manipulation. No systematic differences were found between the confirmation and disconfirmation conditions. Thus, it appears that the manipulation was specific in that it influenced only the crucial trait relationships.

Although the lack of difference between confirmation and disconfirmation subjects with regard to explicit trait relationships cannot be seen as sufficient evidence for the same trait relationships in both conditions (this measure might not be sensitive enough to reveal such differences), subjects' estimates of the number of their own inconsistent ratings appears to be a better measure, since that scale was much more sensitive and subjects probably wanted to be accurate in their estimates. It may be concluded, then, that subjects in the disconfirmation condition thought that they made the same number of inconsistent ratings as subjects in the confirmation condition, when in fact they made more of them.

Some additional evidence suggests that the changes in perception among the disconfirmation subjects were not conscious. In the postexperimental interviews not a single subject reported recognizing any correlations among crucial traits in the stimulus descriptions. In addition, subjects were surprised when they learned about the nature of the manipulation and its hypothesized effects, and they were clearly surprised to find that they had made many more inconsistent ratings than they had estimated.

These results demonstrate that the covariations implicitly contained in the stimulus material influenced subjects' subsequent judgments without their awareness. It also appears that the crucial aspects of the stimulus material were not accessible to subjects' conscious awareness; thus the observed influence of the material was not mediated by consciousness. In fact, the results obtained appear clearer than was expected, especially with respect to trait specificity (i.e., only the manipulated trait relationships were influenced). Initially, the main purpose of this experiment was merely to test in the most general terms the appropriateness of this kind of stimulus material for studying the processing of covariations. That goal was accomplished, but the results also suggested subjects' highly specific sensitivity to the crucial aspects of the material. The results seem to indicate that what influenced subjects' perceptions of new stimulus persons was not a general effect of some inconsistency discovered in the descriptions they had been exposed to, but instead the specific disconfirmation of certain trait relationships.

The next experiment was aimed at replicating and extending the findings just stated.

Experiment 4.2

The same general paradigm was used in this experiment as in Experiment 4.1; there were, however, two major modifications. The first was that the descriptions of stimulus persons containing the crucial covariations were formulated mostly in terms of concrete (although typical) behaviors, rather than in terms of general traits as in Experiment 4.1. This concreteness made the manipulated covariations even more "hidden" than was the case in the study using explicit trait terms. In order to detect the covariation, subjects were required to perform at least one additional cognitive operation, namely, some kind of generalization of the concrete behaviors into general traits. Because the terms denoting the concrete behaviors were used in the stimulus material and the general traits were used in the dependent measures, there was no direct correspondence between the words used in the learning phase and those used in the testing phase.

The second modification was that only one covariation (i.e., the relationship between only two traits) was manipulated in the learning phase and that, in the testing phase, more than one trait dimension related to each of the two manipulated traits were used.

Method

Overview

The learning phase was very similar to the one employed in Experiment 4.1. Subjects were presented with narrative descriptions of six stimulus persons. There were two versions of the stimulus material that differed regarding the crucial covariation pertaining to extroversion–introversion and intelligence. One version presented intelligent introverts and not intelligent extroverts (Condition I), while the other presented intelligent extroverts and not intelligent introverts (Condition II).

After the distractor task, subjects rated 10 real persons they knew on 12 bipolar six-point dimensions; four of these dimensions were related to extroversion–introversion and 3 to intelligence. These ratings provided a measure of the crucial trait relationship in subjects' perception, which was hypothesized to be affected by the manipulation. It should be noted that the manipulation was not expected to modify subjects' images of well-known, real people (some of these images had developed over subjects' lifetimes). It was hypothesized, however, that subjects' memory representations of manipulated categories would be modified (probably temporarily), which, in turn, would affect the way of forming these, in fact stable, images.

Subjects

All subjects who took part in pilot studies and the main study were high school students of both sexes, about 18 years old. Fifty-two persons participated in the main study, they were tested in groups of 10–15 persons, two groups in the Condition I and two in the Condition II.

Six narrative personality descriptions were used, each about 200 words long. They were constructed in the same way as in Experiment 4.1, except that only one covariation was manipulated (between extroversion–introversion and intelligence) and that the descriptions were formulated mostly in terms of concrete events and typical behaviors instead of general traits, which were avoided. The description of each stimulus person contained between two and four facts relevant to each of the two crucial trait dimensions. For example, extroverts attended parties, had many friends, and talked a lot; intelligent people had no problems at school and had sophisticated hobbies. In order to make the covariations less salient, however, introversion–extroversion or intelligence were not salient characteristics of any description of a stimulus person. The intensity of these characteristics was never described as unusual, there were neither geniuses nor mentally retarded people among the stimulus persons described.

The stimulus material was tested as in the pilot studies conducted in Experiment 4.1, and similar results were obtained. Subjects were unable to discover consciously the crucial covariations.

It seems that the task of consciously discovering the covariations was even more difficult in the present study than in Experiment 4.1 since the descriptions contained only concrete behaviors that had to be generalized prior to discovering any co-occurrences. In other words, nothing co-occurred directly across the descriptions because the concrete facts were never the same. What actually co-occurred was not on the level of facts that were directly present in the material, but instead, it was on the level of inferences that had to be made by the subject.

The procedure resembled the one used in Experiment 4.1 up to the end of the distractor task. Then, subjects were asked to fill out rating forms, in which they rated 10 stimulus persons on 12 bipolar 6-point dimensions.

The form was a short version of the rating form used by Lewicki (1983). The stimulus persons were defined by general role definitions, and subjects were asked to choose real persons they knew who matched these definitions. There were seven definitions of positively evaluated persons (e.g., "My mother [the person who acted as mother]" or "My favorite teacher [professor]"), and three definitions of negatively evaluated stimulus persons (e.g., "The teacher [professor] I dislike most"). Four of 12 dimensions were relevant to extroversion–introversion (e.g., "Avoids people—Does not avoid people"), three of them were relevant to intelligence (e.g., "Doesn't have his or her own opinion—Has his or her own viewpoint"), the remaining five dimensions were irrelevant to the crucial traits. Completing the rating form required 120 judgments (10 stimulus persons times 12 dimensions), and took subjects about 25 min. Subjects received instructions to reduce the possible influence of social desirability on ratings: They filled out the forms anonymously, and they were not asked to return the part of the form on which they put down the names of described persons.

At the end of the session each subject was asked about "any co-occurrences between facts or characteristics" of the stimulus persons (presented in the learning phase) he or she had found or could recall. Not one person was accurate.

Results

In order to test whether subjects' ratings were affected by the covariation manipulated in the stimulus material, the summary index of the correlation between dimensions related to extroversion–introversion on the one hand and dimensions related to intelligence on the other hand was computed for each subject. The index was a product moment correlation between the mean ratings (of each stimulus person) on the three dimensions related to intelligence and the mean ratings on the four dimensions related to extroversion–introversion, computed across the 10 stimulus persons (separately in each subjects). The mean of this correlation (computed by means of an r to z transformation) for subjects in Condition I (who "learned" about intelligent introverts and not intelligent extroverts) was .30, indicating that introverts were rated as more intelligent than extroverts. The mean for subjects in Condition II (who "learned" the opposite) was .04. The difference was reliable, $t (50) = 2.69$, $p < .005$ (t was performed on rs transformed into zs).

In order to explore the nature of this difference of correlation coefficients, the groups were compared regarding mean ratings assigned to the positive and (separately) negative stimulus persons on each of 12 dimensions. It appeared that the only reliable differences obtained pertained to dimensions related to extroversion–introversion. Subjects in Condition I (who "learned" about intelligent introverts and about unintelligent extroverts), rated positive stimulus persons as more introverted and negative stimulus persons as more extroverted than subjects in Condition II (ps < .07).

Discussion

The results were consistent with expectations. The groups differed regarding the correlation between crucial traits, and this difference was consistent with the manipulation. The data suggested that there existed some preexperimental tendency in subjects to perceive intelligent people as introverts rather than extroverts (or introverted people as intelligent). This expectation was supported in reanalyses of similar (although larger: 25 × 20) rating forms used in three earlier studies (Lewicki, 1983). In these studies, the mean correlation between dimensions pertaining to extroversion–introversion and intelligence was .24.[5] It seems possible, therefore, that the manipulation—which was consistent with that hypothesized pre-experimental tendency in Condition I and inconsistent in condition II—strengthened the tendency in the former and attenuated the tendency in the latter. These are speculations only, however, since the results obtained with the extended rating forms (Lewicki, 1983) cannot conclusively substitute for the standard control group that was absent in the present experiment.

The data concerning mean ratings on dimensions shed some light on the nature of the obtained difference of crucial correlation. These data might suggest that the connotations of extroversion–introversion (i.e., some aspect of the cognitive representation of this category), rather than of intelligence, were affected by the manipulation, because subjects used this category differently to rate stimulus persons depending on the manipulation. According to this interpretation, after nonconsciously detecting several instances of introversion in the context of intelligence and of extroversion in the context of lack of intelligence (Condition I), subjects might implicitly learn something desirable about introversion and something undesirable about extrovertion (e.g., that it is not nice to talk a lot). This seems probable since intelligence is more clearly saturated with evaluation than extroversion–introversion (Rosenberg & Sedlak, 1972) and thus evaluations of intelligence may be more resistant to change. After such modification of evaluative connotations of introversion–extroversion, subjects were slightly more ready to assign introversion to persons they liked and to deny it to the disliked ones, due to evaluative consistency.

However, another possible explanation cannot be ruled out. Namely, it may be that what subjects implicitly learned was not the new connotations for either of the two trait dimensions but instead the mere fact that they covary.[6] Assuming that information about covariation (that is stored in semantic memory) is capable of influencing the relevant impressions a subject forms, the covariation implicitly learned from the stimulus material in the present experiment could make subjects rate stimulus persons consistent with the manipulation. This, in turn, could be accomplished only by modifying ratings assigned to stimulus persons on either one dimension (or both). Why only the ratings of extroversion–introversion were affected remains unclear; it is possible that this characteristic is perceived as less stable or important than intelligence, and this makes it more susceptible to change. However, these are speculations only.

The results of this study are certainly consistent with the notion that some covariations among features or events may be detected and that the covariations detected in this way may nonconsciously influence semantic memory. According to this interpretation, this influence has been assessed in the experiment from subjects' subsequent perceptions that were affected by representations of the relevant concepts (i.e., by semantic memory).

The effects observed in Experiments 4.1 and 4.2 seem to be in fact nonconscious. The previously stated reasoning about semantic memory, however, is open to the criticism that there is no clear evidence for the influence of concepts on the observed shifts in subjects' ratings of the new stimulus persons. It might be argued that in the experiment just described, the manipulation has created a more or less conscious, concrete image of a person, based on certain facts that one could learn from the stimulus descriptions. Such an image might be based mainly on a specific, individually most meaningful or salient stimulus description, and some aspects of that image might still be available[7] to the subjects when they are rating new stimulus persons, and those aspects might be more or less consciously projected onto the new images of persons rated. This hypothesized process, which does not involve changes in memory representations of concepts, could be sufficient to produce the systematic, although modest, effects obtained in the experiment (cf. Chapter 2, discussion of "abstract" vs. "exemplar" memory representations of IPAs).

In order to address more directly the issue of the process of nonconscious processing of covariation between certain features and its influence on memory representations of these features, the dependent measure in an experiment should involve making semantic judgments, rather than forming images of concrete stimuli.

Experiment 4.3

If the experiment is to demonstrate the nonconscious changes in concepts, one should not refer to the subject's explicit judgment (i.e., yes or no response) verifying a certain semantic statement, since such a measure would not be sensitive enough to capture the phenomenon, as suggested by the results of Experiment 4.1. On the other hand, however, enhancing the manipulation in order to obtain a stronger effect that would be visible in explicit semantic judgment would, in turn, make the crucial covariation easily noticeable to subjects. Their responses to the semantic statement would then depend directly on variables that are of no interest here, such as how subjects think they are supposed to react to the experimenter's "transparent" manipulation. The possible solution seems to be not to strengthen the manipulation (being, therefore, prepared not to find effects for explicit yes or no responses), but instead to measure response times in order to determine whether the manipulation affects processes underlying subjects' responses.

Prior to stating specific hypotheses, let us consider two theoretically different forms in which nonconscious detection of certain covariations among stimuli might affect semantic memory and three major models proposed for structural representation of object categories or traits.

Forms of Changes in Semantic Memory

The influence of nonconsciously detected covariation on semantic memory may take either of two hypothetical forms that are theoretically independent. The first of these forms is relevant to so-called "prestorage models" of semantic memory (Smith, 1978), according to which semantic memory contains ready to use information about relations between concepts (i.e., such information does not have to be generated or "computed" when necessary, but instead it already exists there and may be accessed). In the first of these hypothetical forms, information about the detected covariation between two stimuli x and y is incorporated into semantic memory without any direct modifications in the meaning of x and y. Regardless of the issue of how the stimulus categories x and y are structurally represented in semantic memory (discussed in the section entitled "Models of Structural Representation of Trait Categories"), detection of their covariation might be somehow integrated with the existing information concerning the x–y relationship. Eventually the relationship between x and y that results from all of the information included in semantic memory might be changed. It may either be strengthened or attenuated, depending on whether the detected covariation confirmed or disconfirmed the previously existing relationship. We shall refer to this form as the "covariation incorporation form."

The other possibility is relevant to "computational models" of semantic memory (Smith, 1978), according to which information about relationships between concepts is not constantly "present" in semantic memory, but instead it has to be computed when necessary, based on the contents of relevant representations. This hypothetical form assumes that a possible consequence of detecting covariation between categories x and y may be changes in the meaning of either one or both stimuli in the direction of making them more understandable or subjectively consistent with the context in which they were found. Such changes would, in turn, result in bringing the meaning of x and y closer. We shall refer to this form as the "meaning change form."

The two forms do not seem contradictory, and they might be complementary.

Models of Structural Representation of Trait Categories

The major models for representing trait categories will be discussed briefly in terms of their predictions concerning response time in the above outlined experimental conditions. We will assume the conditions to be analogous to those in Experiment 4.1. Subjects are exposed to the disconfirming covariation. In other words, subjects are presented with stimulus material in which x is negatively related to y. This disconfirming covariation is not consciously recognized by subjects, and their response to the question as to whether x is positively related to y is expected not to be affected by the manipulation and, therefore, to be "yes." The processing time, however, for generating this response is of interest here.

Featural Model. According to this model, trait categories are structurally represented by bundles of more basic semantic features (Rips, Shoben, & Smith, 1973; Smith, Schoben, & Rips, 1974). In order to verify a statement concerning the relationship between two categories, the relative amount of feature overlap is assessed. Processing time depends on a two-stage process. If the overlap is below one criterion level or above a second, the processing is terminated, and the response is given, "no" or "yes" respectively. If the overlap, however, falls between the levels, a second stage process is executed, and the response time is longer. The theory predicts that the greater the feature overlap, the faster the "yes" response is made.

The feature comparison model gives no means to discuss the "covariation incorporation form"; the model provides, however, clear expectations concerning the "meaning change form." Namely, detecting disconfirming covariation would modify bundles of features representing the x and y categories in the direction of decreasing the existing amount of feature overlap, and this, according to the model, would make the response, "yes," slower.[8] The same could be predicted from McCloskey and Glucksberg's (1979) version of the featural model.

Exemplar Scanning Model. Traits are represented in this model as sets of objects possessing certain characteristics (Walker, 1975). In order to verify a statement concerning the relationship between two traits, a sample of objects is examined in respect to trait co-occurrence. If a sufficient proportion of exemplars confirms the statement, a "yes" response is made.

Again, this model does not account for the hypothetical "covariation incorporation form"; it might, however, predict the direction of changes in response time for the "meaning change form." The model predicts that the length of time a person takes to verify a certain statement increases with the number of exemplars that have to be examined. It might be hypothesized, therefore, that changes in the meaning of either one or both of the traits (i.e., the sets of objects) induced by the detected disconfirming covariation would—in terms of the exemplar scanning model—result in defining the particular trait or traits by means of a set of objects that confirms the relationship to a lesser degree than was the case with the previous set defining that trait. This, in turn, would increase the number of exemplars that would have to be examined to give the response "yes," and thus would make that response slower.

Semantic Network Models.   In these models, object categories are interrelated by paths constituting a semantic net. The speed of processing a relationship between two traits depends on the accessibility of the path linking the two traits (Holyoak & Glass, 1975) and/or on the process by which the path is evaluated, for example, in terms of possible counterexamples or disconfirming superordinate connections (Collins & Loftus, 1975).

This class of models seems to provide room for both hypothetical forms by which a detected disconfirming covariation between x and y might influence the $x-y$ relationship existing in semantic memory. Information about such a covariation might be incorporated into a semantic network ("covariation incorporation form") by means of either making the existing pathway between the traits x and y weaker, or making the opposite connection stronger. Either one would result in increasing the overall processing time to give the response, "yes." Consequences of the "meaning change form" would be similar both structurally and in terms of processing time.

Each of the above classes of models proposed as structural representations of object categories leads to the expectation that if the detection of a covariation between traits x and y that disconfirms the existing $x-y$ relationship is to affect semantic memory, it should increase processing time for a "yes" response when verifying a semantic statement concerning the $x-y$ relationship. However, even without adhering strictly to any of the proposed models, the above expectation could be substantiated on a more general level. Assume that the detection of a disconfirming covariation between the traits x and y provides evidence that is contrary to the information existing in semantic memory. If the new evidence is not to be rejected immediately, but instead is to be included somehow in semantic memory, it will make the task of verifying the statement concerning the x–y relationship more ambiguous and more complicated, since such a task requires a decision based on either contradictory or weak evidence. This, in turn, will lead to increased processing time.

In the present experiment, subjects were provided with evidence that disconfirmed existing trait relationships. Namely, they were exposed to a set of stimulus persons in which x was correlated negatively with y. This disconfirming covariation was hypothesized, following the results of Experiments 4.1 and 4.2, to be nonconsciously processed by the subjects, to affect semantic information stored in their memory, and eventually to increase the length of time it took subjects to confirm the statement concerning a positive relationship between the traits x and y.

Method

Overview and Design

In this experiment subjects were exposed to stimulus material that was similar to that employed in Experiment 4.1, but this time each version disconfirmed one stereotypic trait relationship. Two trait relationships were manipulated in the experiment, and there were two versions of the stimulus material, that is, two experimental conditions. In each condition, one of those trait relationships disconfirmed and the other confirmed the stereotype. Thus, unlike in Experiment 4.1, the present design made it possible to separate the effects of the two manipulated covariations. There was no condition with two disconfirmed or two confirmed trait relationships. Following a distractor task, subjects verified statements concerning the manipulated trait relationships and their processing time was measured.

Subjects

Seventy-two undergraduates voluntarily participated in the experiment. They were recruited in a way designed to minimize the probability that the subjects knew each other, and therefore it may be expected that very few, if any, knew the procedure before entering the lab room. None of the subjects reported hearing anything about the experiment. Less than 5% of the people being asked to participate refused for any of a variety of reasons. Subjects were randomly assigned to two experimental conditions separately by sex.

The stimulus material was adapted from Experiment 4.1. The same six descriptions of stimulus persons were used, each about 200 words long, but they were modified regarding the crucial trait relationships and the entire material was tested again in a series of pilot studies, the same as in Experiment 4.1.

Two relationships between trait dimensions were manipulated: the relationship between active–passive and demanding–not demanding, and that between persistent–easily discouraged and self-confident–not self-confident. The third trait relationship manipulated in Experiment 4.1 was confirmed in both versions. Subjects in one experimental condition (Condition I) received a version of this material in which the former trait relationship confirmed the stereotype and the latter disconfirmed the stereotype. That is, all active stimulus persons were also described as demanding, while passive stimulus persons were not demanding. On the other hand, all persistent stimulus persons were described as not self-confident while all those who were easily discouraged were self-confident. Subjects in the other experimental condition (Condition II) received exactly the same six personality descriptions, except that the former trait relationship disconfirmed the stereotype and the latter confirmed the stereotype. In that version, all active stimulus persons were described as not demanding and all passive persons as demanding, and persistent persons were self-confident while the easily discouraged were not self-confident. The location and order of these traits were systematically altered across the six stimulus persons, but the two pertaining to the manipulated trait relationships were never located close to one another. Subjects in a pilot study were unable to recognize the correlations. The stimulus descriptions were constructed so that there were no correlations among traits in different crucial pairs. Similarly, the other characteristics of the stimulus persons were chosen so as to have no clear relationship to any of the manipulated traits; they therefore did not create additional confirmation or disconfirmation effects.

The process of testing these stimulus descriptions regarding the equivalence of the two versions included the same set of pilot studies as described in the context of Experiment 4.1.

Procedure and Apparatus

Subjects participated individually. The first part of the experiment was introduced to the subjects as a form of psychological training or practice in forming impressions of people. The experimenter, blind to the nature of the manipulation, read the descriptions. The subject was asked to try to imagine the personalities of the persons described, but not to relate these images to impressions of any real persons he or she knew. The experimenter also told subjects that they did not have to remember the descriptions because they would not be asked about anything connected with these descriptions. Subjects then completed a 15-min distractor task, the same as in Experiment 4.1, designed to interfere with their short-term memory.

Following the distractor task it was explained to the subject that he or she would be asked to verify general statements of the form: "X people are usually y." It was also explained that the answer "yes" would mean that the sentence being verified was closer to the truth than the opposite sentence (i.e., "X people are usually *not-y*" or "*Not-x* people are usually y"), and that the answer "no" would mean that the opposite would be closer to the truth. Subjects were asked to decide as quickly, yet accurately, as possible. The sentences were projected with a programmed projection tachistoscope onto a translucent sheet of acrylic in front of the subject. The onset of the slide, by means of an electronic shutter, triggered a microprocessor timer accurate to the nearest millisecond. Measurement of the response time ended either when the subject pressed one of two keys ("yes" or "no") on a control box or when a 10-s maximum had been reached. The timer registered subjects' yes or no responses and response times. There was a 3-s interval between the presentations, during which the display was blank.

Each subject verified five statements. The third and the fifth were the crucial ones: "Active people are usually demanding" (C) and "Persistent people are usually self-confident" (E), and they were counterbalanced for order. The first and the second presentations were mostly for the purpose of practice; the fourth was aimed at separating the crucial statements. Those three statements were separately counterbalanced for order, and they read: "Intelligent people are usually industrious" (A), "Sincere people are usually trusting" (B), and "Brave people are usually popular" (D).

Each subject was then interviewed as to whether he or she had recognized any systematic relationships among traits in the stimulus material and was then thanked for his or her participation. Sixty-six subjects (92%) reported not having recognized any systematic relationships. Six subjects claimed to have recognized some correlation, but no one did it accurately; that is no one was able to point out the traits that were actually correlated across the descriptions.

Results

The results of this experiment could not be analyzed by means of a repeated measures ANOVA, since there were considerable differences between trait relationships regarding which subjects and what number of subjects responded "yes" and "no." Therefore, the response time for each statement had to be analyzed separately. Two subjects who were unable to meet the requirement of responding within the 10-s limit were excluded from the analyses.

Separate V^2 [9] analyses completed for each of the five statements revealed no differences (significant at the .05 level) between the conditions, with regard to the frequency of "yes" or "no" responses. As shown in Table 4.1, a majority of subjects responded "yes" to each statement, including the two crucial ones, which was consistent with the common stereotype.

Response times were then analyzed, separately for "yes" and "no" responses. No response time differences significant at the .05 level were found between the conditions for any of the three nonmanipulated trait relationships: Statements A, B, and D (see Figure 4.1). Reliable response time differences were found only for the manipulated trait relationships. The response "yes" to the statement "Active people are usually demanding" (Statement C in Figure 4.1) required a longer time for subjects in the condition exposed to material disconfirming that statement (Condition II) as compared with subjects exposed to the material confirming that statement (Condition I); t (52) = 2.63, $p < .005$. The response, "yes," to the other manipulated statement, "Persistent people are usually self-confident" (Statement E in Figure 4.1), again required more time for subjects exposed to the material disconfirming that statement (Condition I) than for subjects exposed to the material that confirmed the statement (Condition II); t (50) = 2.75, $p < .005$. These results are consistent with the hypothesis that "yes" response times would be longer after exposure to disconfirming material.

A surprisingly high rate of "no" responses was obtained, which were never present in the pilot study (see Note 1) or in Experiment 4.1. It seems possible that those responses resulted mostly from subjects' disorientation and inability to cope with the time pressure created by the conditions of this experiment.[10] It also might have been due in part to the subjects' assumption that both "yes" and "no" responses would be required in their task.

Table 4.1

Frequency of "Yes" Responses to Each of Five Statements
in Experiment 4.3

Experimental condition	Statement				
	A	B	C	D	E
I	23(66%)	26(74%)	27(77%)	22(62%)	28(80%)
II	20(57%)	29(83%)	27(77%)	27(77%)	24(69%)

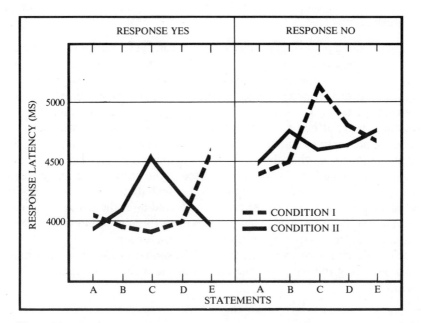

Figure 4.1   Mean response time for the five statements in two experimental conditions of Experiment 4.3. Note that the order of statements presented in the figure does not reflect exactly the actual order in which the statements were presented to the subjects, since both the crucial statements (C and E) and the noncrucial ones (A, B, and D) were separately counterbalanced for order.

There were no hypotheses concerning processing time for the "no" response. It appeared, however, that among subjects who decided to answer "no" in response to the statement "Active people are usually demanding" (Statement C in Figure 4.1), those in the group exposed to material disconfirming that statement ($N = 8$) responded faster than did those in the group exposed to the confirming material ($N = 8$), $t(14) = 2.33, p < .05$ (two-tailed test). There was, however, no analogous significant difference for the other crucial statement (see Figure 4.1, Statement E), $t(16) = .18$, ns.

Close examination of reaction time (RT) patterns in individual subjects revealed large individual differences in subjects' susceptibility to the manipulation. Some subjects had RT patterns conforming perfectly to the predictions, while others had completely undifferentiated patterns of RT. These differences may have been due to unspecific factors like motivation to participate in the study, fatigue, or ability to focus attention on the stimulus material throughout the entire learning phase. They could also be due, however, to the initial, individually differentiated, status of subjects' perceptions of the manipulated covariations. (This possibility is explored in Experiment 4.6.)

Discussion

The obtained pattern of processing times for "yes" responses conforms exactly to the predictions and is consistent with the hypothesis that the semantic information contained in the stimulus material has been processed and has affected subjects' memory representations of relevant concepts. However, exactly what kind of information contained in the stimulus material had been detected and to what extent it was nonconsciously processed remains unclear. More sensitive measures than the ones employed of what the subjects consciously detected and what and when they remembered could not be used in the above experiment. Such testing, if administered first, could have affected subjects' responses to the main dependent measures, and, if collected after the dependent measures, could have been affected by responses to them or could be simply too late (i.e., too distant from the stimulus material).

The following two experiments were designed in order to determine more precisely the nature of the effects of the manipulation on subjects' memory.

Experiment 4.4

This experiment was aimed at exploring subjects' memory for the stimulus material at the moment analogous to the one in which the subjects in Experiment 4.3 completed the dependent measures. In order to maximize the chance of discovering that subjects were consciously aware of some of the crucial features of the stimulus material, subjects were exposed to specific forced-choice questions about the crucial traits, rather than to open-ended questions. The questions were labeled as a "memory test" in order to additionally motivate subjects to give their best answers.

It is possible that the effects obtained in Experiment 4.3 were due to the fact that the crucial traits in the stimulus material were actually consciously recalled by subjects in response to the task of verifying a general statement concerning those traits, but the traits were recalled not as they had covaried in the material but instead as they had been assigned to a particular one-stimulus person (e.g., the one subjectively most salient). Such a kind of recall might subsequently affect subjects' responses due to the availability heuristic (Kahneman & Tversky, 1973) or some similar phenomenon. In order to test such a possibility, in the present experiment subjects were asked not for the covariation between the two traits across the stimulus descriptions, but instead for the two traits in at least one stimulus person (the one they could recall).

Method

Subjects

Forty-eight undergraduates participated in the study. They were recruited from various parts of the campus in order to minimize the probability that subjects knew each other, since it was even more important in the present experiment than in Experiment 4.3 that subjects did not know the procedure before entering the lab room.

Procedure

The procedure up to the final assessment of the dependent variable was similar to the one employed in Experiment 4.3 except that the lab room was different and there was no reaction time apparatus. The initial instructions were the same, the stimulus material was presented by the same experimenter, and the same distractor task was employed. Then, however, subjects were asked whether they were willing to answer two questions concerning the stimulus descriptions. It was briefly explained that some people are able to memorize material even when they are not trying to and that the study was concerned with just that kind of memory. It was further explained that this was why the subjects had initially received the instruction not to memorize the descriptions and were informed that they would not subsequently be questioned on the material. Subjects seemed to accept this explanation, and each of them agreed to participate in the memory test.

Each of the two questions asked had the same format: "I am interested only in one specific aspect of the descriptions, namely in traits x and y. Do you remember how those traits were assigned to at least one of the stimulus persons, that is, whether the person was x and whether the person was y?" (x and y were the elements of one of the crucial trait pairs). If the subject was unable to answer (which happened in the majority of cases), he or she was asked to concentrate and try again, and if that did not help, to guess.

Subjects then received the question concerning the second crucial trait pair, formatted in the same way. The two questions were counterbalanced for order. Finally, subjects were briefly interviewed as to their feelings while answering the questions and then thanked for their participation.

Results and Discussion

Each response was coded as either consistent or inconsistent with the common stereotype concerning the given two traits. If subjects remem-

Table 4.2

Frequency of Consistent and Inconsistent Responses in Experiment 4.4

| Experimental condition | Question | | | |
| | C | | E | |
	Consistent	Inconsistent	Consistent	Inconsistent
I	17	7	17	7
II	17	7	16	8

bered the stimulus descriptions well, in Condition I they should provide consistent answers to Question C (active–demanding) and inconsistent answers to Question E (persistent–self-confident), while in Condition II their responses should be reversed. The frequencies obtained for both types of answers are presented in Table 4.2. Those results show a very clear tendency for subjects to respond consistently with the stereotype in both conditions. However, there are no differences between the conditions (Question C: $V^2 = .00$, ns., and Question E: $V^2 = .10$, ns.). There were also no effects of the order in which the questions were asked. Thus, it may be concluded that there is no evidence that subjects were aware of the crucial aspects of the stimulus material at the moment analogous to the one in which the dependent measures were taken in Experiment 4.3.

Most subjects reported difficulty in recalling the stimulus descriptions, and some of them felt it was due mostly to the fact that the stimulus persons had been numerous and different (e.g., some of them were active and some of them were passive) and that the descriptions were "confounded" in their memories. Subjects' feelings stimulated the idea of conducting an experiment in which subjects' memory at consecutive stages of listening to the stimulus material could be reconstructed.

Experiment 4.5

It is still probable that subjects were momentarily aware of some crucial aspects of the stimulus material while being exposed to it and that they had some consciously registered reflections relevant to those crucial aspects. Those reflections might be difficult to access after completing the distractor task. In the present experiment, therefore, subjects in different groups were questioned at different stages of listening to the material, that is, after listening to the first, second, third, fourth, fifth, or sixth stimulus description. The general purpose was to capture momentary awareness effects and to determine what precisely subjects have memorized at those different stages, as far as the crucial trait pairs are concerned.

Method

Subjects

One hundred twenty-four undergraduates participated in the study. They were recruited in the same way as in Experiment 4.4, and they were randomly assigned to 12 experimental conditions (i.e., 2 versions of the stimulus material × 6 levels of the number of stimulus descriptions presented).

Procedure

The procedure was similar to the one employed in Experiment 4.4 with the following differences. Subjects were tested by five different experimenters (all of them were female undergraduates). Each of them contributed about equally to each of the experimental conditions (and there were no experimenter effects on the dependent measures). There was no distractor task separating the presentation of the stimulus material and the "memory test." Approximately one-sixth of the subjects were presented with one stimulus person description, one-sixth were presented with two versions, and so on, up to six. After hearing all of the descriptions he or she was to hear, the subject was questioned in the same way as in Experiment 4.4. Then each subject, except for those who were presented with only one or two stimulus descriptions, was asked whether "you have noticed any co-occurrence between the traits x and y, across the descriptions presented." There were two such questions (one for each of the crucial trait pairs), and they were counterbalanced for order.

In order to avoid some artifact connected with the experimenters' becoming gradually more experienced (or possibly more tired) in presenting the stimulus material, the order of testing subjects from each of the 12 experimental groups was separately randomized for each experimenter.

Results

Responses to the first two questions, having to do with recall of the crucial traits in at least one stimulus description, are presented in Table 4.3. These were the same questions as in Experiment 4.4, and the responses were coded and analyzed in the same way. In response to Question C, there was a tendency for subjects to provide consistent answers

Table 4.3

Frequencies of Consistent and Inconsistent Responses in Experiment 4.5

Question–Condition	Number of stimulus descriptions presented											
	1		2		3		4		5		6	
	C^a	I^b	C	I	C	I	C	I	C	I	C	I
Question C												
I	8	2	10	1	9	1	8	2	10	1	7	2
II	7	4	6	6	6	4	7	3	7	2	6	5
Question E												
I	4	6	4	7	4	6	10	1	7	4	7	3
II	9	2	9	3	10	0	7	2	7	2	7	3

[a] C = Consistent response.
[b] I = Inconsistent response.

for each of the six groups that had been exposed to different numbers of stimulus descriptions. However, this tendency was also more pronounced in Condition I than in Condition II in each of the six groups, which indicates an effect of accurate recall. That is, in each group there is a higher frequency of consistent responses (see Table 4.3, Columns C) in Condition I than in Condition II, and a higher frequency of inconsistent responses (see Table 4.3, Columns I) in Condition II than in Condition I. This effect is not significant within the subgroups with different numbers of descriptions when each is analyzed separately. However, when the number of observations is increased by aggregating groups, the effect approaches significance. For the groups with one and two presentations taken together, $V^2 = 3.13$. $p < .08$; for the group with three and four presentations $V^2 = 1.17$, ns.; for the group with five and six presentations $V^2 = 1.17$, ns. In the aggregated group with one, two, and three presentations $V^2 = 5.42$, $p < .02$; in the remaining group (with four, five, and six presentations) $V^2 = 1.39$, ns. Those comparisons indicate an effect of the manipulation; that is, there was a tendency to recall accurately the crucial aspects of the stimulus descriptions. This effect, however, was present only in the groups exposed to one, two, or three stimulus descriptions and disappeared while listening to the subsequent three descriptions.

The responses to Question E revealed an analogous pattern (i.e., the opposite pattern to the one revealed for Question C) for each of the first 3 groups, that is, for the group with one, two, and three stimulus descriptions (see Table 4.3). The pattern of responses in the three remaining groups is less clear. Aggregated frequencies indicate the effects of accurate recall. For the group with one and two presentations $V^2 = 5.62$, $p <$ .018; for the group with three and four presentations $V^2 = 1.76$, ns.; for the group with five and six presentations $V^2 = .02$, ns. In the aggregated group with one, two, and three presentations $V^2 = 12.42$, $p < .001$; in the remaining group (with four, five, and six presentations) $V^2 = .09$, ns. The results of these comparisons replicate those obtained for Question C. The effect of accurate recall was again present only in the groups exposed to one, two, or three stimulus descriptions and disappeared in the remaining groups.

Responses to the two questions concerning perceived covariation did not reveal any systematic differences between conditions in either the four separate groups (i.e., with three, four, five, and six presentations) nor for the aggregated groups. The patterns were similar to the one obtained in Experiment 4.4, and they indicated the same strong tendency to respond consistently with the common stereotype.

Discussion

Assuming that this experiment has provided an adequate reconstruction of subjects' memory concerning the crucial aspects of the material in the course of listening to the stimulus descriptions, it might be concluded that subjects were initially consciously aware of the co-occurrence of the crucial traits in single descriptions, or at least that they were able to recall them when questioned. This awareness or ability to recall, however, has subsequently been clearly attenuated or has even disappeared as the number of stimulus descriptions increased.

This apparently paradoxical effect seems to indicate that subjects did not compare subsequent stimulus descriptions with earlier ones in terms of the co-occurrence of traits, since if they were doing something like that, their responses to the questions would become more and not less accurate as the number of stimulus descriptions increased. The observed decrease in the accuracy of the subjects' responses might be due to the fact that what they actually recalled was not a generalization based on the entire set of stimulus materials, but was instead an image of a certain individual stimulus person (probably in most cases the first one). This one image, if not related to the others, may have become less salient and more difficult to recall as the number of additional images increased. Those other images could simply work as distractors. However, the simplest explanation—that the subjects became gradually more tired and less careful listeners—also cannot be excluded.

The above interpretation, which assumes that subjects were not comparing the co-occurrence of traits across descriptions, is consistent with the finding that subjects' responses to the explicit questions concerning covariation between the crucial traits across the descriptions were the same for the two conditions, that is, inaccurate, and based mostly on common stereotypes.

It was striking that subjects were so poor in their ability to recall the stimulus descriptions. In almost all groups, even in the group presented with only one stimulus description, the tendency to respond consistently with the common stereotype appeared to be stronger than the tendency to respond accurately (see Table 4.3). This indicates that subjects were not certain about their specific memories and preferred to base their responses on either their private theories of which traits should go together or on their general impressions of a certain stimulus person, which could be in some respects more consistent with such theories than with the facts.

One possible reason for this pattern of results may be found in the specific formulation of the instructions. Namely, the learning phase of the experiment was introduced to subjects as a "psychological training." It was promised that they would not be questioned on anything connected with the descriptions and were told not to memorize them. Instead, they were asked to try to imagine the persons described. Such an instruction might make the subjects more creative thinkers but also less careful listeners, and eventually it might shift subjects' impressions in the direction of being more subjectively consistent but more distant from some facts (e.g., those inconsistent with the stereotype).

In order to test this explanation, 16 new subjects were presented with exactly the same instruction, except that two sentences were deleted. In one, subjects had been asked not to memorize the descriptions and in the second, it had been promised that they would not be asked about anything connected with the descriptions. Thus, these subjects were in the same conditions as were the subjects in Experiments 4.3, 4.4, and 4.5, except that they could suspect some memory test or at least the necessity to utilize the facts contained in the descriptions. Following this instruction, the subjects were presented with only one stimulus description (8 subjects with Version I and 8 subjects with Version II), and then they were asked to recall the crucial trait pairs. Not one subject responded inaccurately. This result may be helpful in understanding subjects' inability to recall the material in Experiments 4.3, 4.4, and 4.5, and their being not consciously aware of the trait covariations it contained. Subjects were simply not set to memorize the details (a different instruction would make them do so), and their conscious images of the stimulus descriptions were biased by the common stereotypes.

General Discussion

In Experiment 4.3, it was demonstrated that after being exposed to stimulus material containing certain systematic covariations among traits, subjects showed the predicted reaction time effects while verifying semantic statements concerning those trait relationships. The effects indicated that subjects processed information about covariation and developed relevant IPAs. The results of Experiment 4.4, in which subjects were motivated to report the crucial aspects of the stimulus material, failed to demonstrate that subjects were consciously aware of those aspects of the material that actually affected their response times. In Experiment 4.5, an attempt was made to reconstruct the effects on subjects' momentary awareness while listening to the stimulus material. It appeared that subjects were aware of the co-occurrence of traits in single stimulus descriptions, or at least were momentarily able to recall them when questioned. This awareness or recall ability, however, was present only at the beginning of the stimulus material and subsequently disappeared. The results also suggested that while listening to the stimulus material subjects were neither comparing nor relating earlier to subsequent stimulus descriptions but instead were trying to imagine separate stimulus persons. Additional analysis suggested that subjects were not trying to memorize the facts contained in the description of a stimulus person but instead were trying to form a general impression. Since the procedures used in Experiments 4.4 and 4.5 seemed to encourage subjects to report what they had remembered and seemed to motivate them to do so, it appears that subjects were neither momentarily (while listening to the material) nor subsequently aware of the covariations between traits.

Proving the nonconsciousness of a certain cognitive process is always a very difficult task, since it requires demonstrating that something does not exist. From a formal viewpoint, the conclusive demonstration of nonexistence is never possible, and it always might be argued that some small degree of consciousness actually existed but that the procedure was not sensitive enough to capture it. The only possible way seems to be to provide the subjects with the best possible conditions in which to recall and report whatever they have noticed that is crucial in the stimulus material, and Experiments 4.4 and 4.5 apparently have met those conditions.

This set of findings indicates that subjects nonconsciously processed covariation contained in the stimulus material and the cognitive representation of that covariation was capable of specifically influencing subjects' cognitive processes for at least 15 min after the covariation had been processed and stored.

Experiment 4.6

It was suggested in the discussion of Experiment 4.3 (in which RT effects of manipulated covariation were obtained) that the large individual differences in subjects' susceptibility to the manipulation could be due to the apparently individually differentiated initial status of the covariation manipulated. Subjects may have been more or less ready dispositionally (i.e., independent of the manipulation) to affirm a statement that two particular traits covary. Two theoretically independent reasons for these individual differences can be taken into account.

The first refers to the *functional* or working relationship between the two traits. In other words, the degree to which a given pair of trait categories (relevant to the manipulated covariation) was initially interrelated in a subject's semantic memory might reflect either the preexisiting relation between the cognitive representations of the two concepts (according to the *prestorage models* of semantic memory, Smith, 1978), or the similarity of the contents of the two representations (*computational models*). This issue could be explored by determining how subjects understand the two concepts (i.e., the trait dimensions) in question. However, it is possible that subjects would have insufficient insight into their "working" understanding of the two concepts or that it would be difficult for subjects to formulate the mechanisms by which they came to understand these concepts; moreover, such explanations would be open to various response sets or other artifacts. Therefore, some indirect measure of how the two concepts work in perception might be more appropriate. Such a measure could be derived from the structure of the subject's perception, for example, correlations between trait ratings assigned by the subject to some stimulus persons (Lewicki, 1983).

The second reason operates exclusively on the level of declarations, and it reflects a subject's dispositional readiness to affirm a statement that two traits are related that is not accounted for by the reasons included in a "working" relation between the two traits. Factors such as stereotypes, perceived logical relations (i.e., perceived necessary conditions or consequences), and social desirability (i.e., motivation to satisfy the suspected demands of the experimenter) may contribute to subjects' readiness to affirm a certain statement concerning a relation between two particular traits, although the readiness may be independent of the degree to which subjects actually employ the relation in forming impressions of people. For example, one may not actually perceive men as more brave than women but still be more ready to affirm a statement that "Men are brave" than that "Women are brave" (as measured by response latency). This might be due to a subject's belief that the former is more "appropriate" to say, that it is more consistent with "what people usually say about men and women," that it makes more logical sense since men are stronger and usually have more power, or finally that the experimenter would prefer such an answer.

The above distinction has not been taken into account in research on semantic memory (Smith & Medin, 1981), since the distinction seems irrelevant to the kind of simple semantic statements that are usually investigated by memory researchers: for example, asking subjects to verify whether a canary is a bird or whether it is an animal. The distinction between declarative and functional reasons for individual differences in processing covariations, however, seems to be of major importance in the area of social cognition. Research has demonstrated that there may be considerable differences between the structure of subjects' explicit, direct estimations of trait relationships and the structure of their person perception. For example, Rosenberg and Sedlak (1972) compared the structure derived from multidimensional scaling of adjective similarity estimations with an analogous structure derived from naturalistic descriptions of stimulus persons. The two resulting structures were basically different in many respects (cf. Rosenberg & Sedlak, 1972, Figures 3 and 5). The results also indicated that subjects' explicit estimations of trait similarity were much less individually differentiated than were the covariations between traits derived from their perception of the stimulus persons.[11] In another study (Lewicki, 1981), it was shown that these two different aspects of implicit personality theory (i.e., declarative & functional) are related to different factors. For example, the former is much more sensitive to the instructional set, perceived goals of the experiment, and so on than is the latter.

The present experiment[12] was a conceptual replication of Experiment 4.3, which demonstrated RT effects of manipulating covariations in descriptions of stimulus persons. It attempted, however, to control for the two aspects of the preexperimental characteristics of the manipulated covariation discussed earlier. One month prior to being exposed to the stimulus material containing the manipulated covariations, subjects filled out rating forms in which they rated a number of stimulus persons on a number of trait dimensions, including the crucial dimensions relevant to the covariations manipulated later in the experiment. Based on these ratings, the closeness of the preexperimental trait relationships were estimated, separately for each subject. These measures were expected to capture individual differences in the working (functional) relationships between the traits.

The declarative aspect of subjects' preexperimental readiness to affirm the statement concerning crucial covariation was included as an independent variable in the experiment. One of the two manipulated covariations was chosen as logical and stereotypic (the relationship between being "ambitious" and being "active"), the other as much less logical or stereotypic (the relationship between being "frank" and being "persistent"). Both trait relationships were quite weak in terms of subjects' perceptions: The mean correlations between the trait dimensions in the rating forms were .24 and .28, respectively. The variance, however, was much higher in the nonstereotypic trait relationship. Stereotypic trait relationships were found to have less individual variability in general than the less stereotypic ones.

Two possibilities concerning the difference in internal validity between the stereotypic and nonstereotypic trait relationship were taken into account. The stereotypic trait relationships, being less individually differentiated, might provide better conditions to reveal the effects of the experimental manipulation. On the other hand, however, most subjects might react to such a question very fast (due to the stereotypicality of the trait relationship), which could produce a floor effect and eventually supress any effects of the manipulation. Thus, the stereotypic trait relationship was included in this experiment as an exploratory measure.

Method

Overview

The design and procedure were basically similar to those employed in Experiment 4.3, except that rating forms were filled out by the subjects one month prior to the main experiment. The experimental session consisted of a learning phase, in which subjects were presented with six personality descriptions containing the crucial covariations (constructed in a manner similar to Experiment 4.3) and a testing phase, in which subjects made crucial semantic judgments and in which their response latencies were measured.

Participants were 58 high school students (men and women), about 18 years old. One group (Condition I) was presented with the stimulus material in which all "active" stimulus persons were "ambitious" (while "passive" stimulus persons were "not ambitious"), and all "persistent" stimulus persons were "not frank" (while "easily discouraged" stimulus persons were "frank"). The other group (Condition II) was presented with the version of the material in which the two crucial trait relationships were reversed.

Material and Procedure

The rating form that subjects filled out during the first session was a shortened version of the form used previously to measure the interrelations between dimensions in person perception (Lewicki, 1983), but it was longer than the version employed in Experiment 4.2. The form consisted of 14 real and known stimulus persons[13] that were to be rated on 18 bipolar, six-point dimensions, including the four that would be manipulated in the next phase of the experiment. Completing the rating form required 252 ratings (14 stimulus persons × 18 dimensions) and took respondents about one hour. Sessions were run in groups of 10–15 participants (see Lewicki, 1983, for more details about the rating form).

The next experimental session was about one month later. Subjects were tested individually by experimenters different from those involved in the first session. Since the two sessions were very different, it is unlikely that subjects thought that the two sessions were related. The procedure was very much like the one employed in Experiment 4.3 in terms of the general design and the instructions subjects received. The six personality descriptions, however, were different in order to incorporate the new manipulated trait relationships, and they were longer (about 240 words each). The process of constructing and testing this stimulus material was the same as in Experiment 4.3. The descriptions were displayed on a nine inch CRT in all capital letters (block), 4 mm high, white on a black (i.e., no illumination) background.

The learning phase was followed by the distractor task designed to interfere with subjects' short-term memory and also to train subjects to respond to questions displayed on the CRT. Subjects responded to eight questions like "Are things made of wood heavy?" by pressing the "yes" or "no" buttons on a control box. Subjects were instructed not to take time to consider their responses but instead to react following their "first association or intuition." The meaning of "yes" and "no" responses were explained as in Experiment 4.3. After the distractor task, subjects took part in the testing phase, which was designed in a manner similar to that employed in Experiment 4.3; however, in this study there was a total of 10, instead of 5, semantic judgments to be made. The fourth and the eighth judgments were the crucial ones, and they referred to the two manipulated trait relationships. Both the crucial and noncrucial questions were separately counterbalanced for order (as in Experiment 4.3). Only the more desirable endpoints of the four manipulated bipolar trait categories were used in the crucial questions; they read, "Active people are usually ambitious" and "Frank people are usually persistent."

At the end of the session, each subject was interviewed as to whether he or she had recognized any systematic relationships among traits in the stimulus material. As in previous studies, no subject was able to recognize the traits that were actually correlated across the descriptions.

Results

The means of standarized "yes" response latencies to each of 10 statements are displayed in Figure 4.2. No significant differences between conditions were found for any of the eight nonmanipulated trait relationships. Contrary to the hypothesis, however, the same was true for the first of the two manipulated trait relationships, the stereotypic one (ambitious–active, Figure 4.2, Judgment no. 4), $t(52) = .86$, ns. The stereotypic status of that trait relationship was confirmed in that almost all subjects (93%) responded "yes" to that statement, and their response time was relatively short.

The second manipulated trait relationship, the nonstereotypic one (persistent–frank, Figure 4.2, Judgment no. 8), however, produced a reliable difference between experimental groups that was consistent with the hy-

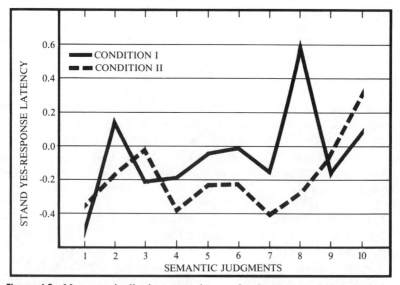

Figure 4.2 Mean standardized response latency for the 10 semantic judgments in two experimental conditions of Experiment 4.6. Crucial statements are no. 4 (ambitious–active) and no. 8 (persistent–frank). Note that the order of statements presented in the figure does not reflect exactly the actual order in which the statements were presented to the subjects, since both the crucial statements and the noncrucial ones were separately counterbalanced for order.

pothesis, $t(31) = 2.17$, $p < .030$. The response latency for subjects from Condition I was longer than for subjects from Condition II. Only 57% of subjects responded "yes" to that trait relationship, confirming that it was not a stereotypical one.

Since only about half the subjects responded "yes" to this question, the analogous comparison could be completed for "no" response latencies. There were no specific hypotheses concerning these responses; the result, however, was consistent with Experiment 4.3, and it seemed consistent with the nature of the manipulation. Subjects in Condition I, who were exposed to stimulus material in which persistent stimulus persons were not frank, made faster "no" responses to the question of whether persistent people were frank than subjects in Condition II, who were exposed to persistent and frank stimulus persons, $t(28) = 1.42$, $p < .10$.

The preexperimental measures of the crucial trait relationships appeared to be unrelated to subjects' reactions to the manipulation.

Discussion

The present experiment was only partially successful. The inclusion of a stereotypic trait relationship did not produce conclusive results. Almost all subjects showed a tendency to respond very fast to this apparently "easy" question, and this tendency seemed to suppress any hypothesized effects of the manipulation regarding the trait relationship. The nonstereotypic trait relationship, however, provided predicted and reliable effects that replicated the pattern obtained in Experiment 4.3, even for "no" response latencies. Thus, it can be concluded that the failure of one of the manipulated trait relationships was a consequence of the specificity of the stimulus material employed and that, in general, the present results can be considered a positive replication of Experiment 4.3.

It is difficult to determine why the preexperimental measures of the manipulated trait relationships (which had been proved to be valid, Lewicki, 1983, 1984b) were unrelated to subjects' susceptibility to the manipulation. A possible cause could be the very small number of observations per cell. Fifty-eight subjects had to be divided into four groups (2[Condition I vs. Condition II] × 2 [response "yes" vs. "no"]), which created difficulties in assessing the influence of the preexperimental measure of the manipulated trait relationship.

According to the arguments presented in Chapter 2, all possible types and modalities of stimuli that are being encoded in any form by a perceiver are potentially subject to processing in terms of covariations between events or features. This reasoning was supported in Experiment

3.4, in which subjects included in their nonconscious search for covariations incidental auditory information that belonged to a different modality than the stimuli on which subjects focused their attention while completing the search task. The next two experiments are concerned with nonconscious processing of covariations that also involves auditory information but in a somewhat more natural setting.

Experiment 4.7[14]

In Chapter 2 it was argued that, parallel to the encoding of the explicit meaning of some information received, various aspects of the context of that information are being processed and can be nonconsciously found (detected by the subject) to covary with the explicit information. If the information is a verbal message, one of the components of the context that may be subjected to nonconscious processing in terms of covariation might be the pitch level of the speaker's voice. This feature seemed to fit well the general research paradigm employed in our studies on nonconscious processing of covariation, since it can be manipulated easily in the stimulus material and still not become salient to the subjects.

In the learning phase of the present experiment, subjects were exposed to auditory stimulus material consisting of a number of self-descriptions recorded by a number of speakers and containing a consistent co-occurrence between the pitch level of the speaker's voice and the content of what he said. In the testing phase, subjects were asked to rate new stimulus persons, who differed regarding the pitch level of their voices, on dimensions relevant to the content of the self-descriptions to which they had been exposed in the learning phase. It was expected that the ratings would be nonconsciously biased by the covariation manipulated in the learning phase.

Method

Overview and Design

In the learning phase, subjects were presented with self-descriptions recorded by eight stimulus persons: four of them had voices with a low pitch; four others had high-pitched voices. The pitch of the stimulus persons' voices covaried with two characteristics: being warm and being capable. Half of the subjects were presented with an arrangement of the stimulus material in which all four persons with higher pitched voices were warm, while all four persons with lower pitched voices were capable (Condition I). The other half of the subjects were presented with an arrangement in which all four persons with higher pitched voices were capable, while four persons with lower pitched voices were warm (Condition II). After a distractor task, subjects rated four new stimulus persons. Some of the dimensions on which they had to rate these new stimulus persons corresponded to the content of the self-descriptions from the learning phase. The new self-descriptions, however, contained no relevant information concerning the crucial traits and, in making their ratings, subjects had to rely on their "intuitions."

After the ratings were completed, subjects filled out a questionnaire pertaining to the basis of their judgments of stimulus persons as they perceived it. At the end of the experiment, each subject's ability to consciously differentiate pitch levels of human voices was assessed in an additional test. This was done in order to explore the relationship between conscious sensitivity to pitch levels of the human voice and nonconscious processing of this particular kind of information in the experiment.

Subjects

One hundred six undergraduates (men and women) participated voluntarily in the experiment. Less than 3% of the people asked to participate refused for any of a variety of reasons.

Stimulus Material

Eight self-descriptions were presented in the learning phase. Each of them was very short (20–25 s) and consisted of three or four sentences implying either warmth (e.g., liking pets and small children, having very close relations with friends, etc.) or capability (having best grades at school, having sophisticated hobbies, etc). Four analogous self-descriptions, neutral with regard to two crucial traits, were also presented in the testing phase. Thus, each subject was presented with a total of 12 voices (6 low and 6 high pitched). Two arrangements of the material were presented in the learning phase: in one of them, stimulus persons with higher pitched voices presented themselves as warm, and those with lower pitched voices presented themselves as capable (Condition I); in the other arrangement, the relations were reversed (Condition II). The testing phase material was the same in both conditions.

Stimulus persons' voices were selected by a music professor from the pool of 60 members of a male chorus: the lower pitched voices were either high-basses or low-baritones; the higher pitched voices were either high-baritones or low-tenors. There were no atypical voices in the sample (e.g., low-bass or high-tenor), and the voices selected for the two groups did not seem distinctively different to nonprofessional listeners (especially when talking and not singing).

In order to control for a possible idiosyncratic correlation between the pitch level of voices and their timbre or some other characteristic, the stimulus material was recorded by two independent groups of 12 persons each. Each version was presented to half the subjects from each condition.

Procedure

Subjects were tested in groups of six to nine persons in one large experimental room that was divided into individual booths. Each subject was located in a separate booth that allowed him or her to concentrate and to perform the tasks with a minimum of external distraction. Subjects heard all the instructions and stimulus materials through stereo headphones.

The learning phase was introduced to the subjects as a kind of "psychological training" designed to help subjects concentrate before "the main part of the experiment." They were told that they would listen to a number of persons chosen as remarkable (i.e., especially positive in some respect) from a large pool of extensive case studies prepared recently by M.A. level students of clinical psychology in partial fulfillment of course requirements in personality. The stimulus material (i.e., the recorded text) was announced to subjects as "short excerpts from the tape recording of what the person said in the interview and that was found by the clinician as particularly accurate and characteristic of the person's personality." This was explained in detail for two major reasons: First, to induce subjects to listen carefully to the descriptions by stimulating interest in the information as being about real people and thus to lead subjects to perceive the material in a manner in which they perceive real-life episodes; second, to prevent subjects' becoming suspicious regarding the artificial pattern followed by the stimulus material, which could be the case if subjects thought the material was fabricated.

After the learning phase, subjects received instructions concerning the testing phase and rating forms. As opposed to the stimulus materials, all instructions were read by a woman. The break between phases of the experiment was 3.5 min long, and thus it could be considered a distractor task that interfered with subjects' short-term memory.

In the testing phase, subjects were presented with four new self-descriptions recorded by new stimulus persons. After each presentation, subjects had to rate the person on six 6-point trait-dimension scales. They did not know these dimensions in advance, however; the forms they received were not labeled, the dimensions were defined in sequence by the female experimenter, and subjects had only 5 s for rating the stimulus person on each dimension, which was very little time. The time pressure was intended to increase the chance that subjects would report only their first impressions and to make the conscious creation of consistency between the ratings more difficult. Except for the two crucial ones, the dimensions used to describe each stimulus person were different, but even the crucial dimensions were labeled for each of the four stimulus persons in a slightly different way and located at different positions in the rating form. Thus, while listening to a new stimulus person, subjects could not anticipate which traits of that person they would be asked about.

After the testing phase, subjects filled out a form containing very detailed questions about their feelings during the experiment. These questions were expected to make the question, "What did you base your ratings on," less salient. The latter was a forced-choice question including the following alternatives: "speed of speech," "pronunciation," "content of the message," "timbre of voice," "intonation," "pitch level of voice," "intuition," "I cannot specify," and "other." Subjects could indicate up to three of the alternatives. A vast majority of subjects indicated the "content of the message," "intuition," or "I cannot specify" alternatives. Out of 106 subjects, only 3 checked the crucial alternative (pitch level of voice), and they were excluded from the analysis. Postexperimental interviews suggested, however, that even they did not discover the covariation manipulated in the stimulus material.

At the end of the session, subjects' ability to consciously differentiate pitch levels of human voices was assessed. They were exposed twice to the recordings of all 12 voices they had heard in the experiment. When listening to the recording for the second time, subjects were asked to rate each voice on a 2-point scale, as either higher or lower than the mean of all 12 voices. Subjects were then divided into two groups according to the accuracy of their judgments.

Results and Discussion

Mean ratings of warmth and capability assigned to lower and higher pitched voice stimulus persons for subjects in the two experimental conditions are displayed in Figure 4.3. The means indicate a clear general tendency to assign more warmth to higher as opposed to lower pitched voice stimulus persons, which may suggest the existence of some stereotype.[15] Consistent with the manipulation, however, this tendency was

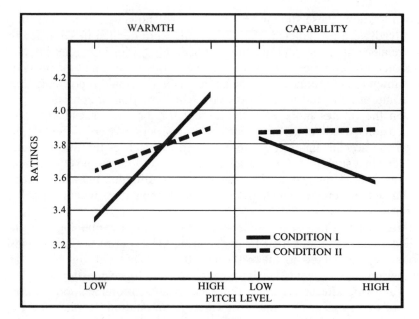

Figure 4.3   Mean ratings of warmth and capability in two conditions of Experiment 4.7.

more pronounced in Condition I than in Condition II. The ratings of capability suggested a general tendency in the reverse direction; subjects assigned more capability to lower as opposed to higher pitched voice stimulus persons. Consistent with the manipulation, however, this tendency was more pronounced in Condition I than in Condition II.

These data were analyzed in a 4-way ANOVA, with condition (I vs. II) and version of the stimulus material (first vs. second set of voices) as between-subjects factors, and trait (warmth vs. capability), and pitch level of stimulus person's voice (low vs. high) as within-subjects factors. The version factor produced no significant effects in this experiment. There was an interaction between condition, trait, and voice, $F(1, 99) = 5.77, p < .01$, which suggested that the above effects of the manipulation were reliable. Planned comparisons (contrasts) indicated that ratings of both traits (warmth and capability) contributed about equally to this interaction.

Including gender as a factor in the ANOVA design revealed that ratings of warmth were influenced by the manipulation only in women, while ratings of capability only in men (see Figure 4.4). Planned comparisons (contrasts) revealed in women an interaction between condition and voice, but only for ratings of warmth, $F(1, 99) = 3.12, p < .07$, and not for

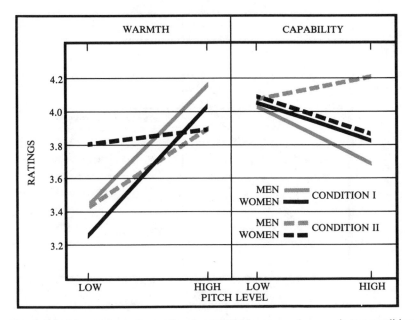

Figure 4.4 Mean ratings of warmth and capability by men and women in two conditions of Experiment 4.7.

capability, $F < 1$. In men, the pattern was reversed; there was an interaction for capability, $F(1, 99) = 3.04$, $p < .08$, but not for warmth, $F < 1$. It may be argued, therefore, that the manipulation of both traits (i.e., warmth and capability) was successful, although not for all subjects at the same time. Women appeared to be more sensitive to covariation involving warmth and men to covariation involving capability. This seems to be consistent with both common intuition and empirical evidence; women focus more than men on traits related to emotional life, while men focus more than women on traits related to capabilities (Carlson, 1971). This difference might influence both the processing of self-descriptions and the interpretation of rating scales. For women, for example, facts relevant to warmth included in the self-descriptions could be more meaningful and easier to understand and to transform into the general trait "warm." They also might be more able to differentiate various degrees of warmth and, thus, to make better use of rating scales related to being warm.

In order to assess the role of the general ability to differentiate pitch levels of human voice in the effects obtained, this variable was included in the ANOVA design. The means are displayed in Figure 4.5. An apparently paradoxical pattern of results was obtained, suggesting that subjects

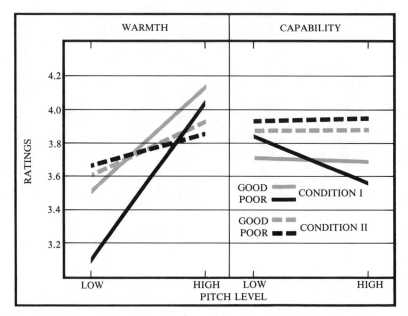

Figure 4.5 Mean ratings of warmth and capability by subjects with good and poor ear for music in two conditions of Experiment 4.7.

with poorer ability to differentiate pitch levels were more sensitive to the manipulation. Planned comparisons (contrasts) revealed a reliable inter-action between condition, trait, and voice in subjects with a poorer ear, $F(1, 99) = 4.28$, $p < .05$, and no such interaction in the remaining group, $F < 1$.

This unpredicted effect seems to be important. First, it provides one more argument supporting the notion that the effects obtained in this experiment were not mediated by subjects' conscious awareness, since if they were, subjects with poorer ability to differentiate pitch levels would show weaker and not stronger effects, indicative of processing the covari-ation. This result also seems to be consistent with results obtained by Reber (1976, see Chapter 1).

Additionally, it seems probable that in the group with better ability to differentiate pitch levels (as compared to those who could not), subjects had more preexisting IPAs involving pitch level of human voice, and these may have interfered with the development of the IPAs manipulated in the experiment.

The results of this experiment were generally consistent with expecta-tions and suggested that subjects nonconsciously processed the manipulated covariation and stored it in an IPA form, because that covariation nonconsciously influenced their subsequent judgments. These encouraging results stimulated us to further explore the process observed in this experimental situation. Two issues were addressed in the next experiment: How many consistent instances of the kind employed in the previous study (Experiment 4.7) are sufficient to be transformed into an IPA, and how long lasting are effects of that kind of manipulation. Unexpectedly, however, the next experiment provided more than evidence related to these two questions alone; in addition, unexpected data cast some doubt on whether we had actually understood what had happened in the previous experiment (4.7).

Experiment 4.8

Method

The basic procedure employed in the previous study remained unchanged; however, in order to address the issue of minimum number of instances and the question of time stability, the experimental design was changed by introducing two new independent variables. Two hundred forty subjects were tested in the experiment.

The number of instances factor was manipulated on three levels. Subjects in three different groups were provided with 4, 8, or 12 self-descriptions, respectively. This means that they were able to process 2, 4, or 6 consistent instances regarding each of two manipulated traits. Thus, the second group was exposed to the same number of instances as in Experiment 4.7. The content of 8 of the 12 self-descriptions employed in this experiment was the same as before; four additional self-descriptions were constructed following the same rules.

The second new variable pertained to the temporal stability of the effects of the manipulation, and it had two levels. A testing phase was administered either immediately after a short distractor task (as in the previous study) or after a one hour delay.

Since not all the persons who had recorded the stimulus material for Experiment 4.7 were available, the new stimulus material was recorded by a new set of 16 persons selected by the music professor following the same rules as before. It should be explained at this point that making these recordings was not an easy task, since the persons selected to be our "actors" were in fact only members of a chorus and not professional actors. At times it required dozens of frustrating attempts on the part of our actors until one recording was finally ready and could be considered to sound more or less natural. Taking into account these difficulties and the fact that we had already demonstrated in Experiment 4.7 that there were no differences between two versions of stimulus material recorded by completely independent groups of people, we decided to use only one version of recordings in this study. This saved us a lot of time and effort and also, unexpectedly, helped us to obtain some important new data.

Results

The predicted and reliable effects of processing covariation concerning warmth were obtained, and they consistently replicated the data from Experiment 4.7. However, ratings of capability revealed a pattern of results that was just the opposite of the predictions and of the results obtained in Experiment 4.7. Specifically, subjects from Condition I, who had been exposed to stimulus material in the learning phase in which capable persons had lower pitched voices, rated the capability of persons with lower pitched voices higher (and not lower) in the testing phase than subjects from Condition II. Thus, subjects "learned" just the opposite of what they were exposed to concerning the trait of capability. Moreover, this paradoxical effect was reliable and highly stable across levels of the "number of instances" and the "delay" factors.

After checking all possibilities for errors in coding the data and arranging the stimulus material, we started to look for similarities, separately for each condition, between the voices of persons from the testing phase and those persons from the learning phase who presented themselves as capable. Nothing clear was revealed; however, the results appeared to be too consistent to be produced by chance. It appears then, that there was some uncontrolled variable involved in stimulus persons' voices that was inversely related to pitch level and that provided more salient or important information than pitch level. This uncontrolled variable could be some aspect of pronunciation, accent, or nuance of voice; none of them, however, seemed to be salient in the stimulus material. Moreover, subjects' responses to the postexperimental interview were the same as in Experiment 4.7, and they did not indicate that subjects followed any systematic rule, relating the learning and the testing materials while making their judgments.

The delay factor appeared to have no influence on the data. The pattern of ratings obtained for the group of subjects who were tested after one hour was almost exactly the same as the group tested immediately, including the unpredicted effect for the trait of capability. This similarity suggests that the respective IPA was stored in long-term memory.

Reliable effects were produced by the number of instances factor. No systematic effects of the manipulation were found for the group exposed to 4 instances; significant effects emerged, however, in the group exposed to 8 instances and in the group with 12 instances. The pattern of means was again very similar in the two groups, including the unpredicted effect for the trait of capability.

Discussion

The predicted results were obtained for only one of two traits manipulated in this experiment (warmth). The other trait also produced highly consistent results, but the pattern of the results was opposite to predictions. Nevertheless, these results, as a whole, provide evidence for the process of nonconscious acquisition of covariation. They also contain, however, an important warning pertaining to the manipulation of quasinatural types of social stimulus material. Such material consists of a very large number of features that, on the one hand, seem to be easily encoded by subjects and nonconsciously processed in terms of covariations, but, on the other hand, these features are not very salient to designers of experiments who can rely only on their consciously controlled processing. Experiments employing these kinds of stimuli have to be very carefully designed regarding control over such factors, which in most cases are likely to attenuate or even destroy predicted effects. Due to the particular chance arrangement of the stimulus material in the present experiment, these factors emerged in a quite robust way. It seems that one cannot easily manipulate the pitch level of the human voice without controlling other features of the voice, and this is not easy. Possibly we were lucky that such factors did not destroy the effects of the manipulation in Experiment 4.7. The strong and consistent effects obtained in that experiment led us to believe that the nature of the manipulated variable is much more simple than it may actually be. It is also likely that if we had a number of versions of the stimulus material in Experiment 4.8, the predicted pattern might emerge in only one of them, but, due to the degrees of freedom lost, the pattern of results would not be reliable in any of them. Thus, it may have been quite fortunate that there was only one version employed in the present experiment, and that its results seem instructive.

Experiment 4.9[16]

The final study to be presented in this chapter investigates the mediating role of permanently accessible categories in the acquisition of internal processing algorithms. It has been suggested that such categories are nonconsciously processed to a larger degree than less accessible categories (Bargh, 1982; Logan, 1980; Nielsen & Sarason, 1981; Posner & Snyder, 1975), and, therefore, they are more likely to be used in nonconscious processing of covariations (see Chapter 2).

A new experimental procedure was employed in the present study. The focused-attention paradigm was employed using a dichotic listening task and the simultaneous presentation of visual stimuli. Synchronized auditory stimuli were presented to both ears with subjects being instructed to attend to one ear and shadow (i.e., repeat loudly) what they were hearing from that ear while ignoring stimuli presented to the other ear. Additionally, a series of pictures, synchronized with auditory stimuli, was presented and subjects were also asked to ignore them.

Considerable research has demonstrated that subjects in dichotic listening tasks are able to keep the contents of the rejected channel out of consciousness. These contents, however, are still processed nonconsciously. For example, they may trigger specific automatic attention responses (Bargh, 1982; Kahneman, 1973; Nielsen & Sarason, 1981; Posner & Snyder, 1975). Research employing dual-task procedures (where subjects performed some kind of shadowing as a main task and were instructed to ignore simultaneously exposed visual stimuli) has indicated that although the shadowing prevented subjects from consciously attending to visual stimuli, these stimuli were still processed and retained in long-term memory. Subjects performed at a greater than chance level in a subsequent recognition test (Allport, Antonis, & Reynolds, 1972; Kellogg, 1980; Rollins & Thibadeau, 1973).

The present procedure combined the preceding two experimental paradigms and, therefore, it could be referred to as a "triple-task" paradigm. Subjects were asked to shadow the words from the attended auditory channel while ignoring both the unattended auditory channel and the simultaneously presented pictures. The attended channel contained neutral words, while the unattended channel contained some neutral and some threatening words. The pictures displayed schematically presented persons with three different types of objects (an umbrella, a jug, or a letter). The manipulated covariation pertained to the contents of the unattended auditory and visual channels: One of the three objects systematically co-occurred with the threatening words presented in the unattended channel.

Subjects were expected to process this covariation and to develop a tendency to encode the crucial object as a cue to expect some threat. This hypothesis was evaluated in the testing phase in which subjects rated some new schematic stimulus persons (carrying one of the three types of objects) on dimensions including ones related to threat. This phase of the experiment took place either right after a short distractor task or one hour later. In the latter condition, after completing the shadowing task, subjects returned to their usual activities and they did not expect to be tested again.

Additionally, subjects' permanent accessibility of categories related to threat or chronic expectation of threat was measured using peer ratings and the Manifest Anxiety Scale (Taylor, 1953). Following the discussion of the contribution of the nonconscious processing of covariations phenomena to the development of stable personality dispositions (see Chapter 2), it was expected that subjects with higher accessibility of categories related to threat would process the crucial words from the rejected channel to a larger extent and, therefore, would develop a stronger, specific IPA.

Method

Design

Subjects in all conditions were exposed to the same set of 180 neutral words in the shadowing auditory channel. The unattended channel also contained 180 words that were logically divided into nine segments of 20 words each. Half of the subjects were exposed in the unattended channel to a list of words in which the second, fifth, and eighth segments contained words related to threat, and all other segments contained neutral words (experimental conditions). The other half of the subjects were exposed to an analogous list except that the three crucial segments (i.e., the second, the fifth, and the eighth) were neutral (control conditions); thus, both the attended and the unattended lists exposed in this group were totally neutral.

Nine pictures were exposed during the shadowing session (three with each of the three objects), and the intervals of their presentation matched the logical segments of the lists. Three sequences of presentation of the nine pictures were employed. The first sequence was: letter, umbrella, jug, letter, umbrella, jug, letter, umbrella, jug. Thus, the umbrella matched the three crucial segments of the unattended list. The second sequence was the same except that the letter was moved from the beginning to the end of the sequence, and, therefore, the jug matched the three crucial segments. In the third sequence, the same modification was pursued one step further (i.e., the umbrella was moved to the end), and, therefore, the letter matched the crucial segments of the unattended list.

These manipulations, varying the contents of the unattended channel (experimental vs. control) and the sequence of presentation of the pictures, were completely crossed in the design, creating six experimental conditions (three experimental and three control). Additionally, half of the subjects from each of these conditions rated new stimulus persons immediately after the shadowing session and a short distractor task, while the other half made their ratings after a 1-hr delay. Finally, the brain hemisphere (i.e., the ear to which the attended channel was presented) was varied and treated as a factor in the experiment. This factor did not produce any effects in any of the dependent measures, and it will not be included in the analysis.

There was one additional group of subjects tested in the experiment. They completed the same shadowing task as subjects in experimental conditions, and then their recognition memory for threatening words from the unattended channel was tested with the pair forced-choice recognition test (recognition condition).

Subjects

Seventy-two male high school students, about 18 years of age, participated in the study (76 were tested but 4 appeared to have difficulties with the shadowing task, and the data obtained from these subjects were excluded from the final analysis). Thirty additional students were tested in the recognition condition. The experimental sessions were conducted in schools, and none of the students asked to participate refused. The recruitment of subjects and the organization of the experimental sessions were designed to assure that subjects did not know the procedure before entering the lab room. Additionally, subjects for the recognition group (which was unexpectedly asked to recognize the words from the to-be-ignored channel) were recruited from a separate high school.

Stimulus material

Tapes. The list of words presented in the attended channel consisted of 180 neutral, two- or three-syllable nouns (e.g., table, shirt, morning). They were read fast (the average was 1.5 words per second) by a female professional radio announcer. In order to perfectly synchronize the two channels, the final versions of the tapes were generated with professional recording equipment. Each synchronized pair of words started simultaneously. The breaks after each word were made of the same length as the preceding word. (The breaks allowed subjects to shadow the words.)

The lists of words presented in the ignored channel consisted of 180 verbs. They were read by a male professional radio announcer with the same speed as the words from the attended channel, and the breaks between the words were generated in the same way. The control and experimental versions of the list differed only in the second, fifth, and eighth segments. In the control version, these segments contained neutral verbs (e.g., to work, to sleep, to learn). In the experimental version, they contained verbs related to psychological and physical threat (e.g., to harm, to suffer, to fear). In both versions, the verbs contained in all the remaining segments were the same, and they were neutral. All verbs presented in both versions were of the same number and length of syllables as their counterparts (nouns) in the attended channel (and words from both channels were synchronized).

Additionally, a training tape was prepared. It contained 50 pairs of words with the neutral nouns in the attended channel and the neutral verbs in the ignored channel. The timing of the presentation of words and

Figure 4.6 Stimulus persons exposed during the learning phase (first three rows) and testing phase (last row) of Experiment 4.9.

the voices of speakers were the same as in the tapes used in the main part of the experiment.

Pictures. A total of 12 pictures of schematic stimulus persons with three types of objects were used in the experiment. Nine of them were presented during the shadowing task—three with each of three objects, and three others were rated by the subjects in the testing phase (Figure 4.6). Each of the nine schematic stimulus persons presented in the learning phase, as well as the three stimulus persons used during the testing phase, were in a different position that made focusing attention on the objects more difficult (i.e., position of the stimulus persons was an additional distracting factor). These pictures had to be emotionally neutral, and they were selected in a pilot study with 30 subjects who rated 30 pictures (10 with each of the three objects) on six bipolar trait dimensions pertaining to emotional connotations of the pictures. Twelve pictures that appeared to be most neutral were selected as the stimulus material.

Rating Scales. Four 6-point bipolar trait dimensions were used as rating scales in the testing phase. Three of them were selected as related to perceived threat: "Warm—Cold," "I don't trust him—I trust him," and "Hostile—Not hostile." The fourth one ("Intelligent—Not intelligent") was unrelated to threat and was introduced to explore any potential effects of evaluative generalization.

Procedure and Apparatus

The experiment was introduced to subjects as an investigation of the ability to concentrate during confusing situations. Subjects were run individually in a small, silent lab room divided into two booths. In the first of them, subjects completed the shadowing task, and then they moved to the second booth where the testing phase took place. After arriving at the lab room, the subject was seated at a table in the first booth and introduced to the nature of the task and the requirements of the shadowing procedure. Subjects wore stereo headphones during the shadowing.

The shadowing started with the practice session during which the training tape was used. No pictures were exposed during the training. Shadowing of the training tape was repeated until the subject achieved a criterion of one errorless shadowing of the entire list of words. After achieving this criterion, subjects were reminded of the nature of their task, and the main session was begun. The pictures were introduced to subjects as an additional distracting factor that they had to ignore. Thus, while shadowing, subjects were instructed to ignore both the unattended auditory channel and the pictures. However, they were asked not to close their eyes but to direct them at the pictures at all times. They were asked to ignore the contents of the pictures "psychologically" but not "physically."

The pictures were displayed on cardboards (18 cm × 25 cm) located vertically in front of the subjects. They were changed manually (following the precise timetable) by the trained experimenter who sat at the same table. The presence of the experimenter was necessary to ensure that subjects would not close (or half close) their eyes and that they look at the pictures. Because shadowing is a very attention-consuming task, subjects had an obvious tendency to avoid visual distraction by not looking at the pictures during the shadowing task. (Usually, subjects close their eyes when performing dichotic tasks.) Each picture was exposed for approximately 20 s. As compared to presenting the pictures on the CRT, this procedure also had the additional advantage that the presence of the experimenter provided one more distracting factor making subjects' conscious discovery of the manipulated covariation even less likely. Subjects' performance in the shadowing task was recorded; distortions, substitutions from the ignored channel, and omissions were treated as errors.

After completing the shadowing task, subjects were interviewed on the difficulty of the task, the strategies they used, and their memory for the ignored stimulus materials. Subjects' responses indicated consistently that they perceived the task as requiring a lot of effort and very difficult. It was also clear that subjects followed the instructions and that they neither tried to memorize the pictures nor to attend to the to-be-ignored auditory channel. (The latter was not only additionally tested in the recognition group, but it was also supported by low-error rates achieved by the subjects in the shadowing task [see following discussion].) The interview was designed not only as a way to learn about subjects' subjective experiences while shadowing, but it was also considered a distractor task that separated the learning and the testing phase of the experiment.

After the interview, half of the subjects were thanked for their participation (the condition with the delayed testing phase), and they were not told that they would be asked to participate in the testing phase 1-hr later. The other half of the subjects received instructions concerning the rating of the three new stimulus persons (the testing phase) immediately after the interview. Then they moved to the second booth where the three testing phase pictures (see Figure 4.6, last row) were displayed on the wall in front of the subject such that the subject could compare them. Subjects were asked to imagine what the schematic persons were doing and their personalities and then to rate them on the provided scales. The time for completing the ratings was not limited, but most subjects did it in a few minutes. This concluded the experimental session.

Subjects in the condition with the delayed testing phase were unexpectedly approached by the experimenter 1-hr after the shadowing session and asked to participate in an "additional short session." They received the same instructions and completed their ratings in the same conditions as the other half of the subjects.

The MAS was administered about 1 month before the experiment during group sessions in which the data concerning subjects' expectations of threat as perceived by peers were also collected. The latter measures will not be described in detail because, although they were highly correlated with the MAS scores, the MAS scores produced stronger effects, and only they will be included in the analysis.

Subjects from the recognition group were exposed to the same stimulus materials during the shadowing session as subjects from the experimental conditions. Immediately after completing the shadowing task, however, instead of the interview, they were unexpectedly given a recognition test that consisted of pairs of threatening words. One word in every pair came from the crucial segments of the ignored list of words they had been exposed to during the shadowing task. The words that accompanied the crucial words in each pair were selected over the course of a series of pilot studies showing that they involved an equal degree of threat and had an equal probability of being chosen in nonexperimental conditions.

Subjects in the recognition group claimed that they could not complete the test since they totally ignored the to-be-ignored channel. They were told, however, that even if they totally ignored that channel, they probably preserved some small degree of awareness for words from it, and they should try to complete the test. Subjects were also asked not to omit any items and to guess if necessary. No evidence was obtained for better than chance recognition of words from the ignored channel (an average of 46% of crucial words were checked).

Results

Ratings

Subjects' ratings of stimulus persons presented in the testing phase were analyzed in a 2(condition: threatening words ["experimental"] vs. neutral words ["control"]) × 2(delay of the testing phase: one hour vs. no delay) × 2(rated object: crucial [exposed during the crucial segments of the tape—II, V, VIII] vs. noncrucial [exposed during the remaining segments][17]) × 4(rating scales[18]) ANOVA with repeated measures on the two last factors. The means indicated no differences between subjects in the experimental and control conditions regarding their ratings of the stimulus persons with noncrucial objects. The stimulus persons with the crucial

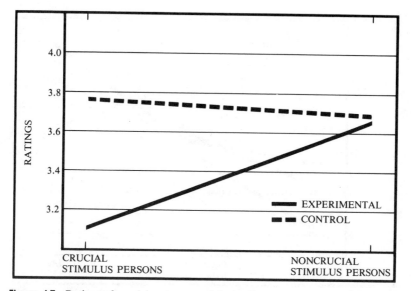

Figure 4.7 Ratings of crucial and noncrucial stimulus persons presented in the testing phase of Experiment 4.9.

objects, however, were rated lower (i.e., as representing more threat) by the subjects of the experimental condition as compared to control subjects (Figure 4.7), which was consistent with the expectations. The effect was reliable as shown by the interaction of condition by rated object (crucial vs. noncrucial), $F(1, 64) = 4.91$, $p < .028$. Planned comparisons (contrast) revealed that experimental subjects rated stimulus persons with crucial objects reliably lower than stimulus persons with noncrucial objects, $F(1, 64) = 10.11$, $p < .003$. When only three scales pertaining to threat were taken into account (i.e., intelligence was excluded from the contrast), the effect was even stronger, $F(1, 64) = 13.33$, $p < .001$. Excluding any other scales did not increase the effect, which suggested that the scale of intelligence was less responsive to the manipulation than the scales specifically related to threat. This finding was additionally supported by a marginally significant interaction of the factors of rated object and scale within the experimental group ($p < .07$) and in a series of planned comparisons.

Since the same sequence of objects on pictures was "rotated" in each group, the effect of each specific object could be estimated, as well as the effect of the distance in time of each object from the exposure of the crucial segments of the nonattended list of words. The latter involved transforming the two-level factor of crucial vs. noncrucial object em-

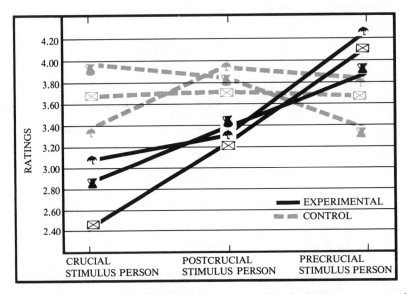

Figure 4.8 Ratings of crucial, postcrucial, and precrucial stimulus persons presented in the testing phase, in three groups differing according to the sequence in which the pictures were presented during the learning phase of Experiment 4.9. The symbols of letter, umbrella, and jug indicate which object was presented during the crucial segments of the ignored channel.

ployed in the above analysis, into a three-level factor: crucial object (i.e., the one displayed simultaneously with the crucial segments of the tape [II, V, VIII]), precrucial object (i.e., the one displayed simultaneously with the segments that preceded the crucial segments (I, IV, VII]), and postcrucial object (i.e., the one that was displayed right after the crucial segments [III, VI, IX]). The mean ratings of crucial, postcrucial, and precrucial objects, in groups with each of three sequences of presentation of pictures (i.e., with letter, umbrella, or jug as a crucial object) are displayed in Figure 4.8. The means indicate no effects for segment in the control groups and a very consistent effect for segment in all three experimental groups, suggesting that the influence of the crucial segments of the list of words presented in the unattended channel spread at least to the next segment. These effects were analyzed in a 5-way ANOVA: 2(condition: experimental vs. control) × 2(delay of the testing phase: one hour vs. no delay) × 3(sequence of presenting the pictures, with: letter, umbrella, or jug, presented during the crucial segments) × 3(rated object: precrucial, crucial, or postcrucial) × 4(rating scales) with repeated measures on the last two factors. This analysis yielded a marginally significant

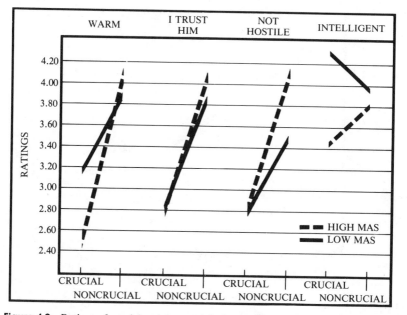

Figure 4.9 Ratings of crucial and noncrucial stimulus persons by subjects with high and low MAS scores in experimental condition of Experiment 4.9.

interaction of group, sequence, and rated object, $F(4, 120) = 2.04$, $p <$ .09, suggesting that the effects of the segment were different in the control and experimental groups. Separate analysis within the experimental group revealed a strong interaction of sequence and rated object, $F(4, 60) = 4.77$, $p < .002$, indicating that the specific effects observed in the experimental conditions are reliable. This analysis demonstrates high sensitivity of the experimental paradigm employed in the present study— each of the consistent curves displayed in Figure 4.8 is based on scores of only 12 subjects.[19]

Permanent Accessibility of Category of Threat

Although subjects' MAS scores were not controlled in the design of this experiment, the scores were symmetrically distributed, allowing for the inclusion of MAS as a 2-level factor (generated by a median split) in the ANOVA. A 5-way ANOVA: 2(condition: experimental vs. control) × 2(delay of the testing phase: one hour vs. no delay) × 2(MAS: below vs. above the median) × 2(rated object: crucial vs. noncrucial) × 4(rating scales) with repeated measures on the two last factors was performed. Although the interaction of conditions, MAS, and rated object was not

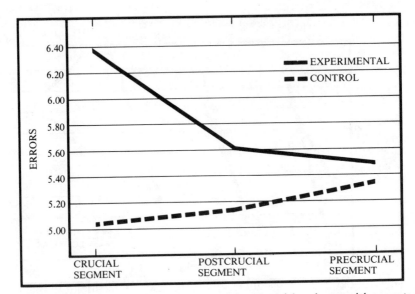

Figure 4.10 Errors in shadowing during crucial, postcrucial, and precrucial segments of the ignored channel.

significant, $F(1, 64) = 1.75$, $p < .18$, planned comparison revealed an interaction of rated object and MAS in the experimental condition, which was very close to the conventional significance level, $F(1, 64) = 3.16$, $p < .07$. Examination of the means (Figure 4.9) indicated that for each of the four rating scales, the effect of the manipulation was stronger in subjects with a more accessible category of threat (i.e., with the higher MAS scores) than in the remaining subjects. Moreover, the means suggest that in subjects with a more accessible category of threat, the effect was generalized to the scale of intelligence for which the ratings in the remaining subjects showed the opposite effect.

Delay of the Testing Phase

None of the above analyses revealed any effects for the factor of delay on subjects' ratings. The ratings of crucial stimulus persons in the experimental conditions decreased reliably in both delay and no-delay subgroups (ps $< .05$). Thus, no evidence was obtained for decay of the experimental effects during the one hour delay.

Errors in Shadowing

Shadowing errors were analyzed in a 2(condition: experimental vs. control) × 3(segment of the ignored channel: crucial [II, V, VIII], precrucial [I, IV, VII], postcrucial [III, VI, IX]) ANOVA with repeated measures on the last factor. This analysis yielded no main effects and no interactions. Planned comparisons (contrasts), however, revealed a slight effect of the segment in the experimental condition, $F(2, 68) = 2.12, p < .12$. The means (Figure 4.10) indicated that subjects in the experimental group made more errors during the crucial as compared to the noncrucial segments. The difference between the error rates in crucial and precrucial segments (in the experimental group) was reliable, $F(1, 68) = 4.31, p < .04$. Number of errors did not correlate with any of the subjects' ratings.

Qualitative analysis of the errors revealed that most of them were distortions. Substitutions from the ignored channel occurred in only four subjects (three from experimental conditions and one from the control condition). Since none of these substitutions referred to the crucial segments, the results of these subjects were not excluded from the analysis.

No effects of the MAS factor on the number or type of errors in shadowing were found.

Discussion

The results obtained demonstrated a consistent and specific bias in perception of testing phase stimulus persons produced by the covariation that had been manipulated in the learning phase. Subjects' impressions of the novel stimulus persons presented in the testing phase followed the relation between the objects presented in the learning phase and the context in which they were presented (i.e., contents of the respective segments of the ignored auditory channel). The experimental paradigm employed in this study (i.e., the "triple-task") made the conscious detection of the manipulated covariation virtually impossible, and, therefore, subjects were not able to control nor to articulate the information that they processed and the rule (i.e., the bias) they followed in their perception of the testing phase stimulus persons.

Subjects in this experiment behaved as if they had learned about the relation between presence of certain objects and threat. The phenomenon observed clearly involved a process of generalization since in the manipulation employed, the only link between information about the threat and the displayed objects was their co-occurrence in time. In other words, threat played only the role of a background that was logically related to neither the objects nor to the stimulus persons displayed on the pictures. Nevertheless, subjects processed and retained these two rationally unrelated variables as related, and they apparently generalized this relation, since in the testing phase their impressions of new stimulus persons were specifically biased depending on the objects that these persons carried.

The question arises at this point as to the particular form of memory representation of the covariation processed by the subjects. Is it represented in memory in the form of a set of exemplars (e.g., pairs of particular words and particular stimulus persons with objects, Medin & Schaffer, 1978; Walker, 1975), or in the form of relations between abstract features (e.g., the relation between a category of an object and a threat, Smith, 1978)? Thus, is the cognitive process leading to the influence of the covariation (stored somehow in memory) on subjects' perception of novel stimuli an "analogy (similarity to instances) mechanism" or a "rule abstraction mechanism" (Elio & Anderson, 1981, p. 416). This question cannot be answered conclusively at this point; however, the abstraction mechanism seems to fit the present data better. The effect of the crucial segments was not confined strictly to the simultaneously displayed object, but it appeared to spread to the object displayed next in the sequence (see Figure 4.8). This may suggest that the words included in the crucial segments activated some general category (i.e., made it temporarily more accessible) or created a certain specific state (e.g., a state of a slightly increased feeling of fear or an expectation of negative experiences). Eventually, this general category or feeling activated in certain segments of the learning phase was processed as being related to certain objects. Thus, the influence of the processed covariation on subjects' perception of novel stimuli might be described in terms of Tulving's (1974) conception of cue-dependent recall: the crucial object exposed in the testing phase played the role of the nonconscious retrieval cue[20] that activated or brought to subjects' short-term memory the general category or feeling induced in the learning phase. It should be noted, however, that the phenomenon observed in this experiment cannot be explained in terms of a cue-dependent decrease in subjects' mood during the testing phase because the effects obtained were specific. Although subjects perceived all three stimulus persons at the same time, the perceptual bias was confined only to the stimulus person with the crucial object and (except for subjects with high MAS scores) to the crucial scales.

The results obtained provided not only a consistent demonstration of the perceptual bias produced by an IPA, but they also supported the notion that this kind of processing may play a role in the development of stable perceptual dispositions. First, the data indicated that the perceptual bias produced by the manipulated covariation did not disappear after one hour of unrelated activity. This kind of durability of the bias suggests that it is a long-term memory phenomenon and that it provides room for operation of self-perpetuating mechanisms (discussed in Chapter 2) capable of strengthening the bias and making it more durable.

Additionally, the mediating effect of permanently accessible categories revealed in the present study suggests that nonconscious processing of covariations may contribute to increases or maintenance of a relatively higher degree of accessibility of certain categories. Higher accessibility of a certain category was shown to facilitate processing of covariation relevant to this category, which, in turn, may make this category even more accessible because it would make it more likely to be activated. In other words, processing and retention of covariations relevant to a given category provides new cues capable of activating this category in future perceptions and thus increasing its overall accessibility.

The research presented in this chapter demonstrates aspects of the processing of covariations that make it a potentially powerful and ubiquitous mechanism of acquisition of stable personality dispositions.

Notes

1. In the pilot study 80 subjects answered four versions of "either/or" questions about each of the three crucial trait relationships. For example, the four questions referring to the first trait relationship were" (1) People who are active are more likely to be: demanding or not demanding? (2) People who are passive are more likely to be: demanding or not demanding? (3) People who are demanding are more likely to be: active or passive? (4) People who are not demanding are more likely to be: active or passive? The order of these 12 questions was randomized across subjects. There was near perfect agreement among subjects regarding these relationships; only two subjects out of 80 (2.5%) did not answer all of the 12 trait-inference questions according to the common pattern.

2. Stimulus persons within each of these two categories (fictitious and real) were differentiated regarding the amount of subjects' knowledge about stimulus persons and other characteristics, and there was a set of related, specific hypotheses concerning the differences between the stimulus persons in their susceptibility to the manipulation. None of them has been confirmed, however, so they will not be presented.

3. A more detailed discussion of possible effects on the level of consciousness and a series of additional studies addressing the issues of changes in subjects' memories in the course of listening to the stimulus material and momentary awareness effects are presented in the context of Experiments 4.4 and 4.5. The stimulus material employed in that experiment was only a slightly modified version of the present material.

4. No correlation was found between the reported and real number of inconsistencies in either group.

5. The generality of that tendency to perceive introverts as more intelligent than extroverts is confined to the particular trait dimensions defining the two categories in the particular rating form. Especially, introversion–extroversion is open to different interpretations stressing its different aspects.

6. These two possible mechanisms underlying the obtained effect of manipulated covariation are relevant to the distinction between "computational" and "prestorage" models of semantic memory to be discussed in the next experiment.

7. What I mean here is that memory traces of some aspects of the stimulus persons the subjects were presented with during the learning phase might be easier to access or activate than any other at the time when subjects were rating new stimulus persons.

8. Predictions for the "no" response seem less clear. Processing time for such a response could again be slower if the overlap falls between two criteria and the second stage

of processing is executed or faster if the overlap falls below the lower criterion. This ambiguity does not seem, however, to be a problem here, since due to the nonconsciousness issue mentioned above, only processing time for the "yes" responses is of interest for our reasoning.

9. The V^2 is the χ^2 corrected for sample size as recently suggested by Kendall and Stuart (1979), and Rhoades and Overall (1982). All the V^2 analyses reported in Experiment 4.3, 4.4, and 4.5 fit case II, as discussed by Kendall and Stuart (1979).

10. There was no evidence that some subjects gave responses consistent with the stereotype across all or most of the statements, while others showed a pattern of giving counterstereotypic responses. Thus, there was no support in the data for the above interpretation.

11. Dealing mostly with subjects' explicit (i.e., declarative) knowledge, which is different than the working knowledge actually influencing their perceptions, seems to be one of the major factors responsible for the poor external validity of the research on so-called implicit personality theories (Lewicki, 1981; Ostrom, Lingle, Pryor, & Geva, 1980; Schneider, Hastorf, & Ellsworth, 1979).

12. This experiment was conducted by M. Czyzewska (1984) as part of a doctoral dissertation submitted to the Department of Psychology at the University of Warsaw.

13. There is evidence suggesting that the perception of real and known persons is indicative of an individual's perceptual dispositions (Lewicki, 1981, 1983, 1984b; Gara & Rosenberg, 1979, 1981), since such perception is less likely to activate artificial response sets than the task of rating fictitious stimulus persons. Additionally, employing fictitious stimulus persons is difficult for procedural reasons, since rating numerous fictitious persons on the numerous dimensions required in order to capture reliable correlations would be an extremely boring task for subjects.

14. Experiments 4.7 and 4.8 were made in cooperation with Piotr Bielawski, Anna Otffinowska, and Janusz Tworzynski.

15. An informal survey was conducted (as part of this study) that indicated that people usually think that a low (and not high) voice implies being warm, which is contrary to this finding, and to the results of Experiment 4.8.

16. This experiment was conducted in cooperation with Dorota Szczepan.

17. There were two different objects presented during the noncrucial segments of the tape. Ratings of the noncrucial object were an average of the ratings of these two different objects.

18. The ratings were transformed so that high numbers always indicated desirable ratings (i.e., less threat or more intelligence).

19. This does not mean, however, that each curve is based on 12 single scores, because each of these 12 subjects made 12 separate ratings.

20. Tulving (1974) argued that cued recall gives not only better results than free recall but even better than recognition.

CHAPTER 5

Processing Covariations (III): Experiments with Small Children

Introduction

It was argued in Chapters 1 and 2 that the actual performance of pre-school children and their ability to acquire a working knowledge in various domains considerably outstrips the concepts and categories that they are able to consciously "understand" or verbalize. It was also argued that their high, nonconscious sensitivity to covariations and their ability to process them and to store them in long-term memory in the form of internal processing algorithms (IPAs) is responsible for this discrepancy. The following experiments were designed to explore the nonconscious sensitivity to covariations in small children.

The experimental paradigm employed in these studies was analogous to the one employed in the experiments presented in Chapter 4. First, there was a learning phase, during which subjects were exposed to stimulus material containing a covariation; second, after a distractor task, subjects were tested on whether they had acquired the respective IPAs (i.e., whether they influenced subjects' behavior). Since subjects in these experiments were small children, the entire procedure was designed as a play or game. Its first phase attracted subjects' attention to the crucial aspects of the stimulus material, and, after the distractor, the second phase always involved some guessing game that provided the opportunity to assess whether an IPA had been acquired.

Experiment 5.1[1]

In the learning phase, subjects were exposed to a succession of matrices consisting of colored squares and small pictures of simple objects. The crucial covariation pertained to locations of colored squares in relation to certain categories of objects across the sequence of matrices. In the testing phase, following a distractor task, subjects were presented with similar frames, but these frames were covered with colored covers. The subjects' task was to guess where a certain object was located. The covers had the same design of colored squares as the frames from the learning phase, and thus they provided a basis for accurate guessing, assuming that the manipulated covariation was processed and stored in the form of an IPA.

Method

Subjects and General Conditions

Seventy-one 5-year-olds (boys and girls) from a number of day-care centers participated in the study. Subjects were selected on the basis of not being color blind. The experiment was conducted in the respective day-care centers; however, the procedure required subjects to be run individually in a separate room, which could have frightened subjects if they had not been acquainted with the experimenters. Therefore, before the sessions started, the experimenters spent two days with each group of participants, assisting in their routine programs and getting acquainted with the children. This was designed to make the children comfortable and relaxed during the experiment, which was introduced as "a new fascinating game." The data were gathered by two independent teams of experimenters (two persons each). Each team contributed equally to each experimental condition.

Stimulus Materials and Procedure

The stimulus material employed in this experiment was similar to the "matrix scanning paradigm" (see Chapter 3); however, instead of reaction times, subjects' choices were assessed at the end of the experiment (as in the last phase of Experiment 3.4). In the learning phase subjects were exposed to a succession of eight 4 × 4 matrices, divided into four quarters. The four squares in the center of the matrix were empty and colored red, green, blue, and yellow, while the remaining squares contained small black and white pictures. The pictures presented simple, well-known objects belonging to four categories (homes, cars, flowers, and trees). Objects from each category were located in separate quarters of the matrix. Thus, in a given matrix, each category of objects was associated with a different color (Figure 5.1), since they were located in the same quarter. The entire succession of eight matrices was arranged so that there was a systematic covariation between object categories and colors.

The matrices were located on cardboards (40 cm × 40 cm), and they were presented on a table in front of the subject. Subjects were also provided with a set of 12 cards (10 cm × 10 cm each) displaying the same pictures as those displayed in the matrix. Their task was to cover each picture on the matrix with a card containing its matching picture. They were asked to do it as fast as they could. The four colored squares in the middle of the matrix always remained uncovered. After each successful or partially successful completion of the task, the subject was praised and presented with the next matrix. This phase was expected to provide subjects with an opportunity to nonconsciously learn about the crucial covariation.

After a total of eight trials, there was a 5-min-long distractor task con-

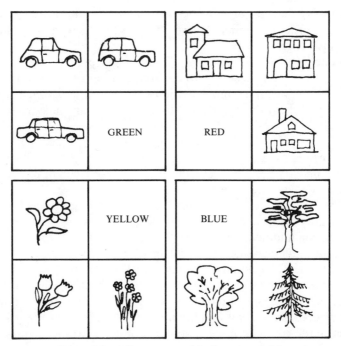

Figure 5.1 A frame exposed in Experiment 5.1.

sisting of a standard conversation with the subject and the presentation of some cartoons.

The testing phase was introduced to a subject as "a guessing game." The subject was exposed to a succession of four matrices, but in this phase they were covered with cardboard covers. The covers were divided into 16 squares, analogous to the squares of the covered matrix. The four squares in the center of the cover were colored exactly as the center squares of the covered matrix; the remaining 12 squares, however, were blank and consisted of small, closed windows that could be opened independently. The subjects' task was "to guess under which window a house is located," and they were asked to do it quickly. The nature of this task was explained to subjects with the help of a blank matrix and a blank cover with windows. The testing session began when the experimenters were sure that a subject completely understood the task. After the first unsuccessful guessing trial, a subject could try for a second time.

It would have been better for the design of the present study if subjects could not have opened the windows they had chosen, since it would have freed us from uncontrolled effects of direct feedback during the testing phase. However, this was impossible, because without feedback regarding the accuracy of their guessing, subjects would have found the task meaningless, and the level of their motivation would probably have decreased. In order to minimize these effects, subjects were only allowed to try the task twice.

In order to avoid the potential effects of any preexisting associations between colors and objects, two covariations between categories of objects and colors were manipulated in two different experimental groups. In neither of them did the covariations seem "realistic" or stereotypic (e.g., yellow houses and green trees). The houses co-occurred with a green color in experimental Condition I, and with a blue color in Condition II. The matrices used in the testing phase were different from those of the learning phase; they were the same in both conditions, and they contained no consistent covariation.

At the end of the session participants were questioned regarding whether they had based their guessing on the arrangement of colored squares in the middle of the cover. This turned out to be the most difficult part of the session, since the vast majority of the subjects could not understand these questions, although we tried to design them to be as simple as possible. After a number of trials we refined the questions so that they could be understood. Judging from the responses, it appeared that subjects did not pay any attention to the arrangements of colored squares on the covers. They did not remember the arrangements of colors and objects from the learning phase, and they tried to follow the instruction to "guess." They seemed to be totally naive subjects, and we found no evidence suggesting that subjects consciously detected the nature of our manipulation. After running and interviewing these 71 children, we concluded that it was probable that, even if they consciously discovered and remembered the covariations manipulated in the learning phase (which was not the case), they would not consciously attempt to employ them in the testing phase. It was clear that they tried to follow the explicit instruction to guess.

Pilot Study

The main purpose of the pilot study was to explore subjects' memory for the co-occurrences of colors and objects presented in the learning phase. Thirty 5-year-olds were tested using exactly the same procedure as in the main study up to the testing phase, half with each version of the stimulus material. Instead of the testing phase, they were shown a matrix with pictures, but with the four center squares left blank (white). Then, using very simple words, subjects were informed that in all the matrices they had seen before colors co-occurred with objects. Their task was to recall which color co-occurred with "homes" Because we expected that some subjects would have problems with naming the colors, we presented four colored cards, and subjects could respond by indicating the color or locating the respective card in the square matching the quarter with homes. Subjects' responses were completely independent of the manipulation. Actually, the majority of subjects in both conditions picked red, supposedly the most attractive or most salient color for children, although this color was not associated with homes in any of the conditions.

Results and Discussion

The index of subjects' accuracy was the number of successful guesses; thus, since four matrices were presented in the testing phase, accuracy was measured on a 5-point scale (0 through 4). Two versions of that index were employed, depending on whether only the first or the first and second guesses were taken into account. Because there was no objective evidence for lack of preexisting associations between homes and some colors, the analysis did not employ as H_o any theoretical point of reference (e.g., 25% accurate responses in the first trials), but instead the two conditions were compared regarding the number of accurate responses using the same reference point for accuracy in both conditions. Two separate analyses were performed. First, only responses consistent with the stimulus material presented in Condition I were considered "accurate,"[2] or second, only responses consistent with material from Condition II were considered "accurate." It was expected that in Condition I there would be more Type I accurate responses, while in Condition II there would be more Type II accurate responses. The advantage of this type of analysis was that it could provide information regarding the relative "difficulty to learn" of each of the two covariations manipulated in the experiment. For example, if a difference between conditions would emerge only when employing the Condition I accuracy criterion, but not when employing the Condition II criterion, it would indicate that the covariation manipulated in Condition I was easier to process than that manipulated in Condition II.

The results were consistent with the expectations. Mean accuracy scores, based on subjects' first responses to each matrix, revealed that subjects in Condition I ($M = 1.31$) were more accurate than subjects in Condition II ($M = 0.90$), using the Condition I criterion of accuracy, $t(69) = 2.62, p < .02$, and that they were less accurate ($M = 0.88$) than subjects in Condition II ($M = 1.26$), using the Condition II criterion of accuracy, $t(69) = 2.90, p < .01$. The same results were obtained when using accuracy scores based on the first two responses to each matrix.

It should be noted that the testing phase in this experiment could also be considered as an uncontrolled learning phase, since every successful response, that is, locating the house, provided an additional experience supporting some new or old covariation, and every unsuccessful response provided implicit information that "it's better to try some other algorithm." Therefore, we tried to trace individual sequences ("histories") of responses in each subject. No consistent patterns were found that would indicate any learning effects during the testing phase. Additional V^2 analyses performed on subjects' first responses in the testing phase (i.e., the first guessing regarding the first matrix) indicated that there were predicted and reliable ($ps < .05$) differences between conditions, indicating that the IPA acquired in the learning phase reliably influenced subjects' first choice in the guessing game.

The results of this experiment seem to be clear. It can be assumed that participants in this experiment were naive subjects, and they were completely unaware of the covariation manipulated in the learning phase. On the other hand, however, the choices they made in the testing phase (i.e., the guessing game) indicated that they had acquired the manipulated covariation, and that they had stored it in the form of an internal processing algorithm. In the next experiment, we attempted to demonstrate the process of acquisition of a somewhat more complicated IPA.

Experiment 5.2[3]

In the present study we employed stimulus material similar to that used in Experiment 5.1, but we manipulated two independent covariations simultaneously. The testing material was arranged so that completely accurate responses could be provided only if subjects simultaneously followed both covariations; however, we could also assess whether they followed each of these covariations independently.

Method

Subjects and General Conditions

Seventy-five 5-year-olds (boys and girls) from several day-care centers participated in the study. The experiment was conducted in the centers, and subjects were tested in a separate room. The procedure was similar to the one employed in Experiment 5.1; as before, the experimenters spent two days with each group of children in order to get acquainted with them. The data were gathered by two independent teams of experimenters (four persons each). Each team contributed equally to each experimental condition.

Stimulus Materials and Procedure

The logic used to construct the stimulus material and the dependent measures were the same as in the previous study. However, not one but two different covariations were manipulated; the nature of the stimuli was somewhat more complex since it involved cues from outside the matrix.

As before, in the learning phase, subjects were exposed to a succession of eight 4 × 4 matrices divided into four quarters. The quarters, however, were separated by wider distances in order to stress the fact (i.e., make it clear to subjects) that they represented distinct units (i.e., choice alternatives during the testing phase). Each of 16 squares contained a picture of a different well-known object, and one of them was a house (Figure 5.2). Prior to each presentation the matrix was covered. Subjects' task, after uncovering the matrix, was to find a house among the pictures and to point to it with a finger as soon as possible.

Two independent covariations were manipulated in this stimulus material. The cover of the matrix was either red or blue, and its color covaried with the location of the target in either the left or right half of the matrix (i.e., in either the upper or lower left quarter, or in the upper or lower right quarter). Subjects sat at a table, and each covered matrix was sepa-

Figure 5.2 A frame exposed in Experiment 5.2.

rately brought to them by the experimenter, who approached subjects
from either the left or the right side of the table. The experimenter's
position, in turn, covaried with location of the target in either the upper or
lower half of the matrix.

There were two experimental conditions that differed regarding the
specific arrangement of these two covariations. In Condition I, a red
cover co-occurred with the location of the target in the left half of the
matrix, and a blue cover with the right half. A left position of the experimenter co-occurred in this condition with the location of the target in the
upper half of the matrix, and a right position with the lower half. Condition II was arranged in the "opposite" way.

In the testing phase (after the distractor task that was the same as in
Experiment 5.1), subjects were presented with a series of four matrices.
Each matrix was covered with either a red or blue cover and, when
bringing each matrix, the experimenter approached the subject from either the left or right side. There were 16 small, closed windows in the
cover; they reflected positions of the pictures in the matrix, and they
could be opened independently. This phase of the study was introduced to
the subjects as a "guessing game"; their task was "to guess under which

window a house is located,'' and they were asked to do so as quickly as possible. Subjects were allowed two trials for each matrix. As before, the nature of this task was explained to the subjects with the help of a blank matrix with a blank cover. In order to avoid potential experimenter's nonverbal influence on subjects' choices, different experimenters conducted the learning and the testing phase, and the one who conducted the testing phase was blind to the experimental conditions.

The postexperimental interviews provided results similar to those obtained in Experiment 5.1. Participants in this study were completely unaware of the nature of the manipulation.

Pilot Study

An additional 20 children were tested in order to explore whether, at the begining of the testing phase, subjects were able to recall the arrangement of crucial elements (color of the cover and/or position of the experimenter and location of the target) in at least one concrete instance (i.e., matrix) presented in the learning phase. The problem was analalogous to that described in Experiment 4.5. Various ways of formulating these questions were explored in this study; no evidence was found, however, for subjects' remembering any of the crucial arrangements. They were focused entirely on the ''search task,'' and they paid no conscious attention to the context.

Results and Discussion

The analysis of Experiment 5.2 was basically the same as that of Experiment 5.1, however, in order to assess the independent influence of each of the two manipulated covariations, as well as their joint effect on subjects' choices, several versions of the criteria for ''accurate'' responses were employed. The two experimental conditions were compared regarding the mean number of ''accurate'' responses based on 12 different versions of accuracy scores that are conceivable by combining the following possibilities for defining accuracy: (1) accuracy regarding the manipulations used in the first or in second experimental condition; (2) accuracy of the first response, or the first *and* second responses; (3) accuracy with regard to the upper or lower half of the matrix, with regard to the left or right side of the matrix, or with regard to both.

The results were consistent with expectations. Mean accuracy scores, based on subjects' first responses to each matrix and based on the criterion of the ''correct quarter'' (i.e., correct choice of both upper or lower and left or right half of the matrix) revealed that subjects in Condition I

(M = 1.55) were more accurate than subjects in Condition II (M = .70), using the Condition I criterion of accuracy, $t(73)$ = 4.25, $p < .001$, and that they were less accurate (M = 0.71) than subjects in Condition II (M = 1.46), using the Criterion II criterion of accuracy, $t(73)$ = 3.36, $p < .002$. This pattern was found in analyses based on all of the versions of accuracy scores ($ps < .05$), as well as in V^2 analyses of the accuracy of subjects' first responses to the first matrix ($ps < .05$).

The process demonstrated in this experiment could be described as either nonconscious simultaneous acquisition of two independent IPAs that subsequently, in the testing phase, "cooperated" or at least did not interfere in producing consistent responses, or nonconscious acquisition of one "higher level" IPA. In the latter case the algorithm would be represented by the covariation of three variables rather than by the simple two-variable covariation we dealt with before (e.g., "when the cover is blue, choose the right upper quarter, but only if the experimenter approaches you from the left side; however, choose the right lower quarter when she approaches you from the other side"). Obviously, the design of this experiment did not provide the means to discriminate between these two possibilities. On a more general, functional level of interpretation, however, both of them seem to suggest the same. They indicate that more than one covariation may be simultaneously and nonconsciously processed and stored in the form of an IPA (either as a single, complex one, or as a set of simple ones). The functional "higher order" IPA acquired in the present study may be considered as a simple laboratory analogue of the complicated systems of high-order IPAs discussed in Chapter 2 that were hypothesized to be basic structures responsible for the acquisition of language and semantic knowledge in general, including various cognitive and behavioral dispositions.

Five-year-olds proved to be very good subjects for investigating nonconscious cognition. They appeared to be sensitive to the manipulation, but still naive on the level of their conscious awareness, thus requiring less precautions for avoiding the effects of "transparent manipulations" than when dealing with adult subjects. We will return to experiments with small children in Chapter 7, which deals with another phenomenon of nonconscious generalization of experience.

Notes

1.   The cooperation of Malgorzata Charkiewicz and the participants in a seminar on cognitive developmental psychology at the Department of Psychology, University of War-

saw, in the preparation of the stimulus materials and conducting this study is gratefully acknowledged.

2. ''Accurate'' response does not, in this context, represent a successful response (i.e., finding the house).

3. The cooperation of Grazyna Nasiadko and the participants in a seminar on cognitive developmental psychology at the Department of Psychology, University of Warsaw in the preparation of the stimulus material and conducting this study is gratefully acknowledged.

CHAPTER 6

Processing Covariations (IV): The Two-Stage Model*

Introduction

All the experiments on processing covariations presented in Chapters 3, 4 (except Experiment 4.3), and 5, employed dependent measures that pertained exclusively to whether the respective internal processing algorithms worked. The dependent measures could only indicate whether an IPA was developed and powerful enough to influence a subject's judgment or behavior. Such indices are very conservative as far as the existence of the phenomenon of nonconscious detection and processing of covariation is concerned, and they may produce the impression that the phenomenon is less general and less ubiquitous than it may actually be. It seemed reasonable to expect that between the initiation of the process of development of an IPA and the establishment of the IPA that would be strong enough to influence judgments, there would be intermediate stages that cannot be detected by indices based exclusively on whether the IPA works.

Uncontrolled factors that interfered with the experimental situation in the studies presented so far (e.g., various uncontrolled nonconscious processes), might have inhibited in some subjects the process of development of an IPA. Thus, at the time when the dependent measures were administered, some subjects seemed not to have detected the covariation, although in fact they had, but the development of the IPA may only have been in the early stages and the IPA may not have been strong enough to

* I am grateful to Malgorzata Ciepluch, Wlodek Daab, Ewa Engelking, Barbara Engelking, Jola Falkowska, Ewa Kot, Justyna Kubicka, and Malgorzata Parzuch, who contributed to the preparation of research presented in this chapter and tested the subjects in all pilot studies and in Experiments 6.1–6.6, 6.8, and 6.9. Portions of this chapter are adapted from Lewicki, 1986.

influence judgments. The other possibility is that some of these subjects, whose behavior was found unchanged by the manipulation, had processed all the crucial instances referring to the manipulated covariation, but for some reason (e.g., inconsistency of the covariation implied by the manipulation with some preexisting IPAs) the new IPA was not activated. The latter does not mean that the manipulated covariation had not been detected and processed. In fact, it might have been detected and processed, but the evidence in question was found insufficient to produce the working IPA, due to its inconsistency with some preexisting structures of semantic memory.

This reasoning suggests that if a more sensitive measure of subjects' processing of the manipulated covariation was available, the results of the preceding experiments would have been much stronger, since such a measure could capture not only strong IPAs but also such instances of processing of the manipulated covariation that, for these or other reasons, had not been concluded with the establishment of a strong IPA. The starting point for the research presented in this chapter was to search for a new measure of nonconscious detecting and processing of covariations that would be capable of capturing not only cases of strong IPAs (as in the previous studies), but also such cases in which an IPA was developed but was not strong enough to influence judgments.

The general idea of the experimental paradigm employed in the studies to be presented was inspired by J. R. Anderson's (1976, 1983) theory of retrieval processes from long-term memory, and by Glucksberg and McCloskey's (1981) question–answering model. Neither of these two theories has mentioned processing of covariation, both of them, however, suggest a supposedly very sensitive measure for the investigation of whether a subject's memory contains any cognitive representation of knowledge relevant to a question. Therefore, if questions could be formulated so that the only kind of relevant information would be information about the covariation manipulated in the experiment (regardless of whether its representation was strong enough to influence subjects' choices or not), this method could provide a sensitive measure of whether the development of an IPA was initiated. This would allow investigating such nonconsciously acquired knowledge about the manipulated covariation that has not (or has not yet) gained the status of a strong IPA.

Let us look closely at the question–answering model of Glucksberg and McCloskey (1981). The model postulates that answering questions involves a two-stage process:

> In the first stage a preliminary memory search is conducted to determine whether anything relevant for answering the question is known. If no relevant information is found, a rapid don't know decision is made. If, however, relevant facts are re-

trieved, these are examined in detail to determine whether they specify an answer to the question. If the retrieved information proves to be insufficient, however, a slow don't know response is made. (p. 321)

In a series of studies, Glucksberg and McCloskey determined that, consistent with their model, the response latencies were considerably longer when the stimulus material the subjects were exposed to prior to answering the questions contained any sort of information relevant to the question, than when it contained no such relevant information. It was true even when the relevant information was confined to a statement that nothing relevant was known about the issue. For example, response latency to the question of whether it was true that "John has a chair," was longer when the subjects had learned that "John has a chair," or "John does not have a chair," and even when they had learned that "It is unknown whether John has a chair," than when they had not learned anything relevant to the relation between John and a chair (i.e., when they had learned only about somebody else possessing a chair and about John possessing something else).

These results suggest that latency of response to a question might provide a sensitive measure of whether anything relevant to the question had been registered by a perceiver in the stimulus material he or she was previously exposed to. If there exists in memory some relevant information, then response latency is longer (see also Anderson, 1983). This "paradox of the expert" (Anderson, 1983, p. 28)[1] is counterintuitive, since it implies that when one knows the answer to a question, then responding takes longer than when one does not know the answer. It should be noted, however, that the model refers exclusively to the retrieval processes that are not mediated by conscious awareness. Obviously, people do not consciously decide to initiate the "second stage" of processing. Moreover, they are not aware of the very moment of triggering the second stage, nor have they access to any criteria that have to be met before the second stage is triggered. In the testing phase of the Glucksberg and McCloskey experiment, subjects employed knowledge that was overlearned during the learning phase and that could be easily recalled without the help of any conscious strategies or mnemonic devices.

It may well be expected, however, that if subjects in these experiments had to employ any consciously controlled retrieval or inferential strategy in order to retrieve or generate the relevant information, the response time pattern would not conform to the one predicted by the Glucksberg and McCloskey model. Consider, for example, a situation in which in order to respond to a testing phase question, subjects had to evaluate serially (i.e., by means of some consciously controlled strategy) the items they had memorized in the learning phase. (This might be due to some complicated nature of the testing phase question and/or to poor memorization of the material.) In such a case the response time pattern would most likely not conform to Glucksberg and McCloskey's predictions. Moreover, the response time pattern could even be "reversed," since response latency would be longer in a case where all items had to be evaluated, that is, in a case where there is no relevant information in the memorized material.

The Glucksberg and McCloskey model (and the above reasoning concerning response latency patterns expected when retrieval strategy is consciously controlled and when it is not consciously controlled) may be employed in processing information about covariation since a covariation may also be considered a case of information relevant to some questions. Namely, if a perceiver has registered and memorized a covariation between categories x and y and has not memorized a covariation between categories x and z, then he or she would possess information relevant to a question as to whether an exemplar of category x is y and would not possess such information concerning a question whether an exemplar of category x is z. Eventually, his or her response latency to the former question would be longer than to the latter one (consistent with the Glucksberg and McCloskey model).

An advantage of this method of determining whether a covariation has been processed is that it potentially might reveal the existence of a memory trace of the previously registered covariation that cannot bias subjects' subsequent perceptions directly (i.e., a weak IPA). Thus, even if the memory trace of the nonconsciously processed covariation failed to influence subjects' subsequent judgments, the method was hypothesized to be sensitive enough to detect the mere existence of the trace of the covariation.

It should be noted, however, that the previously stated response time pattern can be expected only if the underlying retrieval processes work as in Glucksberg and McCloskey's experiment, that is, when the relevant information (about covariation) is accessed without employing any consciously controlled retrieval or inferential strategies. This condition is met when subjects are not aware of possessing the information about the covariation.[2]

This reaction time pattern cannot be expected, however, when subjects are aware of the covariation and employ the covariation in the course of a controlled process generating their responses (i.e., when the responses are inferred on the basis of the covariation following a consciously controlled process of reasoning).

The difference between the response latency patterns (expected when processing of covariation is consciously controlled vs. nonconscious) will be shown in an example that also introduces the specific paradigm used in the following experiments.

The stimulus material consisted of photos and short descriptions of six stimulus persons. Three of them were long-haired, and they were presented as being very kind; three others were short-haired and were presented as being very capable. The material was arranged so that these covariations were not salient and thus nonaccessible to subjects' conscious awareness. In the testing phase, subjects were exposed to photos of some other stimulus persons (either long- or short-haired) and asked either whether the person was kind or whether she was capable. Based on the previously stated reasoning it might be expected that if the covariations present in the material were nonconsciously detected and memorized by the subjects, the response latency to the questions relevant to the covariations would be longer than the response latency to the irrelevant questions. For example, response latency to the question as to whether a stimulus person was kind would be longer when the specific person was long-haired (since subjects possessed the relevant knowledge that long-haired persons are kind) than when she was short-haired (since nothing was "learned" about the kindness of short-haired persons). Response times for the questions about capability would be affected in an analogous (i.e., "reversed") manner.

It might be expected, however, that in the case that subjects were aware of the covariation and employed a consciously controlled strategy of generating responses consistent with these covariations, the above response latency difference between relevant and irrelevant questions would not occur, since such a consciously controlled strategy would not follow the two-stage process postulated by Glucksberg and McCloskey and would take the same amount of time for each combination of question and haircut, regardless of its relevance to the manipulated covariation. Such a consciously controlled algorithm could be, for example, as follows. First, determine whether the question pertains to kindness or capability; if it pertains to kindness, then check if the hair is long; if it is long, answer "yes"; if it is short, then either employ some other algorithm, or at once give a random response, either "yes" or "no." The order of steps in this example is arbitrary (e.g., one might start with checking the hair), and there could be many other possibilities of how it could proceed. None of them, however, seems to predict longer processing time for responses to questions relevant to the knowledge one is trying to employ, as was predicted by the Glucksberg and McCloskey model.

The following three experiments (6.1, 6.2, and 6.3) explored response latency patterns in conditions in which subjects were not consciously aware of the covariation manipulated in the stimulus material. Next, the data obtained were compared to response latency patterns revealed in analogous experiments that differed, however, from the former ones in that subjects were able (Experiment 6.4), instructed (Experiment 6.5), or instructed and motivated (Experiment 6.6), to employ consciously controlled strategies to conform their responses with the covariation.

Experiment 6.1

Since the experimental procedure employed in this experiment turned out to be highly effective and was employed (with small modifications) in six subsequent experiments, it is presented here in detail.

Method

Overview

The stimulus materials were six slides presenting faces of young women, accompanied by brief descriptions read by the experimenter. The women differed in their haircuts: three had long hair and three had short hair. The descriptions differed in what traits they referred to: three of them focused exclusively on the kindness and helpfulness of the stimulus person and three others on her capability and effectiveness. There were two versions of stimulus material. One group of subjects was exposed to the stimulus material in which all three women with long hair were kind and all three with short hair were capable (Condition I); the other group was exposed to the material in which all three long-haired women were capable and all three short-haired ones were kind (Condition II). In other words, the former group received no information relevant to the capability of long-haired women or to the kindness of short-haired ones; the latter group received no information relevant to the kindness of long-haired women or to the capability of short-haired ones.

After a distractor task subjects were asked about the kindness and capability of a different set of four stimulus persons presented on slides; half of them had long and half of them had short hair. Latency of responses to these questions was measured. Based on the model presented above, it was hypothesized that if a given covariation present in the stimulus material was registered in memory, it would make the response latency to the relevant questions longer, since it would provide the relevant information that would have to be "examined in detail to determine whether they specify an answer to the question" (Glucksberg & McCloskey, 1981, p. 321).

An important difference between Glucksberg and McCloskey's and the present study is that in the former the relevant information was explicitly contained in the stimulus material, and in the latter it was contained implicitly, that is, it could influence subjects' response time only if it had actually been registered. In this sense the present study provided a test of whether the subjects had registered the covariation.

Subjects

Fifty-four undergraduates participated in the study. There was an equal number of men and women; none of them were psychology majors. The subjects were recruited in various parts of the campus in order to minimize the probability that they knew each other, since it was important in the present experiment that subjects did not know the procedure before entering the lab room. They were randomly assigned to two experimental conditions (i.e., the two versions of the stimulus material), separately by sex.

Stimulus Material

Slides.   The process of selecting the slides was based on anthropological advice and the opinions of a number of judges (men and women undergraduates). The aim was to obtain two sets of faces that would differ exclusively in their haircut and not in other characteristics (like race, anthropological type, color of hair, size and color of eyes, proportions and shape of face, general attractiveness as estimated by men and women, and type of dress). Finally, 10 photos (black and white) of women (undergraduates) were selected out of a pool of about 50 photos. Six of them were used in the learning phase and 4 in the testing phase (in different arrangements). The photos were slightly different in degree of "close-up" in order to make comparisons between them more difficult. The haircuts within each of the two subsets (i.e., long and short hair) were differentiated in order to make the difference between the sets less salient; that is, it was not so that simulus persons all had either very short or very long hair. The photos are displayed in Figure 6.1 and they are arranged so that the two rows represent the two levels of haircut (long and short) and each column represents the pair of faces considered by the judges as similar both "physically" and "psychologically." The latter was positively verified in a pilot study with 70 undergraduates who rated each of the 10 photos on five 6-point, bipolar trait dimensions (kind, capable, persistent, frank, physically attractive). The pilot study subjects were tested individually, and both the order of the photos and of the trait

Figure 6.1 Stimulus persons (Experiment 6.1).

dimensions was randomized across subjects. The overall means for long- and short-haired photos indicated a trend for short-haired stimulus persons to be perceived as slightly more capable ($p < .11$); there were no differences, however, even approaching the .10 significance level for the other four dimensions).

There were four permutations of the 10 slides employed with regard to which of them was used in which phase (learning or testing) and in which order they were presented. The sets were the same in both experimental conditions, and each slide served about an equal number of times in the learning phase and in the testing phase. The short-haired and long-haired slides were presented alternately, both in the learning and in the testing phase. (These orders of slides appeared to affect none of the dependent measures.)

Descriptions. It was made clear to the subjects that the stimulus persons were psychologically unusual and that the descriptions would focus only on those special features. The descriptions were very short (three sentences each) and pertained exclusively to either kindness or capability: The stimulus persons were presented as either very kind and helpful or very capable and effective. The descriptions are quoted fully in the Appendix.

Procedure

Subjects participated individually. The session began with a training with the reaction time apparatus. Questions referring to whether certain people a subject knew (such as mother, friend, professor) possessed certain personality characteristics were presented in the rear projection screen, and subjects were asked to respond quickly and accurately by pressing either the "yes" or the "no" key on a control box.

The next part of the experiment was introduced to subjects as "a kind of psychological training which helps you concentrate before the experiment." Slides of 6 of the 10 stimulus persons were then presented in the rear projection screen (48×72 cm and about 150 cm distant from a subject) by a programmed projection tachistoscope. Each slide was presented for 15 s and there were 2.5 s long intervals between presentations, during which the display was blank. The trained experimenter read the descriptions in such a way that she finished reading each description 1–2 s after the offset of a slide. That is, the text was always a little longer than the exposure of a slide, and subjects could never watch a slide without being distracted by the text being read. (As compared to presenting text from a tape recorder, this method has the advantage of better attracting a subject's attention.)

Subjects were also told that the stimulus persons were "real" and that they were chosen as "remarkable" (i.e., especially positive in some respect) from a large pool of extensive case studies prepared recently by students of clinical psychology. This was explained in detail to make the subjects serious about the stimulus material and to prevent subjects' becoming suspicious about the artificial pattern that was followed in the stimulus material (e.g., about the rules of matching slides and descriptions), which could be the case if subjects thought the material was fictitious.

The experimenter was blind to the sequence of slides that was exposed to each subject; thus she did not know to which slide a given description referred (long or short hair). Subjects were asked to imagine the personalities of the persons described and displayed, but not to relate these images to their impressions of any real persons he or she knew that might resemble a stimulus person physically or psychologically. The above instructions were introduced as "requirements of successful training."

It should be noted that the above time sequence (16–17 s long presentations of material and 0.5–1.5 s long intervals) left subjects no spare time to think or make conscious comparisons, and so on. The descriptions had to be read fast to fit their 16–17 s limits.[3]

There was a distractor task separating the learning phase from the dependent measures, designed to interfere with subjects' short-term memory. This distractor was a standard "conversation" initiated by the experimenter, which lasted approximately twice as long as the entire presentation of the stimulus material (i.e., about 3 min).

Next, subjects were presented with the four remaining slides; each of them was exposed two times: once accompanied by the one-word question "KIND?" and once by the one-word question "CAPABLE?"; thus, there was a total of eight exposures in this phase of the experiment. The two exposures of the same slide were separated by two to four other exposures. The one-word questions covered the lowest one-seventh of a slide and were printed in uppercase block letters (9 cm high), black on white. The onset of the slide triggered a microprocessor timer, accurate to the nearest ms. Measurement of the response latency ended either when the subject pressed one of two keys "yes" or "no" on a control box, or when a 10 s maximum had been reached (which never happened). The timer registered subjects' "yes/no" responses and response times. There were 3 s long intervals between presentations, during which the display was blank. Subjects were told not to consider in detail their responses, but they were told instead to respond as quickly as possible following only their "first thought" about the stimulus person.

At the end of the session subjects were asked whether they "were able to discover a co-occurrence between the psychological characteristics of the stimulus persons presented during the first stage of the experiment and any of their visual characteristics." Over 75% of the subjects responded "yes" and explained that there was something special but difficult to describe in their faces (e.g., "those intelligent girls simply looked brighter"). Most of the subjects mentioned the stimulus persons' gaze and said that some of them possessed "those typical eyes of the dependable person" or "a sharp gaze of a bright person." Not one subject mentioned haircut or anything connected with hair.[4]

A potential shortcoming of the measure, regarding what subjects were able to consciously discover, was that it could be employed only after the dependent measures had been obtained and not directly after exposure of the stimulus material. Therefore, an additional pilot study was completed.

Pilot Study

Thirty-two undergraduates, recruited in the same way as in the main study, were tested individually by the same experimenter following the same procedure up to the distractor task, which was not employed. Instead, subjects were asked directly for co-occurrences between the visual and verbal data they were able to discover in the stimulus material. The responses closely resembled the ones obtained in the main study—not one subject mentioned haircut.

In the next pilot study (with the same number of participants) the same procedure was employed, except that prior to being exposed to the stimulus material, subjects were asked in the instructions to *search* for covariations between the visual and verbal data. Again, not one of the 32 subjects mentioned the hair. This inability to discover what the covariations are seems surprising. It is understandable, however, when taking into account the fact that subjects believed that the stimulus material was not fabricated by the experimenters, and thus the subjects were trying to look at (or test) only the co-occurrences that made some sense to them, like bright gaze or the like. These results were also consistent with the previous study by Lewicki (1981) in which subjects were unable to discover covariation between haircut and ability in math after seeing as many as 10 stimulus persons (in the present study there were only 6 of them).

It may be expected that if subjects were asked directly whether hair length covaried with kindness and capability, at least some of them would be able to "reconstruct" the crucial covariation, since subjects were probably able to recall at least some stimulus persons. Obviously, this does not mean, however, that they would be able to discover the crucial covariations if they were not helped by an experimenter's specific question.

Results

Mean yes- and no-response latencies to each of two questions (Kind? vs. Capable?), referring to each of two haircut types of stimulus persons (long vs. short), in each of two experimental conditions (I vs. II) are displayed in Figure 6.2. The means indicate that regardless of the specific response (either "yes" or "no"), subjects in each condition responded more slowly to questions that were relevant to the covariation they were exposed to. Namely, subjects in Condition I, who had been exposed to the version of the stimulus material in which long-haired persons were kind, responded more slowly to the questions as to whether long-haired persons were kind than to the analogous questions pertaining to short-haired persons. In this version of the stimulus material, short-haired persons were, in turn, capable and, in this group, response latencies to the question as to whether short-haired persons were capable were longer than to the analogous questions pertaining to long-haired persons. Exactly the reverse, as compared to the above, was the pattern of response latencies obtained in Condition II, in which subjects were exposed to the "reversed" stimulus material (i.e., in which short-haired persons were kind and long-haired ones were capable).

These results were analyzed by means of a 2(Condition: I vs. II) ×

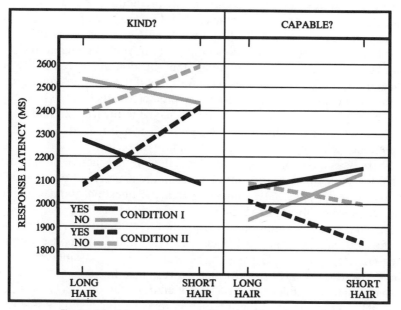

Figure 6.2 Means of response latencies (Experiment 6.1).

2(Question: Kind? vs. Capable?) × 2(haircut: long vs. short) ANOVA with repeated measures on the two last factors. The yes- and no-response latencies were added together since the yes or no factor could not be included in the ANOVA design. (This factor was not controlled and thus not all of the subjects provided both yes- and no-responses to each of the four categories of questions.) There was a significant interaction between the three factors $F (1,52) = 10.14$, $p < .002$, suggesting that the predicted pattern of response latencies was reliable. Planned comparisons (contrasts) revealed that response latencies for each of the two questions (i.e., Kind? and Capable?) contributed about equally to this interaction ($ps < .01$).

The aggregation of yes- and no-response latencies, which made the above analysis possible, seemed justified since the patterns of the means of the response latencies were comparable for both yes- and no-responses (see Figure 6.2), and the predictions did not discriminate between the two types of response. However, the frequencies of yes–no responses were not exactly the same across conditions, questions, and haircuts of stimulus persons (see the following analysis), and thus it seemed worthwhile to test whether the reliability of the predicted effect could be demonstrated in separate analyses for yes- and no-responses. In order to do so, for each subject a difference was computed between the mean response latency to long- and short-haired stimulus persons, separately for each question, and separately for yes- and no-responses. The predictions of the model were that for both yes- and no-responses this difference would be higher for subjects in Condition I than for subjects in Condition II as far as the question about kindness was concerned, and it would be higher in Condition II than in Condition I as far as the question about capability was concerned. All four differences (i.e., for each of the two questions and for both yes- and no-responses) were in the predicted directions (which could well be expected based on the means displayed in Figure 6.2), and all four of them were significant, $ts > 2.00$, $p < .05$, which indicated stability of the effect across both yes- and no-response latencies.

There was only one more reliable effect in the above three factor ANOVA performed on response latencies, the main effect of question, $F (1,52) = 33.75$, $p < .001$, indicating that the question about capability produced generally faster responses.

An analogous 2(condition) × 2(question) × 2(haircut) ANOVA was performed on yes-response frequencies (yes- and no-response frequencies correlated $r = -1$, since there was no other possible response). Similarly to the analysis performed on response latencies, this analysis also revealed a significant interaction of all three factors, $F (1,52) = 5.59$, $p < .025$. As opposed to the interaction revealed for response latencies,

Table 6.1

Means of Yes-Response Frequencies (Experiment 6.1)

Condition	Question			
	Kind?		Capable?	
	Long hair	Short hair	Long hair	Short hair
I	1.23	1.27	0.81	1.19
II	1.42	1.19	1.31	0.73

however, this one appeared to be produced solely by responses to the question about capability. Namely, two-factor ANOVAs (2[condition] × 2[haircut]) found a clear interaction for this question, $F(1,52) = 9.08, p < .004$, and no interaction for the question about kindness, $F(1,52) = 1.08$, ns. Means of yes-response frequencies are displayed in Table 6.1. The means for the question about kindness show no clear effects; the means for the question about capability, however, suggest an effect consistent with the manipulation. Namely, subjects from Condition I, who were exposed to the stimulus material in which short-haired stimulus persons were capable, responded more often "yes" to the questions about capability of short-haired persons than to the analogous questions referring to long-haired persons, while exactly the opposite effect was revealed among subjects in Condition II, who were exposed to the "opposite" stimulus material.

The overall ANOVA on yes-response frequencies also revealed a significant main effect of question, ($F(1,52) = 9.09, p < .004$), indicating that subjects responded more often "yes" to question about kindness, than to the one about capability.

Discussion

The model received full support. For all conditions, questions, and haircut types of stimulus persons, the subjects responded more slowly after being exposed to material implicitly containing relevant information. Since the material could provide such information only if a perceiver registered the covariation it contained, the results indicate that the covariation had actually been registered and processed. Taking into account the evidence that subjects were unable to discover the covariation consciously, these results suggest that nonconscious processing of covariation took place. Moreover, consistent with expectations, the reaction time measure of processing the covariation was clearly more sensitive than the simple measure of yes–no responses.

It seems that after the nonconscious acquisition of information about certain covariations, subjects' cognitive processes leading to answering the questions could look as Glucksberg and McCloskey (1981) proposed. Namely, in the case of questions that were not relevant to the stimulus material a subject was exposed to (e.g., pertaining to the capability of a long-haired person in experimental Condition I), after completing a "preliminary memory search" nothing relevant was found, and thus the subject was ready to make "a rapid don't know decision" (p. 321). Such a response, however, was not available in the present procedure (as opposed to Glucksberg's and McCloskey's, 1981), since if it were, probably all subjects would respond in this way to the majority of questions. Thus, subjects had to give a random yes or no response. In the case of relevant questions, however, relevant information (i.e., covariation detected in the stimulus material) was retrieved in the preliminary memory search, and it led to the initiation of the second stage: evaluation of the relevant facts "in detail to determine whether they specify an answer to the question" (p. 321). This, in turn, led to an increase in response time.

The analysis of yes-response frequencies revealed a specific effect of stimulus material for one of the two traits being manipulated. Namely, subjects seemed to acquire a working IPA based on the covariation between capability and haircut (subjects in each condition acquired a different IPA based on this covariation) and to employ this IPA in subsequent perceptions. This indicates that at least in some subjects the evidence being evaluated in detail during the second phase had been found sufficient to permit an informed answer (i.e., had a form of a relatively strong IPA).

It is unclear why this effect was not present in responses to the questions about kindness. A possible explanation, consistent with the data obtained, might be that responses to questions about somebody's kindness are more open to social desirability factors than responses to questions about capability. Thus, there could be a relatively stronger tendency (than in the case of questions about capability) in subjects in all conditions to respond "yes," which made revealing the effect in question impossible. There is some support for this explanation in the data. First, there were reliably more yes responses to the question about kindness than about capability. Second, response latencies to the questions about kindness were reliably longer, which might be due to the operation of some social desirability "filters" (Erdelyi, 1974), and this difference was especially pronounced for no-response latencies (see Figure 6.2). The latter could indicate that, regardless of the version of the stimulus material and the haircut of the stimulus persons, it was especially difficult for subjects to respond that the person displayed on a slide was not kind.

Experiment 6.2

The present experiment was designed to further explore the relation between the judgmental and reaction time measures of nonconscious processing of covariations, using different stimulus material.

Method

The general design of Experiment 6.1 remained unchanged except that there was no training with the reaction time apparatus. The training employed in Experiment 6.1 might have encouraged the subjects to process the stimulus material in terms of "traits" and promoted processing of covariation. The same set of slides was used, with six of them serving in the learning phase and four in the testing phase, but the four versions of their order (employed in Experiment 6.1) were entirely different. Descriptions were completely new, and they referred to different traits: frank and persistent. Subjects in Condition I were exposed to stimulus material in which long-haired stimulus persons were frank and short-haired ones were persistent, and subjects in condition II were exposed to the "opposite."[5] The stimuli were presented according to a slightly different time schedule, the screen was different, the lab room was different, and it was located in a dormitory. There were different experimenters (all women).

Participants were 80 undergraduates (men and women) recruited in a similar way as in Experiment 6.1.

Results and Discussion

Mean yes- and no-response latencies to each of the two questions (Frank? vs. Persistent?), referring to each of two haircut types of stimulus persons (long vs. short), in each of two experimental conditions (I vs. II) are displayed in Figure 6.3. All the response times appeared to be considerably longer than in Experiment 6.1, which may have been due to the lack of training on the reaction time apparatus in the present procedure. The pattern of means, however, indicated that, analogous to Experiment 6.1, regardless of the specific response (either "yes" or "no"), subjects in each condition responded more slowly to the question that was relevant to the covariation they were exposed to.

An ANOVA was performed on the aggregated yes- and no-response

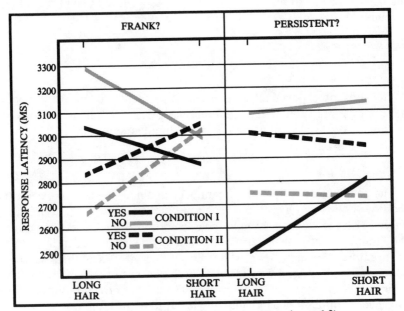

Figure 6.3   Means of response latencies (Experiment 6.2).

latencies, with condition (I vs. II) as a between-subjects factor and question (Frank? vs. Persistent?) and haircut of stimulus persons (short vs. long) as between-subjects factors. The only significant effect was the interaction between all three factors, $F(1,78) = 9.78, p < .002$, indicating that the predicted pattern of response latencies was reliable. Planned comparisons (contrasts) revealed that the interaction effect was stable across the questions ($ps < .01$).

The same design ANOVA performed on yes-response frequencies revealed no effect involving experimental condition; the means for each of the four combinations of questions and haircuts were virtually the same in both conditions.

The response latency data were consistent with the model in every respect, that is, in each of the two experimental conditions, for each of four traits manipulated in two experiments (i.e., kindness, capability, frankness, and persistence) and for each of two possible responses (i.e., "yes" and "no"). Lack of training on the reaction time apparatus in Experiment 6.2 seemed to increase subjects' overall response time as compared to Experiment 6.1. However, it apparently did not affect the sensitivity of the measure.

In this study, the higher sensitivity of the reaction time measure of processing covariation, as compared to the judgmental measure, was even clearer than in Experiment 6.1. For reasons, which are difficult to reconstruct, nonconscious detection and processing of covariation in this experiment was not concluded by forming the strong IPAs (or at least not in a reliably high proportion of subjects). One might suspect that the meaning of the two traits manipulated in this experiment was more difficult to interpret without any context, and that it is advantageous in this paradigm to use clearer and simpler traits like those employed in Experiment 6.1 (this is only a speculation, however).

Despite the fact that the manipulation employed in this study appeared to be too weak to make subjects form strong IPAs, we were still able to demonstrate that the crucial covariation was detected, processed, and stored in memory. Although the memory trace of the covariation was not an active structure capable of influencing subjects' judgments (i.e., strong IPA), it was apparently accessed during subsequent memory search processes and found to be relevant to the testing phase questions. Thus, it may be concluded that if subjects' explicit responses were the only measure available in the experiment, we would not have detected any effects. However, due to the apparent high sensitivity of the reaction time measure employed, we discovered consistent and strong evidence demonstrating that the covariation had actually been processed.

Experiment 6.3

The important question arose at this point as to the nature of the "passive" (i.e., incapable of influencing judgments) cognitive representation of the nonconsciously detected covariation that was registered in Experiments 6.1 and 6.2. Was it a permanent and independent memory structure that could influence the processing of relevant information at a later time? The other possibility was that the passive cognitive representation registered with the reaction time method in the previous experiments was only a temporary phase of the process of development of an IPA. The latter possibility would imply that if the process was not concluded by establishing the strong IPA, the representation would soon disappear (e.g., after leaving the lab room and getting into some different social environment).

The present experiment was designed in order to explore this problem. The major difference between the procedure of the preceding two studies and the present one was that the testing phase was delayed by about 48 hours. If no reaction time effects were obtained after such delay, then the second possibility would be supported.

Seventy undergraduates (men and women) participated in the learning phase of the experiment. They were recruited in a manner designed to minimize the probability that subjects knew each other. The experimental procedure was exactly the same as in Experiment 6.1, except that there was no training on the reaction time apparatus. After the distractor task, subjects were asked to fill out a short questionnaire (Eysenck Personality Inventory), which, as they thought, was the main part of the experiment. They were then thanked for their participation, and no appointment was made for the second phase of the experiment to lead subjects to believe that the experiment was completely finished. Otherwise, the subjects could try to refresh in their memory the stimulus material between the two phases of the experiment, expecting that it might be useful during the second phase, or they could think more (and think more analytically) about the possible nature of the manipulation "hidden" in the first phase. It was important for the present study to prevent subjects from thinking about the stimulus material. The personality inventory was designed to represent a reasonable "main part of the experiment" in subjects' judgments and to justify the fact that they were instructed to "relax" during the presentation of the slides. But most of all, the questionnaire was expected to focus subjects' attention on their scores on the questionnaire and to make them think, after the first part of the experiment, about this questionnaire rather than about the nature of the "relaxation phase."

An undesirable consequence of having no apointments with subjects was that only 48 (69%) could subsequently be located and were able to participate in the testing phase (40–60 hours after the learning phase). The testing phase was the same as in Experiment 6.1.

The response latency pattern was the same as in Experiments 6.1 and 6.2. Again, subjects responded more slowly after being exposed to stimulus material containing relevant information (for both conditions, questions, and haircut types of stimulus persons). The interaction of condition, question, and haircut was significant ($p < .03$). No yes or no response frequency effects were found in this experiment.

There are at least two alternative interpretations of the results obtained regarding the question raised in the introduction to this experiment. First, the passive cognitive representations of the covariations manipulated in the learning phase could have been stable and durable enough to remain available for about two days. It is also possible, however, that these representations were initially active (i.e., they were relatively strong IPAs) and later changed into passive ones. Namely, either both or at least one of the covariations manipulated in this experiment could have been processed so successfully in the learning phase that they were stored in the form of a strong IPA initially and were powerful enough to influence subjects' judgments for some time (but no tests were administered at that time). According to the latter interpretation, the passive state of these representations at the time of taking the dependent measures in this experiment was a natural consequence of their decay over time, and of the fact that there was no supportive rehearsal (like employing the IPA or encountering some new supportive evidence). Thus, according to this (second) interpretation, the passive representations registered in this study had status that is analogous to the experimentally deactivated IPAs in Experiments 3.2 and 3.3 (see Chapter 3 on the "matrix scanning" paradigm). The evidence obtained in those experiments clearly indicated the existence of such nonconscious memory traces of covariation that did not have the status of a strong IPA (did not influence subjects' behavior any more).

Whichever of these alternative explanations is valid, the results of this experiment seem to indicate that the 2-stage model reaction time measure of processing covariation provides more than merely data on a temporary phase of development of the IPA. The data also clearly indicate that the reaction time measure is much more sensitive than measures based on subjects' responses.

Experiments 6.4, 6.5, 6.6

The following experiments were aimed at determining the response latency pattern in conditions in which subjects were consciously aware of the manipulated covariation and employed some consciously controlled strategy of responding consistently with that covariation. Based on the reasoning presented at the beginning of the present chapter, it was expected that such a consciously controlled algorithm of generating consistent responses would not follow the two-stage model of retrieval process and that it would take the same amount of time for each combination of question and haircut, regardless of its relevance to the manipulated covariation.

Since in the present experiments subjects had to employ some consciously controlled strategy, their performance depended directly on their motivation to be accurate or to follow the instructions. Thus, the level of subjects' motivation was a very important factor that could determine the response time pattern. For example, if subjects were not sufficiently motivated to follow the instructions, they might ignore the explicit information they received about covariation, and eventually, their cognitive processes might look as in Experiments 6.1, 6.2, and 6.3. On the other hand, if subjects were instructed and very strongly motivated to respond consistently with the covariation (and fast), their motivation might turn out to be too high and their consciously controlled reasoning might be disorganized; it might turn out that such an experimental setting would be an inadequate analogue of the natural controlled process of generating judgments based on a covariation.

Due to this problem, three versions of the experiment were conducted, in which subjects were enabled (Experiment 6.4), instructed (6.5), and instructed and motivated (6.6) to base their judgments on the explicit information about the covariation they received.

Method

The general design and the stimulus materials employed in these studies were the same as in Experiment 6.1, except for the explicit information about the crucial covariations. Since the explicit information could be expected to work in a different way depending on whether it was presented to subjects before or after exposure to the stimulus material (i.e., it may or may not influence subjects' perception of the six stimulus persons), in each version of the experiment, half of the subjects received the explicit information about covariation before and the other half after exposure to the six stimulus persons.

In the testing phase of all three versions of the experiment subjects were asked to respond rapidly; however, the versions differed regarding subjects' motivation to respond consistently with the covariation.

In Experiment 6.4 subjects were informed that in the material to be presented to them (or which had already been presented) all long-haired persons would be kind (or capable, depending on the condition), and all short-haired ones would be capable (or kind). In the testing phase they were asked to follow the same rule "except for cases in which it would lead to judgments that would seem to you counterintuitive." Thus, in this version of the experiment, the covariation was accessible to the subjects, and they were asked to employ it as a basis for their judgments. It was not insisted, however, that they do so in all cases; therefore, they would not be "alarmed" by failure to be always accurate. Participants were 80 undergraduates (men and women).

In Experiment 6.5, the same procedure was employed, except that subjects were asked to *always* respond in a manner consistent with the rules (i.e., they were not given the explicit option to be inconsistent with the rules). Thus, subjects in these conditions were motivated, more than in Experiment 6.4, to follow the covariations, since any inconsistent response was considered to be an error. Participants were 40 undergraduates (men and women).

In Experiment 6.6, subjects were not only instructed to always respond consistently with the rules (as in Experiment 6.5), but they were additionally motivated to be accurate. Namely, before the testing phase, subjects were informed that this part of the experiment is "a test of the ability to employ newly acquired knowledge." Participants were 64 undergraduates (men and women).

Results and Discussion

The results of each of the three experiments were analyzed by means of 4-way ANOVAs with condition (I vs. II) and time of providing the subjects with the explicit information about the covariation (before vs. after the presentation of stimulus persons) as between-subjects factors, and question (Kind? vs. Capable?) and haircut type of stimulus persons (long vs. short) as within-subjects factors.

Analyses performed on yes-response frequencies revealed that in each of three versions of the experiment, subjects' responses were highly accurate ($ps < .001$). There were no clear differences between the versions.

However, response latency patterns were undifferentiated, and unlike in Experiments 6.1, 6.2, and 6.3, subjects' cognitive processes of generating responses required about the same amount of time for each combination of question and haircut regardless of its relevance to the manipulated covariation. The interaction between condition, question, and haircut type of stimulus persons did not approach significance in any of the three versions of the experiment ($Fs < 1.14$).

The time of providing subjects with the explicit information about the covariation (before vs. after the learning phase) affected none of the dependent measures.

The results obtained in these experiments supported the hypothesis that the controlled retrieval or inferential strategies would not follow the two-stage model of retrieval processes confirmed in Experiments 6.1, 6.2, and 6.3 (in which subjects' retrieval processes were most likely not mediated by any controlled strategies). These data provided additional evidence indicating that the covariation implicitly contained in the stimulus material of Experiments 6.1, 6.2, and 6.3, was detected and memorized nonconsciously and that subjects in these experiments were not aware of its influence on their subsequent retrieval processes and judgments.

Experiment 6.7[6]

Comparison of the very consistent reaction time patterns obtained in Experiments 6.1, 6.2, and 6.3 with the equally consistent results of Experiments 6.4, 6.5, and 6.6 provides strong supportive evidence for the two-stage model of nonconscious retrieval of information about covariation. After obtaining these consistent results, I designed a number of new experiments to learn more about the mechanism of nonconscious process-ing of covariations. Two of these studies will be presented later in this chapter (Experiments 6.8 and 6.9). However, since these new studies employed only slightly modified versions of the procedure and stimulus material used in the above six experiments, let me first report briefly a study (Czyzewska, 1984) that used completely different stimulus material.

This study was designed to test the generality of the specific experimen-tal paradigm employed so far and to verify the two-stage model. It was also designed to test the hypothesis (Chapter 2) that nonconscious pro-cessing of covariation includes not only those traits which can easily be verbalized by the subject and potentially be used in his or her controlled processing of information, but also those traits that are hard to verbalize and are not used in the controlled processing of information (see Chapter 2, discussion of inference from facial features). In all of the experiments on nonconscious processing of covariation reported so far (in Chapters 3 through 6), the manipulated covariations included only such trait catego-ries that were known to the subject and included in his or her common conscious cognition. In the present study the manipulated covariation included a trait dimension that was not known to subjects from their conscious experience and that was not easy to verbalize.

Method

Participants were 120 high school graduates (boys and girls) who had never participated in psychological experiments. The design of the study was analogous to the one employed in the previous experiments on the two-stage process. As usual, the learning phase was introduced to sub-jects as a type of "psychological training." They were asked to relax and try not to memorize the material or relate it to their real-life experiences. Subjects were presented with a sequence of six graphics displayed on a CRT and accompanied by short psychological characteristics. The graph-ics were irregular patterns of small, rectangular figures, and subjects were told that these patterns represented "computer generated structures of elementary, functional units of long-term memory, based on extensive psychological diagnoses." Each of the six patterns was ostensibly based on the diagnosis of a different person. The subjects were not expected to understand this explanation, nor were they able to imagine how such computer diagnosis could be completed. However, they were expected to realize that there was some reasonable relation between the graphics and the short descriptions of psychological characteristics. The "diagnosed persons" were introduced as remarkable individuals: three of them were very kind, three others were very bright.

Each of the six patterns consisted of the same number (36) of small, rectangular figures, and the total area of each pattern (i.e., the sum of 36 components) was kept constant. The patterns were differentiated, however, along a dimension that is not easily labeled with a single term and that will be referred to as "polarization of size of the component figures." Namely, each small, component figure belonged to one of three size categories: small, medium, or large. Three of six patterns presented in the learning phase consisted of 13 large component figures (i.e., 4 square "units" or more), 10 medium (i.e., 2 or 3 "units"), and 13 small (i.e., single "units") component figures; they will be called "polarized patterns" since they contained relatively less medium-size components than the small or large ones. The other three patterns consisted of 5 large, 26 medium, and 5 small components; they will be called "not polarized patterns." In order to make the crucial difference less salient, the patterns differed on dimensions of spread-concentration, symmetry, and overall shape; these characteristics, however, were counterbalanced across the two crucial types of patterns (i.e., polarized and not polarized). The example of the polarized and not polarized patterns are displayed in Figure 6.4.

There were two experimental conditions. In Condition I, polarized patterns represented the kind persons, and not polarized patterns represented the bright persons. Stimulus material presented in Condition II were arranged just opposite.

A series of pilot studies indicated consistently that subjects were unable to discover consciously the crucial covariation manipulated in the stimulus material, even if instructed to search for covariation. Subjects were confused by very salient differences regarding spread-concentration, symmetry, and overall shape of the patterns. It was also revealed that when presented with two sets of patterns simultaneously and informed that the patterns belong to two different categories, subjects agreed that the two sets are different, but they were unable to define or point out the difference (cf. subjects' inability to define the difference between masculine and feminine features, discussed in Chapter 2).

In the testing phase, after the distractor task, subjects were presented with four more patterns[7] (two polarized and two not polarized). This time, however, instead of psychological characteristics there were one-word questions, "Kind?" or "Capable?," displayed on the CRT. Subjects were then asked to respond as quickly as possible to those questions by pushing a button on a control box (as in Experiments 6.1 through 6.6).

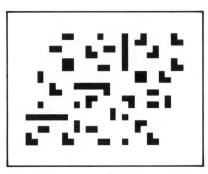

Figure 6.4 "High-polarized" (upper panel) and "low-polarized" (lower panel) patterns exposed in Experiment 6.7.

Results and Discussion

Mean response latencies to each of the two questions (Kind? vs. Capable?), referring to each of the two types of patterns (polarized vs. not polarized) in the two experimental conditions are displayed in Figure 6.5 (yes- and no-response latencies are aggregated since they did not show obvious differences). The pattern of means clearly follows the predictions: Response latencies to all relevant questions were longer. This was confirmed in the three-way analysis of variance that revealed a reliable interaction of all three variables, $F(1,116) = 8.31$, $p < .005$. Contrasts revealed that response latencies to both questions contributed significantly to the effect.

Examination of yes- or no-response frequencies revealed no effects for the question about kindness and a significant tendency to respond consistently (with the manipulation) to the question about capability, $F(1,116) = 7.20$, $p < .008$. This replicated exactly the pattern of results obtained in Experiment 6.1 in which the tendency to respond consistently with the

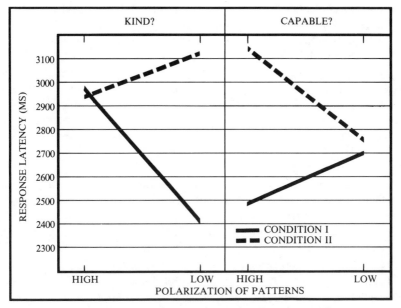

Figure 6.5   Means of response latencies (Experiment 6.7).

manipulation was found only for the question about capability and not to the one about kindness.

The consistent pattern of results obtained in this study demonstrated the generality of the results obtained in Experiments 6.1, 6.2, and 6.3. Moreover, the evidence obtained supported the hypothesis that nonconscious processing of covariations is not confined to variables that participate directly in the conscious cognition. Obviously, an alternative explanation cannot be totally ruled out. Namely, it is conceivable that subjects processed some simple component trait of the manipulated complex dimension (e.g., number of small figures). However, it appears unlikely, since subjects in the pilot study could not verbalize any of such component traits, even when asked directly for differences between the two crucial sets of patterns.

Experiment 6.8

At this point it may be concluded that the data support the idea that information about covariation in a process of judgment or of answering questions is nonconsciously retrieved in a way suggested by the two-stage model proposed by Glucksberg and McCloskey (1981). The question arises, however, as to how in particular the two-stage process of accessing the relevant information stored in memory proceeds. In other words, what particular kind of information is being accessed (or evaluated) at the first stage, and what kind at the second stage? Two possibilities could be considered that are consistent with the data obtained. Each of them, however, implies a different model of storing and accessing information about covariation. Assuming that the second stage of memory search is triggered only if the first stage has determined that there is relevant information stored in long-term memory, the difference between these two models pertains to what "relevant" means in these terms (i.e., what kind of information is capable of triggering the second stage).

The difference between the two models pertains to whether information accessed at the first stage (i.e., the one concerning the existence of relevant data in long-term memory), contains merely a message that there exist items in memory that involve something about x and something about y (first model), or it directly contains a message that data in memory suggest covariation between x and y (second model).

The first model implies that the second stage of processing includes both checking whether the relevant information found during the first stage of processing implies the existence of covariation between x and y, and (in case it does) evaluating this information in terms of whether the evidence suggesting the covariation is strong enough or sufficient to justify a certain judgment. On the other hand, the second model implies that the second stage of processing is triggered only if the first stage of processing concluded not only that there exists in memory information relevant to both x and y, but also that this information implies the existence of covariation between x and y. According to this model, the second stage of processing is confined to the evaluation of data on covariation (e.g., whether the evidence is strong enough or sufficient).

The following study was designed to test these alternative models. The procedure was similar to the one employed in Experiments 6.1, 6.2, and 6.3, except that one additional variable was manipulated. Namely, one half of the subjects were exposed to the same stimulus material as in Experiments 6.1, 6.2, and 6.3 (containing a covariation between features x and y, covariation condition); whereas, the second half of the subjects were exposed to a version of the same material that contained information relevant to both x and y, but there was no covariation present between x and y (no-covariation condition). For example, subjects in the covariation condition were exposed to material in which all three long-haired women were kind and all three short-haired ones were capable. Subjects in the no-covariation condition were exposed to material in which descriptions of all three long-haired women contained information relevant to kindness; there was no covariation, however, between being long-haired and being kind: one long-haired person was presented as very kind, one as fairly kind, and one as not kind. Analogously, in this version one short-haired person was presented as very capable, one as fairly capable, and one as not capable at all.

If the first model is correct, then the increase in response time observed in Experiments 6.1, 6.2, and 6.3, which was connected with locating in the first phase of processing some relevant information and triggering the second stage, would occur in both the covariation and the no-covariation condition. However, if the second model is correct, the increase in response time connected with locating relevant information would occur exclusively in the covariation condition.

Method

Overview

There were four experimental groups (2[Condition I vs. Condition II) × 2[covariation condition vs. no-covariation condition]). The stimulus descriptions presented in the covariation condition were exactly the same as in Experiment 6.1, while the descriptions presented in the no-covariation condition were modified so that they did not contain a covariation but still pertained to the relevant traits.

Subjects

One hundred undergraduates (men and women) participated in the study.

Stimulus Material and Procedure

Stimulus descriptions presented in the covariation condition were the same as in Experiment 6.1, while the ones presented in the no-covariation condition were modified. The modification consisted of making the descriptions differentiated in terms of the degree to which a described person possessed a crucial trait, thus eliminating the covariation. The first of the three descriptions relevant to kindness was left unmodified, the second was modified to make it imply kindness to a lesser degree, and the third was modified to make it imply a lack of kindness. The same was done with the three descriptions relevant to capability. The modifications were produced by means of changing or adding qualifiers. For example, "always ready to make sacrifices for others" was changed into "sometimes ready to make sacrifices for others."

The procedure was exactly the same as in Experiment 6.1, except for absence of training on the reaction time apparatus.

Results

Mean response latencies to each of the two questions (Kind? vs. Capable?), referring to each of the two haircut types of stimulus persons (long vs. short), in each of the four experimental conditions (2[Condition I vs. Condition II] × 2[covariation vs. no-covariation condition]) are displayed in Figure 6.6 (yes- and no-response latencies are aggregated since they did not show obvious differences). The examination of means suggests that the predicted effect is clear only in the covariation condition (left panel) and is absent or almost absent in the no-covariation condition (right panel). This finding was confirmed in the four-way ANOVA (2[covariation vs. no-covariation condition] × 2[Condition I vs. Condition II] × 2[question: Kind? vs. Capable?] × 2[haircut: long vs. short], with repeated measures on the last two factors). As in the previous studies, there was a significant interaction between condition (I vs. II), question, and haircut factors, $F(1,96) = 7.08$, $p < .009$. Planned comparisons (contrasts) indicated, however, that this interaction was due entirely to a clear

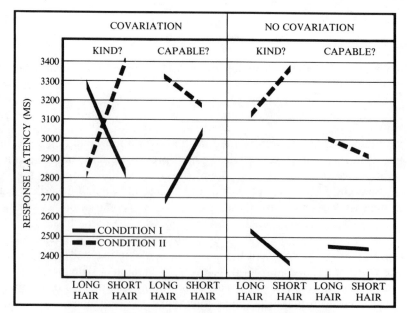

Figure 6.6   Means of response latencies (Experiment 6.8).

interaction effect between these three factors found in the covariation condition, $F(1,96) = 8.06$, $p < .006$. There was no such interaction effect, however, in the no-covariation condition, $F(1,96) = .85$, ns. In this condition the means for the question about kindness (see Figure 6.6) are consistent with the general pattern; planned comparisons, however, revealed no significant effect on that question in this condition, $F(1,96) = 1.40$, ns.

The means of yes-response frequencies revealed no consistent effects in the no-covariation condition ($F < 1$). In the covariation condition the means were consistent with the manipulation only for the question about capability, which replicates the results found in Experiments 6.1 and 6.7. This effect, however, was not significant, $F(1,96) = 2.00$, $p = .16$.

Discussion

The results obtained seem to support the second of the two previously discussed models. The response time data indicated that the second stage of processing was involved only in the case in which the relevant information referred to covariation between x and y and not (as implied by the first model) to data merely relevant somehow to both x and y. This kind of processing seems to be more efficient, in that the time consuming second stage is involved only when there is a considerable chance that it is in fact necessary (i.e., there are fewer "false alarms" involving the second stage). It implies, however, that the first stage involves more than merely looking for data that are generally relevant, but instead it also includes some kind of evaluation of the relevant data in terms of whether they are in fact relevant in a desired way (i.e., whether they refer to covariation or to something else).

It should be noted, however, that both Glucksberg and McCloskey's (1981) model and the present reasoning are first steps in understanding the process, and it must be taken into account that, in fact, it may be much more complicated. It might involve more stages, and describing it as a two-stage process may be a simplification. It also cannot be ruled out that even the type of relevance that was involved in the no-covariation condition produced in fact similar response time effects to the one found in the covariation condition, but that it was much weaker and the procedure employed was not sensitive enough to capture it.

Regardless of the above issue, however, it should be concluded that consistent evidence from Experiments 6.1, 6.2, 6.3, 6.7, and the present study strongly suggests that if there exists in long-term memory information about a certain covariation, it leads to increased processing time while responding to a question relevant to that covariation. Thus, it seems justified to assume that there exists a stage (or stages) of preliminary memory search for relevant information and, depending on the outcome of this stage, some secondary stage (or stages) of evaluating, or some other processing of that relevant information. The results of the present study suggest additionally that the preliminary stage includes not only a search for relevant information but also some preliminary evaluation of that information in terms of whether it implies a covariation, since if it does not imply the covariation the entire processing lasts a much shorter time, even if the information is relevant in some sense.

The question arises, however, as to how an individual comes to acquire the information about covariation at the very beginning of the processes demonstrated in Experiments 6.1, 6.2, 6.3, 6.7, and 6.8. In other words, how does the nonconscious detection of covariation proceed?

Experiment 6.9

Since there is very little relevant data in the research literature that might be directly helpful in forming a model of this mechanism, our preliminary proposition was mostly intuitive and based only on some very general premises concerning human information processing. The first of these premises was that humans are not only able to encode (and used to encoding) separate consecutive (successive) facts or episodes, but are also able to process some metaknowledge about those facts and episodes. In other words, they acquire information that could not be accessed by processing each episode separately but instead could be accessed only by processing entire sets of episodes, for example, the frequency of their occurrence (Howell, 1973). There is considerable evidence suggesting that processing of such information implicitly contained in sets of episodes (like frequency) might require no intention and might be unconscious[8] (see, Hasher & Zacks, 1979; Zacks, Hasher, & Sanft, 1982; but see also Fisk & Schneider, 1984).

Let us consider first the simplest possible case of acquiring such implicit information, for example, information about the frequency of some events. Regardless of how frequency is represented in memory, which is unknown (Zacks, et al., 1982), acquiring frequency data requires at least two kinds of information to be registered with each event, namely, recognizing the event itself and registering that it has happened one time more (the latter process is very similar to incrementing a loop counter in BASIC or FORTRAN). A simple model of acquiring information about covariation might seem to be analogous; two kinds of information must be registered (with the addition that, in order to involve covariation, events in this case have to be defined by a co-occurrence of two features). However, even independent attributes will occasionally co-occur. Moreover, independent attributes that are frequent may co-occur more often than less frequent attributes that are highly correlated. Therefore, in our preliminary model of detecting covariation, a major difference, as compared to processing frequency, was expected. It was hypothesized that a certain number of consistent co-occurrences and a certain ratio of consistent to inconsistent co-occurrences are required in order for any covariation to be finally encoded.

In other words, one or two instances clearly provide information about frequency; however, they would not provide any useful information about covariation of events, since even if two instances are perfectly consistent regarding covariation between some two-bipolar dimensions, its binomial probability is as high as .5. Obviously, even a single instance of co-occurrence has to be memorized, since otherwise every instance would be the first. According to this hypothesis, however, its memory representation would not be accessible to a perceiver in the form of information about general covariation, and thus it would not affect subsequent cognitive processes in the way in which information about covariation would (cf. Experiments 6.1, 6.2, 6.3, 6.7, and 6.8). The model predicts that the previously mentioned "counter of consistent and inconsistent instances" would not register that a covariation has been detected until a number of consistent co-occurrences and a ratio of consistent to inconsistent co-occurrences reaches a certain value (which is an unknown parameter of the process). Up to this point information relevant to potential covariation is stored in a form inaccessible to a perceiver's cognitive processes as information about covariation.

The first experiment designed to test these expectations involved no inconsistent instances, and only the number of consistent instances was manipulated. Subjects in different groups were exposed to stimulus materials containing implicitly different numbers of consistent co-occurrences, beginning with a very small number ($N = 2$). It was predicted that the effect of encoding the covariation would appear at the level of a certain number of consistent co-occurrences.

Method

Overview

The method was basically the same as in Experiment 6.1, except for modifications necessary to manipulate the number of co-occurrences. There were five groups varying in the number of consistent instances that subjects were exposed to, namely 2, 4, 6, 8, and 10. The group with 2 instances was presented with only two slides: one with a short-haired and the other with a long-haired stimulus person, the group with 4 instances was presented with two short-haired and two long-haired stimulus persons, the group with 6 instances was exposed to exactly the same number of stimulus persons as in the previous experiments. The remaining two groups were exposed to two or four additional slides, respectively. This five-level factor was crossed with the factor of condition (I vs. II), which determined the matching between haircut (long vs. short) and traits (kind vs. capable) in the stimulus material. Thus, there were 10 experimental groups (5[number of instances] × 2[condition: long-haired kind and short-haired capable vs. long-haired capable and short-haired kind]).

Subjects

I would like to describe the population from which subjects were recruited in some detail because it turned out to be important in this particular experiment. Eighty men and women, 18–19 years old, participated in the study. Each of them had just graduated from high school and had come to Warsaw to be interviewed at the University of Warsaw prior to being admitted as freshmen. None of them was a resident of Warsaw and during the time of the interviews they were located in a huge complex of dormitories. They did not know each other, and each subject was recruited from a different floor or from a different building. Subjects were randomly assigned to 10 experimental groups (separately by sex). Subjects from all of the groups were run in a counterbalanced order, so that any changes in the experimenter's performance contributed equally to each group.

Stimulus Material

The present design required the preparation of additional stimulus material, since up to 10 descriptions and up to 14 slides had to be presented. The additional 4 slides were selected in a less formal way than before, in the sense that there were no pilot studies, although an attempt was made to follow exactly the same rules, and in making the final choices a number of undergraduates were consulted. The missing four descriptions were designed to follow exactly the pattern of the initial six. Two of the new stimulus persons were described as kind, and two others as capable.

The order of presentation of the stimulus material was determined in the following way. Since there were 8 subjects in each of the 10 experimental groups, initially 8 permutations of 14 slides were designed regarding which 10 of them would serve in the learning phase and which 4 in the testing phase and regarding the order of presentation (as before, each order followed the rule of alternately presenting short- and long-haired stimulus persons). Thus for each subject in a given group, a different arrangement of slides was prepared, based on exactly the same arrangements in all 10 groups. The final sets of slides that were presented to subjects in each group were determined by deleting the necessary number of slides from the subsets used during the learning phase, beginning from the end, to obtain the number of presentations desired in a given group. This arrangement met the condition that subjects in a subsequent group (regarding the number of instances they were exposed to) were presented with exactly the same set and the same order of stimulus persons as the preceding group plus, at the end, with 2 additional stimulus persons. For example, Arrangement 1 was assigned to one subject in each of 10 groups, and each of those 10 subjects was exposed in the testing phase to exactly the same four slides. However, they differed regarding the number of slides presented in the learning phase. Namely, 2 subjects from groups exposed to only 2 instances (i.e., a subject from Condition I, and a subject from Condition II) were exposed only to the first two slides of the learning phase subset of Arrangement 1. The 2 subjects from groups exposed to 4 instances were exposed to the same two slides plus the two subsequent ones, and so on, up to the 2 subjects exposed to the entire subset of 10 slides assigned to the learning phase in Arrangement 1.

Each slide was accompanied by a description. The different covariations between traits and haircut of the stimulus person in each of the two conditions (I and II) was analogous to that in Experiment 6.1. That is, subjects in Condition I were exposed to stimulus material in which long-haired stimulus persons were kind and short-haired ones were capable, and subjects in Condition II were exposed to the opposite.

Procedure

The procedure was basically the same as in Experiment 6.1, except that there was no training on the reaction time apparatus, and the experimenter was male.

At the end of the session each subject was questioned (as in previous experiments) for covariations he or she had discovered between the visual and verbal data, and the responses were again the same. None of the subjects, not even the 16 subjects who were presented with 10 instances, discovered the covariation.

Results

Mean yes- and no-response latencies to each of the two questions (Kind? vs. Capable?), referring to each of the two haircut types of stimulus persons (long vs. short), in each of the two conditions (I vs. II) are displayed in Figure 6.7 (the means were aggregated over the five levels of the "number of instances" factor). As in the previous experiments, the overall pattern of results was again consistent with the general model. Regardless of the specific response (either "yes" or "no"), subjects in each condition responded more slowly to the question that was relevant to the covariation they were exposed to.

A four-factor ANOVA was performed on the aggregated yes- and no-response latencies with number of instances (2, 4, 6, 8, and 10) and condition (I vs. II) as between-subjects factors, and question (Kind? vs. Capable?) and haircut of stimulus persons (short vs. long) as within-subjects factors. Surprisingly, not one reliable effect involving the number of instances factor was found ($Fs < 1.30$). The only significant effect revealed in this analysis was the interaction between condition, question, and haircut, analogous to the one found in Experiments 6.1, 6.2, 6.3, 6.7, and 6.8, and of roughly similar size, $F(1,70) = 7.80$, $p < .007$. Trend analyses revealed no reliable trends indicating that this effect of interaction was not stable across the five levels of number of instances.

Separate planned comparisons (contrasts) were performed for each of

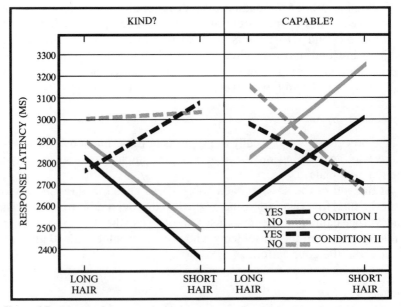

Figure 6.7 Means of response latencies aggregated over the 5 levels of the number of instances factor (Experiment 6.9).

two questions (i.e., Kind? and Capable?). In each of them the effects of the number of instances were not significant ($Fs < 1$). Each of them, however, showed the reliability of the predicted interaction between condition and haircut ($ps < .05$).

Planned comparisons revealed no systematic differences between cells indicating any effects of the number of instances factor, although this method could not be considered sensitive, due to the very small number of observations in each cell ($N = 8$).

No effect of number of instances was found even when the analysis was redesigned in order to maximize its sensitivity to the potential effect of the number of instances factor. Namely, the *middle* group (i.e., the one with 6 instances) was deleted, and the remaining four groups were reduced to two by aggregating the groups presented with 2 and 4 instances, and separately the groups presented with 8 and 10 instances. In an ANOVA (2[number of instances] × 2[Condition I vs. Condition II] × 2[question] × 2[haircut]), again no effect of the number of instances was found, $Fs < 1$. The means in these two extreme groups (i.e., "2 and 4 instances" and "8 and 10 instances") followed the same general pattern (see Figure 6.8), indicating that subjects detected and processed the covariation. Although in neither of these groups did the crucial three-way interaction reach the

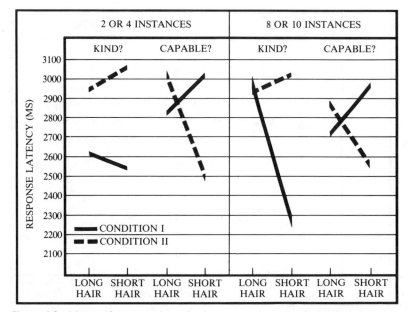

Figure 6.8 Means of response latencies in two groups exposed to different numbers of instances (2 or 4, vs. 8 or 10) of Experiment 6.9.

.05 level of significance (probably due to the small number of observations, $N = 32$), there were trends in the predicted direction in each group, and in each of them of approximately the same strength ($p < .12$, and $p < .09$, respectively). These results indicate that the overall crucial three-way interaction was present in the entire data and was not affected by the number of instances that subjects were exposed to.

An analogous set of analyses was performed on yes-response frequencies. The means, aggregated over the five levels of the number of instances factor, are displayed in Figure 6.9. An overall ANOVA with number of instances (2, 4, 6, 8, and 10) and condition (I vs. II) as between-subjects factors and question (Kind? vs. Capable?) and haircut of stimulus person (long vs. short) as within-subjects factors again revealed no reliable effects involving the number of instances factor. The only significant effect revealed was the interaction between all three of the remaining factors, $F(1,70) = 7.55$, $p < .008$. Planned comparisons revealed that this effect was mostly due to responses to the question about kindness, $F(1,70) = 8.95$, $p < .004$; in the case of the question about capability $F < 1$. Examination of means (see Figure 6.9) indicated that this interaction effect was consistent with the specificity of the stimulus material presented to the subjects. Namely, subjects presented with the stimulus

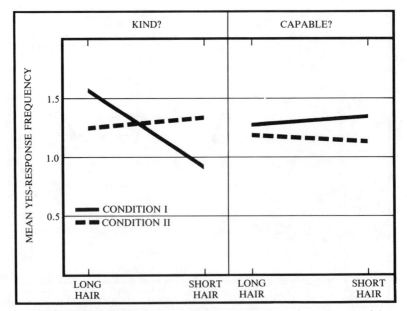

Figure 6.9 Means of yes-response frequencies aggregated over the 5 levels of the number of instances factor (Experiment 6.9).

material in which long-haired persons were kind (Condition I), responded more frequently "yes" to the questions about kindness when stimulus persons had long hair than when stimulus persons' hair was short. For subjects in Condition II, who were exposed to the opposite, the reverse pattern of yes-response frequencies was found.

Planned comparisons did not reveal any systematic effects of the number of instances factor on the above interaction. As noted earlier, however, the number of observations in the single cells was very small. In the analysis with two extreme groups (created in the same way as has been done in the analysis performed on response latencies), again no reliable effects involving the number of instances were found. Moreover, the means (see Figure 6.10) suggested that the "effect of learning" found in the overall analysis is consistent across the two groups differing sharply in the number of instances that subjects were exposed to (i.e., 2 or 4 vs. 8 or 10), $F(1,70) = 4.20$, $p < .05$, and $F(1,70) = 3.43$, $p < .07$, respectively.

Discussion

The results of Experiment 6.9 again provided perfectly consistent confirmation of the two-stage model of nonconscious processing covaria-

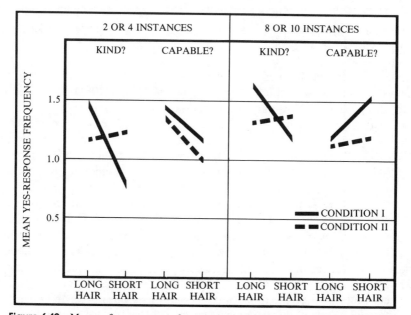

Figure 6.10 Means of yes-response frequencies in two groups exposed to different numbers of instances (2 or 4, vs. 8 or 10) of Experiment 6.9.

tions. The data appeared, however, to be completely in disagreement with our preliminary model of this nonconscious detection process in that the model assumed that a certain, sufficiently high number of consistent instances is a necessary condition to register these instances as information about covariation. The results obtained suggested that even if there is such a threshold number of consistent instances required to involve registration of covariation, this number may be as surprisingly low as 2 or 4. Note, however, that it cannot be concluded that the response latency pattern indicative of processing the covariation was found in the group that was exposed to two instances. The sample size was too low to allow for separate analyses at subsequent levels of the number of instances factor, so conclusions should be confined to the level of combined groups (i.e., 2 or 4 instances). What is clear, however, is that there was no evidence found for any increase of the effects of detecting covariation produced by the increase of number of consistent instances.

These results shed some new light on the nature of the mechanism. It may be possible that the process is very different than human intentional and rational search for co-occurrences, in which the final decision is suspended until a sufficient number of consistent instances is found. It seems that no reasonable controlled process of covariation detection would assume a covariation between short hair and kindness after exposure to two kind short-haired persons. The nonconscious detection of covariation might be more like registering (in some generalized form) a few recent consistent instances, even if from a statistical viewpoint they are too few to justify any generalization. Some theorists postulate the existence of long-lasting effects based on a single piece of experience. In their study of perceptual learning, Jacoby and Dallas (1981) found that it was "surprising that a single presentation of an item has such large and long-lasting effects on its later perceptual recognition. Even low-frequency words have been read thousands of times by most university students, so one additional reading of the word in the laboratory should add little." (p. 336). The effect might be similar with detecting covariation based on limited evidence and its subsequent impact on cognitive processes. This view leads, however, to the conclusion that countless unnecessary processes accompany perception and that the time consuming second phase of memory search for relevant information (Glucksberg & McCloskey, 1981) is in most cases initiated without any rational need, since in most cases the supposedly relevant information about covariation is in fact based on evidence objectively far from being sufficient.

These results raised the objection whether there was in fact any process of detecting consistent covariation that would involve processing the entire set of available relevant evidence, since it might be argued that what influenced subjects' subsequent retrieval processes was mostly the memory trace of the most recent one or two relevant instances. Such memory representation might either be in the form of some abstract set of features or the form of exemplars. In order to check this possibility, one more experiment was conducted. Sixty undergraduates were exposed to exactly the same stimulus material as subjects from Experiment 6.9 who were presented with eight instances (i.e., four long-haired and four short-haired stimulus persons), except that in both conditions the two last slides were reordered and therefore the two last instances were inconsistent with the six previous ones. That is, subjects in Condition I were exposed to three long-haired and kind stimulus persons, to three short-haired and capable stimulus persons (the long- and short-haired persons were presented in the same order as in Experiment 6.9), and, at the end of the entire set, they were exposed to one long-haired stimulus person who was capable and to one short-haired stimulus person who was kind. Arrangement of the material in Condition II was reversed.

The response time pattern obtained was in both conditions the same as in the respective conditions of Experiment 6.9 (and there was a significant interaction of condition, question, and haircut, $p < .05$). This result indicated that these two instances were not able to eliminate the effects produced by the six previously processed instances. This evidence speaks clearly against the objection that the effects obtained in the experiments reported in this chapter might be due to the influence of most recently processed instances. It may be stated that more than one, or the two most recent instances are nonconsciously stored in terms of covariation and that the memory trace of this processing of covariation is relatively resistant to disconfirming evidence (at least if the disconfirming evidence is not abundant).

One more important finding from Experiment 6.9 pertains to the biasing effect of detected covariation on subsequent judgments (i.e., yes or no responses). Such an effect was revealed in Experiments 6.1, 6.7, and 6.8, and here it was found again.[9] Moreover, the effect was consistent across all levels of the number of instances factor, and it was separately found to be significant even in the group exposed to as little as two or four instances. This result provides additional information about the nature of the memory representation of a detected covariation discussed earlier. Namely, it suggests that it is not so that the influence of such a representation on subsequent perceptual processes is confined to affecting the time of processing relevant stimuli (due to the necessity of examining in detail the representation in question, Glucksberg & McCloskey, 1981). Instead, the results indicate that this representation has a form of a relatively strong IPA, since it is powerful enough to bias subsequent judgments, by making them consistent with the covariation to which the representation refers. In terms of Glucksberg and McCloskey's model it might be stated that reliably often the second phase of the question answering process (i.e., examining the relevant representation in detail) resulted in finding it sufficient to specify an answer. What was really startling in the results of Experiment 6.9 was how little evidence was required to produce such a powerful representation, capable of biasing subsequent perceptions (i.e., strong IPA).

The question arises at this point as to the particular form of the memory representation of so few instances that were found to be sufficient for influencing subsequent perceptions in Experiment 6.9. Is it represented in memory in the form of exemplars (Walker, 1975) or in the form of some abstract set of features (Smith, 1978), and thus, is the cognitive process leading to its influence on the final judgment a "rule abstraction mechanism" or an analogy (similarity to instances) mechanism" (Elio & Anderson, 1980, p. 416)? The results of the experiment (reported briefly above) in which the stimulus material contained six consistent and two inconsistent instances suggests a rule abstraction mechanism or at least provides strong evidence against the possibility that the results obtained were produced by the most recent exemplars.

On the other hand, the consistent results of the group exposed to only two or four instances in Experiment 6.9 might suggest some analogy or exemplar mechanism. These results indicated that in the case of lack of any stronger evidence even the memory representation of very few consistent instances is considered relevant, and it may even be sufficient for establishing an IPA. The research program presented in Chapter 7 focuses on this possibility.

Appendix: Stimulus Descriptions Employed in Experiments 6.1–6.6, 6.8, and 6.9

1. She always acts in a way that makes everybody around her feel better. She does a great deal for others, and they can always count on her. She is also a real expert in helping resolve conflicts between people.

2. No one could ever call her self-centered. She does a lot for other people; she is sensitive and helpful. She knows how to treat each individual so as to make him or her feel really good.

3. She is the type of person who is always ready to make sacrifices for others. It is simply a natural thing for her to help other people and to be nice to everybody. She probably thinks more about others than about herself.

4. She is very intelligent and effective. She knows very well how to make the best use of her particular talents, so she usually wins. She likes to be on a tight time schedule and she hates to waste her time.

5. She is bright and innovative. She is better than other people in most of what she does. She is also very hardworking, and this helps her in accomplishing what she decides to tackle.

6. Everything is easier for her than for other people because of her intelligence, but she still pushes herself very hard. She is never afraid of new tasks, because she is the type who is a winner. She is systematic and consistent in carrying out her plans.

Notes

1. In his theory of retrieval processes, Anderson (1983) assumed that knowledge can be represented in terms of propositional networks that consist of interconnected nodes. The nodes represent concepts, and the paths they are interconnected with represent relations between the concepts. When a subject is asked about a relation between two concepts (e.g., whether in the previously memorized stimulus material, the concepts occurred in one sentence) the two respective nodes are activated. Activation spreads down all paths leading from the concepts. A subject is able to recognize the relation between the two concepts when activation from the concepts has intersected. Any intersection will have to be evaluated and will slow the decision process, as compared to the situation when the two concepts are not interconnected (i.e., when the subject has no information relevant to the relation between the concepts). In the latter situation, the model proposes that a subject decides by default that he or she does not know anything about the relation between the concepts after waiting for a certain period of time without achieving intersection. Thus, the model predicts that if a subject is asked a question pertaining to the relation that he or she knows something about, the response latency to that question will be longer than in the case when the subject has no relevant information—what Anderson (1983) calls "the paradox of the expert" (p. 28). This prediction has been confirmed in a number of experiments in which subjects' response latency to questions was found to increase along with the subjects' knowledge of facts relevant to the questions (e.g., Anderson, 1976; King & Anderson, 1976). There are some exceptions. For example, the prediction does not hold for highly familiar concepts (Anderson, 1976) and for well-integrated facts (Smith, Adams, & Schorr, 1978), but these cases are irrelevant to the present research.

2. The above response time pattern can also be expected when subjects are aware of the covariation and are very well-trained in employing it in their judgments (i.e., when the information about the covariation is accesses and utilized without employing any consciously controlled retrieval or inferential strategy as in the Glucksberg and McCloskey (1981) experiments. This possibility will not be discussed further, however, since it is irrelevant to the research reported in this chapter.

3. The descriptions presented in the Appendix can be read in about 12–13 s. However, they are English translations; the original descriptions were in Polish, and spoken Polish requires more words than English.

4. Since a number of subjects had mentioned stimulus persons' gaze, the question arose whether the stimulus persons' hair influenced the appearance of the eyes (e.g., short hair might emphasize the eyes, making them look larger) that, in some sense, would indicate awareness of the covariation between hair length and kindness or capability. In order to check this possibility, another group of 21 subjects rated eyes of each stimulus person on six dimensions: size, darkness, salience (prominence), eye separation, "sharpness" of the gaze, and "trustworthiness" of the gaze (i.e., opposite to "shifty"). No differences were found between long- and short-haired stimulus persons. Obviously, it cannot be totally ruled out that hair length influenced appearance of some other element or aspect of stimulus persons' faces; no evidence was obtained, however, indicating that this was the case.

5.   Only the second version of the pilot study conducted for Experiment 6.1 was employed. Thirty-two subjects were asked to search for covariations between the visual and verbal data during the learning phase. Subjects were tested in the same arrangements as the subjects in Experiment 6.2, except for the instruction to search for covariations. All other instructions and the details of the procedure were the same. Again, not one of the subjects discovered the covariation, and again, gaze was mentioned most often.

6.   This experiment was prepared and conducted by Maria Czyzewska (1984) as part of a doctoral dissertation submitted to the Department of Psychology at the University of Warsaw.

7.   There were six different permutations (i.e., orders of presentation) of the stimulus material employed in the experiment.

8.   See second section of Chapter 1.

9.   The problem of why this consistent effect (i.e., consistent across the 2 and 4, and the 8 and 10 conditions, see Figure 6.10) was found in this experiment for different questions than in Experiments 6.1, 6.7, and 6.8, remains unsolved. It should be noted, however, that Experiment 6.9 was not simply an exact replication of Experiments 6.1 and 6.8. There were potentially important differences between the experiments, which seem capable of producing changes in the way in which the subjects encoded the meaning of the two traits. Namely, the subjects were from different populations, and they were currently in very different real-life situations (i.e., college students tested in the middle of an academic year, and high school students tested at the time of their entrance exams for the university). Experiment 6.9 included 40% new stimulus material; the experimenter was male, and his nonverbal and nonexplicit behavior could be entirely different (e.g., his behavior might increase the accessibility of different categories than was the case in previous experiments).

CHAPTER **7**

Nonconscious Generalization of Single Experiences*

Introduction

The results of the previous study (Experiment 6.9) suggest that in some circumstances even a very limited amount of evidence consistent with some covariation may be detected nonconsciously and stored in a cognitive representation that influences subsequent cognitive processes as if it were information about covariation. Regardless of what the structure of this representation may be, it functions as a piece of a general knowledge, that is, as a kind of internal processing algorithm (IPA). One may speculate that such a cognitive representation of covariation based on a very limited amount of evidence would not be capable of producing "strong" behavioral consequences. That is, it would not affect one's judgments or choices in situations in which other relevant situational or cognitive factors were operating. It would also, probably, have no effects in situations in which one may avoid making a judgment or decision. There are, however, situations in which there is no obvious evidence supporting any of the possibilities among which one must choose, and no possibility to avoid the decision. Based on the results of Experiment 6.9, it might be suspected that in circumstances just described the process of generating the response (e.g., judgment or choice) could be nonconsciously affected by the relevant cognitive representation of such functionally generalized,[1] although very limited, evidence.

* Portions of this chapter are adapted from Lewicki, 1985.

There is some support for this expectation in the previously discussed work of Glucksberg and McCloskey (1981). Although the authors did not investigate the case in which a "don't know" decision was impossible, they hypothesized that

> When it is important to find the answer to a question, an initial failure of the retrieved facts to specify an answer may lead to one or more additional attempts to locate relevant information. These new attempts to find relevant information may simply employ a looser criterion for relevance than that used originally. (p. 323)

This hypothesis was supported in a series of unpublished studies[2] in which Glucksberg and McCloskey manipulated the degree of relevance (i.e., the degree of overlapping between the sentences from a learning phase and questions asked in a testing phase). It appeared that, consistent with the hypothesis of employing a gradually "looser criterion of relevance," response latency to a question was a monotonic function of the degree of its relevance to the previous material (the less relevant the question, the longer the response latency).

The hypothesized process of loosening criteria of relevance is not included in the activation-spreading model of retrieval processes discussed in Chapter 6. However, it could be incorporated easily in this model. Anderson (1983) proposed that "a subject is able to recognize a particular fact when activation from the various concepts has intersected and the level of activation has reached some threshold value" (p. 26). The new attempts to locate relevant information may employ a lower "threshold value" for activation.

The major question that arises at this point is, What is the limiting criterion for the relevance of a fact to make that fact capable of influencing a subject's answer? In other words, when does the process of searching for relevant facts terminate, providing the definite answer that "absolutely nothing relevant is available" and making room for truly random responses? Conceivably, this may never occur, since in making the criterion gradually looser, some single and at least slightly relevant fact would finally always be found. However, would a single instance, similar in some respect, be enough?[3]

Research on categorization suggests that people do recall single specific items or instances and use them to classify novel items (Brooks, 1978; Elio & Anderson, 1981; Medin & Schaffer, 1978). A number of social cognition theories suggest that in the absence of stronger support, people base their judgments on a single, previously encountered similar event or situation (Abelson, 1976; Nisbett & Ross, 1980; Schank & Abelson, 1977; Wyer & Carlston, 1979). There is also evidence indicating that people transform single social experiences (e.g., a single positive or negative feedback) into information about the importance or general desirability of trait dimensions (Lewicki 1983, 1984a).

In a series of studies, Read (1983, 1984) has demonstrated that, if there is no better support for a judgment, people consciously decide to rely on single instances having even a small degree of similarity to a present situation. In these studies, subjects learned about a number of members of a primitive tribe. Some of them had performed a strange ritual, some of them had not. In the testing phase subjects had to make predictions about whether other members of the tribe (presented by means of short descriptions) would also perform the same ritual. Subjects clearly based their predictions on the similarity between the new individual and a certain, concrete individual who had been observed (in the learning phase) to perform the ritual. These experiments are a clear demonstration of categorical decisions (" does that individual belong to the category of those who perform the ritual?") based on single, concrete instances.

There is, however, a problem with these studies that makes the results hard to generalize. Namely, the way of providing the subjects with "an experience of a single instance" was totally explicit and it served as the only possible basis for the judgment they were subsequently asked to make publicly (not anonymously). Under such conditions, subjects' employment of the single instance in their subsequent judgment can be entirely due to demand characteristics or to similar phenomena. For example, the effects could be due to subjects' motivation to show to the experimenter that they listened carefully to the stimulus material, and/or that they were able to discover in the stimulus material even such a nonsalient cue as the single instance indicating how to respond.[4]

In our first study on nonconscious functional generalization of limited evidence, the reaction time experimental paradigm (based on the two-stage model and the spreading activation model of retrieval processes, see Chapter 6) was used. This experimental paradigm has been proven to be a highly sensitive method of testing whether a given memory trace exists and whether it is considered relevant to subsequent judgments (see Chapter 6). It seemed, therefore, an adequate method for the first exploratory experiment on the phenomenon.

Experiment 7.1

In the learning phase of the study, subjects were provided with the experiences of the single instances. In order to avoid problems with demand characteristics, these single instances were provided to subjects via subliminal exposures. In the testing phase, subjects were asked questions that were either relevant or irrelevant to the single experiences they had encountered before. Based on the model of retrieval processes discussed in Chapter 6, it was hypothesized that if the memory representation of the single instance encountered in the learning phase was considered relevant to the question, then response latency to that question should be longer (as compared to an irrelevant question) since the memory representation of the single instance would be "examined in detail to determine whether . . . [it] specifies an answer to the question" (Glucksberg & McCloskey, 1981, p. 321).

Method

Overview

The learning and testing phase appeared very similar to the subjects: A succession of questions was exposed on a CRT. All the questions had the same format, and they required the subjects to choose one of two adjectives that "fits the noun better." Some of these questions had easy and obvious answers (e.g., "Is an elephant big or small?"), some others had no obvious answers (e.g., "Is a sentence short or long?"). The questions exposed in the learning phase were expected to make subjects familiar with the procedure and with the format of the stimulus material, but most of all, they were designed to provide room for exposures of "single instances." These single instances were adjective–noun pairs (e.g., "big tree") exposed subliminally in the brief breaks between the exposures of the questions. In the testing phase (separated by a 3 min long distractor task) subjects were asked questions that were either relevant (e.g., "Are trees small or big?") or irrelevant (e.g., "Are trees young or old?") to the single instances they were exposed to in the learning phase. The subliminally exposed sets of adjective–noun pairs were different in different experimental groups, so the same questions that were relevant for one group were irrelevant for the other group.

Subjects

One hundred twenty-eight undergraduates (men and women) participated voluntarily in the study.

Procedure and Stimulus Material

Subjects participated individually. Stimuli were presented on a 12 in. CRT under the control of a computer that also registered subjects' responses and response times. The location of the chair was fixed, and, when a subject sat straight in the chair, the center of the CRT was about 55 cm distant from the subject's eyes. All words were in upper case letters 7 mm high, and they appeared as black on white. The level of illumination of the white background was kept constant and equal to 4.0 lx.

The first part of the experiment was aimed at making a subject familiar with the task of reading from the CRT. Several instructions and questions were exposed on the CRT (such as whether the subject was comfortable in the chair or whether the letters were sharp) and the subject had to choose his or her answer by pressing the left or the right button on a control box. Subjects were instructed to use the index finger of their dominant hand. Also, the format of the subsequent questions was explained, and a subject was told that he or she would be asked to choose the one out of two adjectives that, according to his or her "feelings, would fit better with the noun." Subjects were asked to decide as quickly, yet accurately, as possible. Then the exposure of the questions began.

A noun was centered 2 cm above the middle of the screen, and the two adjectives were located on one line, 4 cm below the noun, at the same distance from the middle and about 7 cm distant from each other. A subject's response (i.e., pressing either the left or the right button) terminated exposure of the question. There were 2.0–3.7 s intervals between presentations, during which the display was blank. The lengths of the intervals were randomly generated, but their sequence was the same for all subjects. Approximately in the middle of each interval, an adjective–noun pair was subliminally exposed, and subjects experienced it as a very brief disturbance on the screen. Those stimuli were presented in the middle of the CRT for 30 ms and were immediately masked by a string of Xs, of the same length as the words, which remained on the screen for 50 ms.

A total of 28 questions were presented, and four adjective–noun pairs were subliminally exposed: "big tree" or "old tree," "simple sentence" or "short sentence," "country house" or "one-story house," and "low cloud" or "dark cloud." These adjective–noun pairs were located after the fourth, sixth, eighth, and tenth questions. After all of the remaining questions, brief stimuli were presented and masked in the same way, but they consisted of two strings of "A" and "B" letters simulating adjective–noun pairs. After the eighteenth question there was an approximately 3 min long distractor task designed to interfere with subjects' short-term memory. Several long questions in different formats appeared on the CRT (such as whether the subject was tired, or how he or she estimated, in minutes, the time the experiment had taken up to that moment). The last 8 questions, out of the remaining set of 10, were the testing questions, which corresponded to the manipulated four adjective–

noun pairs: "tree: big—small?," "tree: old—young?," "sentence: simple—complex?," "sentence: short—long?," "house: country—town?,"
"house: one-story—two-story?," "cloud: low—high?," and "cloud:
dark—light?."

The design and the order of questions was the same for all subjects, and
the order of the subliminally presented nouns (in the adjective–noun
pairs) was the same and corresponded to the order of the crucial questions. That is, each brief exposure was separated from its corresponding
two questions (i.e., the relevant one and the irrelevant one) by the same
number of other questions (i.e., 14 questions plus the distractor questions). The experimental conditions were created by specific arrangements of the adjectives accompanying the nouns in the subliminally exposed adjective–noun pairs. There were 16 possible arrangements
(permutations) of the adjectives, and 8 subjects were exposed to each of
them. This way, half of the subjects were exposed to each of two adjectives relevant to a given noun; those halves, however, consisted of different subjects for each noun.

Pilot Study

It seemed improbable that subjects were able to consciously recognize
the meaning of words exposed for as brief a time as 30 ms, after which
they were immediately masked; such exposure was probably for most
subjects even below the detection level of stimulus-onset asynchronies
(i.e., below the threshold for determining whether a word or a blank was
exposed (Marcel, 1983a). An additional pilot study was conducted, however, to test for any potential idiosyncrasies of the apparatus employed
that could make the stimuli easier to recognize.

Thirty undergraduates were tested with exactly the same procedure,
except that they were told that during the intervals separating the exposures of the questions, adjective–noun pairs would be exposed very
briefly, and that it was the subjects' task to recognize them. To avoid the
potential effect of "setting the subjects for being unable to recognize the
words," it was explained to them that the words were in fact recognizable. They were also asked "to guess, in case of being uncertain." The
subjects received no immediate feedback from the experimenter after
their guesses.

None of the subjects responded accurately to any of the stimuli. For the
vast majority of presentations participants claimed that they had no idea
what it was, and therefore they were unable to guess. It should also be
noted that their guesses were about equally frequent in the cases when the

real words were exposed and in the cases when the stimuli were in fact the strings of "A" and "B" letters.

Results and Discussion

Separate 2(subliminally exposed adjective [e.g., simple vs. short]) × 2(question [e.g., "sentence: simple—complex" vs. "sentence: long—short"]) analyses of variance with repeated measure on the second factor were performed for each of the four crucial nouns. No reliable main effects indicating that two questions pertaining to the same noun produced different reaction times were obtained. The patterns of means, however, revealed that for each of the four nouns, subjects responded more slowly to relevant than to irrelevant questions (i.e., for each question these subjects for whom the given question was relevant to what they had been exposed to in the learning phase responded more slowly). The interaction effect was reliable only for "sentence," $F(1, 126) = 4.45, p < .05$. However, an analysis on aggregated indices (average reaction time to all relevant questions and average reaction time for all irrelevant questions) provided a highly significant effect, $t_{corr}(126) = 2.69, p < .005$ (one-tailed test), indicating that subjects' overall reaction time to relevant questions was longer than to irrelevant questions.

These results indicate that the experience of the single instance (e.g., "a big tree") was represented in memory in a form that was considered by the subsequent memory search processes as relevant to categorical decisions ("Are trees small or big?"). It is clearly implied by these data that there was an attempt made to "read" and evaluate in detail the representation of the single experience when it was relevant (longer RT), and that such an attempt was not made (or it was given up sooner) when the representation was irrelevant (shorter RT). It should also be noted that these results could not be attributed to some long lasting priming effects (or increased category accessibility effects, Higgins & King, 1981), nor to perceptual enhancement (Jacoby, 1983; Jacoby & Dallas, 1981), since these phenomena would result in shorter (instead of longer) response latencies for previously "activated" categories.

While these data supported the expectation that the hypothesized process of making a criterion of relevance gradually looser may finally go so far as to make an attempt to read (or "examine in detail") a memory representation of a single instance, it is in no way implied by the data that the results of the observed reading or examination of the memory representation of the single instance would influence the final response. It is possible that examining the memory representation of the single instance would always lead to the conclusion that it is not capable of specifying any informed response. If such were in fact the case, the experience of a single instance would not influence the categorical decision.

The specific design of this experiment, however, did not allow examination of the potential biasing effects of such a memory representation of a single instance on subsequent judgments. (This was because the two answers to the testing questions did not have an equal probability of being chosen in the nonexperimental conditions; for example, more subjects chose "big tree" than "small tree.") The experiment that is reported next was designed to allow for the examination of such biasing effects.

Experiment 7.2

As shown in Chapter 6, the reaction time data provide a much more sensitive measure of the existence of relevant memory traces than choice data. In the present study we did not expect any strong effects and, therefore, we were prepared to run two or even three times more subjects than in Experiment 7.1.

Method

Overview

The method employed was basically similar to the one employed in Experiment 7.1; however, the responses themselves, rather than response latencies, were of interest here. Thus, based on an extensive pilot study, the crucial questions (i.e., the ones presented in the set of test questions) were designed so that the two possible answers were equally probably in the nonexperimental conditions, as far as common stereotypes and logic were concerned. Two example questions are, "Is a tree old or big?" or "is a word long or short?" For each question, half of the subjects had been subliminally exposed to the noun accompanied by one of the two adjectives, and the other half had been exposed to the other adjective. In such circumstances each question was, as a whole, equally relevant to subjects in all conditions, and thus no response latency effects were expected. However, the two alternative adjectives were hypothesized not to be equally relevant, and subjects' choice of one of them was expected to depend on condition.

Assume that a subject had no prior preference for choosing either of the two adjectives as fitting the noun better and thus that a preliminary memory search for evidence capable of specifying the answer would fail to find sufficient support for either of the two possibilities. It was hypothesized that, if a "don't know" response was not available to the respondent, the criterion of relevance would be gradually loosened up to the point at which a single instance encountered recently would become sufficient to determine the answer. Although the specific process of loosening the criterion of relevance was not examined in the experiment, the possible final consequence of this process was tested.

Subjects

Undergraduates (men and women) participated in the study for course credit. We were prepared in this study to test many more subjects than in Experiment 7.1; it turned out, however, that reliable effects of the manipulation were found after running as few as 80 subjects.

Stimulus Material

The crucial adjective–noun pairs were chosen based on a pilot study in which 100 undergraduates answered, "based on their feelings," 24 questions of the form "Is x: y or z?", where x was a noun and y and z were adjectives that seemed to fit the noun equally well. Four questions, that provided closest to a 50/50 rate of response were chosen as the crucial ones for the experiment: "flower-pot [small or big]", "tree [old or big]", "word [long or short]", and "down [white or light]". For none of them was the deviation from the even distribution of responses higher than 5%. The remaining 20 questions served in the experiment as noncrucial questions.

The design and the order of questions was the same for all subjects, and the order of the subliminally presented nouns (in the adjective–noun pairs) was the same and corresponded to the order of the crucial questions. That is, each brief exposure was separated from its corresponding question by the same number of other questions (i.e., 14 questions plus the distractor questions). The experimental conditions were created by an arrangement of the adjectives accompanying the nouns in the subliminally exposed adjective–noun pairs. There were 16 possible arrangements (permutations), and 5 subjects were exposed to each of them. Thus, half of the subjects were exposed to each of two adjectives relevant to a given noun; those halves, however, consisted of different subjects for each noun.

Results

Separate analyses performed for each of the four crucial questions revealed that for each of them the majority of subjects had chosen the adjective to which they had been subliminally exposed. The effect, however, was significant only for "flower-pot [small or big]", $V^2(1, N = 80) = 6.79, p < .005$ and for "word [long or short]", $V^2(1, N = 80) = 3.24, p < .05$. For the two remaining questions there were only tendencies in the predicted direction ($.10 < p < .25$).

In order to estimate the overall effect of the manipulation, the number of responses consistent with the stimuli that each subject was exposed to was computed for each subject. The possible range of this index was 0 to 4. The mean for all 80 subjects was 2.70, with a 99% confidence interval of 2.20 to 3.20. This mean was reliably higher than 2.00 (i.e., than the value predicted by H_o), $t(78) = 4.05, p < .001$, which indicated that the manipulation affected subjects' responses by making them consistent with the briefly exposed stimuli.

No response time effects of the manipulation were found, but they were not expected since all questions pertained to relevant data available from the exposure stage.

Discussion

The results were consistent with expectations. While the effect was not reliable for each of the four items, it should be noted that for each of them the direction was consistent with expectations and the overall effect was strong. Thus, these data indicated that a memory representation of a single nonsalient instance was powerful enough to bias a perceiver's subsequent judgments in the absence of any "better" evidence relevant to the issue. Although this experiment did not examine the nature of the retrieval process, it confirmed the implication of the hypothesis concerning the loosening of relevance criteria.

An important advantage of the present procedure was that the effect obtained cannot be attributed to demand characteristics or similar phenomena, as might be possible in the case of a more explicit way of providing subjects with "an experience of a single instance."

The question arises at this point as to what in particular a subject thought or felt while he or she was choosing the answer that was in fact biased by the nonconscious experience of the single instance. The informal postexperimental interviews suggested that subjects thought that they had responded randomly (some of them even thought that "the task was crazy"). It seems that in fact the respondents had no access at all to what actually influenced their responses and that the memory representation of the single instance operated on a level not accessible to their awareness. There might be very few nonconscious experiences based on subliminal exposures in real-life settings. On the other hand, it may be argued that there are numerous such experiences, which are not salient, not well-remembered, and which do not operate entirely on the level of conscious reasoning. The stimuli employed in the above experiments could thus also be considered as laboratory analogues of such real-life experiences.

It was recently demonstrated that subliminal exposures might produce simple familiarity effects (Kunst–Wilson & Zajonc, 1980; Seamon, Brody, & Kauff, 1983a; see Section 2 of Chapter 1). The question arises as to what extent the familiarity or the "mere exposure" effect (Harrison, 1977) could contribute to the results obtained. In the present experiment, subjects were asked to choose a better fitting adjective; it might be argued, however, that what they did was to pick up the one with which they were more familiar. If this were the case, the demonstrated phenomenon could not be discussed in terms of learning relations between some elements (e.g., "which adjective fits better") but only in terms of acquisition of preferences based on familiarity. (This issue is addressed in Experiment 7.3.)

The particular way of providing subjects with an experience of a single instance raises the question of the generality of the observed "one-case based judgment" phenomenon. Namely, the specific adjective–noun pairs presented subliminally in the learning phase referred to preexisting concepts (well-known words). Thus the experience of encountering the single instance consisted of one more exposure to an already well-learned concept. The question arises as to whether the same effect would be obtained if the single instance would be a completely novel experience (e.g., a pair of elements that have never co-occurred before). This distinction seems important since the memory trace of a single instance encoded in the context of a well-learned concept may be different (e.g., better developed and more easily accessible) than the memory trace of a single completely novel instance. The latter case was employed in the next experiment, in which subjects were provided with *new* relations between stimuli.

Experiment 7.3[5]

The present study was different from the two previous ones in two major respects. First, in the learning phase, subjects were exposed to a number of items, and the testing phase questions were relevant to only some of them. This made the present procedure responsive to the alternative "mere exposure" explanation discussed in Experiment 7.2. Subjects were asked to make decisions that made sense to them—their task was to guess where something had been hidden. They were not aware of the fact that the single experiences that they had had before could influence their choices (guesses).

Second, subjects were 5-year-olds. It seemed important to demonstrate the "one-case-based judgment" phenomenon in small children since it would support our general reasoning about early nonconscious development of cognitive dispositions (see Chapter 2). The nonconscious cognitive dispositions (biases) produced by manipulations in all the experiments reported in this book are obviously very weak, and they cannot compete with any reasonable and consciously controlled, relevant knowledge. They can operate (show up) only in conditions where all other relevant factors capable of influencing the judgment in question are eliminated. Due to the "self-perpetuating" mechanisms (see Chapter 2), however, these biases may eventually become strong dispositions, that may be even more powerful than any consciously controlled reasoning. As argued in Chapter 2, in small children there are especially good conditions for the operation of these "self-perpetuating" mechanisms, and therefore incidentally acquired tendencies (like the "one-case-based" generalization) have higher chances than in adults to be eventually transformed into durable and strong IPAs.

Method

The procedure employed in the present study was similar to the one used in earlier experiments with kindergarten children (see Chapter 5).

Sixty 5-year-olds (boys and girls) from a day-care center participated in the study. The experiment took place in the center; however, the procedure required subjects to be run individually in a separate room, a procedure that might have made subjects anxious if they had not been acquainted with the experimenters. Therefore, before the sessions started, the experimenters spent a day with subjects assisting in their routine programs in order to get acquainted with them. The experiment was introduced to them as "a fascinating new game." The experimental setting was organized around the game called "Colorama Disneyland."[6] Subjects were presented with a cardboard matrix with four rows and six columns. Each square of the matrix contained a small black and white picture of a character from Walt Disney films (e.g., Mickey Mouse, Donald Duck, etc.). All pictures, however, were covered by small, plastic blocks. The blocks had different colors and different shapes (e.g., square, triangle, round, polygon, etc.). There were six different colors and six different shapes represented in the matrix, and each block was a unique combination of a color and a shape.

Subjects were presented with this matrix only in the testing phase. At the beginning of the experiment (in the learning phase), subjects were shown four small cards with black and white pictures of Walt Disney characters. The cards differed in shape and color of background (i.e., there were four different shapes and four different colors), and combinations of these features matched 4 out of the 24 small, plastic blocks that covered the pictures in the testing phase matrix. A subject and one experimenter played with these small cards for about four min. The experimenter asked the subject a number of questions about each picture and made sure that the subject was able to recognize each cartoon character and that he or she looked at each picture for about one min.

After a short distractor task (a conversation with the experimenter), subjects were presented with the cardboard matrix, and they were asked (by a different experimenter who was blind to experimental conditions) to guess where Mickey Mouse (or some other creature) was "hidden." After either one (if successful) or after two trials (even if both of them were unsuccessful), a subject was asked to guess where some other creature was hidden, and again a maximum of two guesses could be made. Each subject was asked about two of the four characters he or she had played with in the learning phase. There were six experimental groups, and each group was asked about a different pair of creatures.

As in the previous experiments with kindergarten children (see Chapter 5), subjects were interviewed on whether they tried to base their guesses on their memories of the shape and background of cards they were presented with in the learning phase. As in earlier studies (see Chapter 5) there was no evidence for this suspicion; the subjects not only did not try to draw analogies, but they did not even remember the relations between the creatures they saw in the learning phase and the colors and shapes of the cards.

Results and Discussion

Subjects' first guess was found to be consistently influenced by the single experience of a relation between the target creature and features of the card on which the creature had been presented. Subjects showed a clear tendency to pick up first a plastic block of the color that was the same as the color of the respective card they had played with. Twenty-one of 60 subjects picked up the right color in their first move (10 was predicted by the H_o), $Z = 3.78$, $p < .001$. Fifteen subjects picked up the right shape in their first move (10 was predicted by the H_o), $Z = 1.64$, $p < .10$. These effects could not be accounted for by any general preferences or tendencies on the part of subjects to choose certain colors or shapes, since colors and shapes were counterbalanced in this experimental design.

A consistent pattern of responses was not found, however, in the subjects' second series of guesses. Subjects showed a significant ($p < .01$) tendency to pick up blocks that were of the same color (but not same shape[7]) as the ones they had picked up in the first series. This effect was more pronounced among those subjects who were successful in their first series of guesses than among unsuccessful subjects, which might suggest that the former "learned" (based on the single experience) which color guarantees success in general; the difference was not reliable, however ($p < .13$).

It might be assumed that there were at least two types of unsuccessful subjects in this experiment. The first type were those who for some reason did not retain the knowledge available to them in the learning phase (because of being tired, distracted, etc). The second type were those who had had strong preexisting preferences for certain colors, and they continued to exercise these preferences throughout the entire experiment, regardless of what new information they had learned. It might be speculated that at least some of the unsuccessful subjects who picked up the same color in the second series as in the first one were those who belonged to the second type of subjects.

Obviously, subjects' first guess provided better (than the subsequent ones) testing conditions since the first guess was free from any possible distractive feedback from the results of the earlier guesses (which were not controlled in the experiment). The results of subjects' first guess were consistent with predictions, and they provided a demonstration of the "one-case-based" judgment phenomenon.

Additionally, these results cannot be accounted for by a priming or category accessibility effect (Higgins & King, 1981; Srull & Wyer, 1979, 1980), since a number of alternative "categories" (i.e., associations of creatures and colors or shapes) were made accessible by the manipulation in the learning phase, and only the crucial one has influenced subsequent judgments. The present results also cannot be accounted for by the "mere exposure" effect (Harrison, 1977), since again, subjects were made familiar with as many as four combinations of color and shape, and only one of them (i.e., the crucial one) influenced subsequent performance.

The general idea of this experiment was replicated in the next study, which employed more naturalistic stimulus material.

Experiment 7.4

Method

In the learning phase of this experiment subjects were exposed to three photos of young women, and each photo was accompanied by a psychological characteristic (10 sentences long). As in a number of previous experiments, this initial phase of the experiment was introduced to subjects as a form of psychological training. They were asked to imagine the stimulus persons but not to try to memorize the material. The stimulus persons were presented as real and chosen as remarkable (i.e., very positive) in some respect: All of them were college students, but one of them was very capable in foreign languages, one very capable in math, and one was especially gifted in biology. There was only one sentence about the specific capability in each description (i.e., 10% of the material). The rest pertained to various personality characteristics, unrelated to the capabilities.

There were two experimental groups: In one of them the gifted math student had her hair put back, while the other two did not; in the other group, the other two students had their hair put back, while the math student did not. Thus, the groups differed regarding the single feature of the single math student they were presented with in the learning phase.

Then the subjects participated in a distractor task that was introduced as "the main part of the experiment," that is, they were asked to fill out a short personality questionnaire (Eysenck's Extroversion–Neuroticism inventory). Subjects were asked to hurry up. The last part of the experiment was the testing phase that was introduced to subjects as "a test of psychological intuition." They were asked to rate two new photos of young women (one had her hair put back, the other did not) on six 6-point trait dimensions: warmth, persistence, frankness, extroversion, math capabilities, and ear for music.

Only the rating of math capability was of interest. It was hypothesized that if subjects had no stronger support for their judgments, their memory search for relevant information might finally include the single, previously encountered instance (i.e., the gifted math student presented in the learning phase). It was also expected that if other aspects of similarity between the faces of the learning phase math student and a given testing phase student were controlled, the feature manipulated in the experiment (i.e., the hair type) would influence the ratings.

A major problem, however, involved in the preparation of the stimulus material was how to control these other aspects. This was especially important in the present procedure, since, unlike in previous experiments with natural faces (see Chapter 6), in the present experiment subjects' judgments were expected to be influenced by the relation between only two single faces. Other features of these two faces might turn out to be in fact more influential than the manipulated feature. In order to counterbalance (between groups) the influence of these uncontrolled features, the same models who played the "put back hair roles" in one group had their hair not put back in the other group, and vice versa.

There were 50 subjects run in each experimental group and there were 50 different permutations of five models (see Figure 7.1) employed in the study. The corresponding (i.e., matching) permutations in the two groups were exactly the same regarding which models were used and in which order they were presented in the learning and testing phases. They were opposite, however, in regard to the hair of each model. The psychological descriptions were presented in the same order for all subjects.

Despite the above counterbalanced arrangement of the stimulus material, several precautions were taken in order to attenuate the effects of the factor of uncontrolled similarity between the faces. The five models were selected with respect to overall similarity. A pilot study with 120 subjects indicated that no one pair among these five models was considerably more alike than the others.[8] Additionally, the photos were not sharp and they were made with a newsprint technology, in order to make the details less salient.

One hundred sixteen subjects (men and women undergraduates) were run individually in the experiment and after finishing the ratings, each subject was interviewed on what he or she based his or her judgments on. Then their memory for the hair of the math student presented in the learning phase was tested, and in order to motivate the subjects, the question was labeled "a test of your perceptiveness."

Subjects' responses strongly suggested that subjects did not attempt to consciously draw analogies between the learning phase and the testing phase stimulus persons. However, 16 subjects succeeded in recalling the hair of the math student (11 of them were women), and following a conservative strategy they were excluded from the analysis. Each excluded subject was immediately replaced with another run according to exactly the same permutation of models. Finally, results from two pair-matching groups of 50 subjects each were obtained.

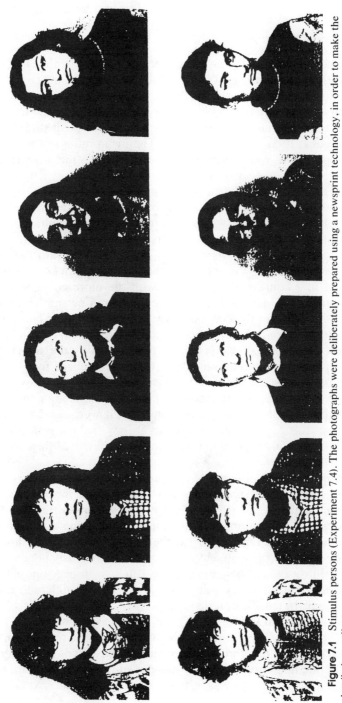

Figure 7.1 Stimulus persons (Experiment 7.4). The photographs were deliberately prepared using a newsprint technology, in order to make the details less salient.

Results and Discussion

The two experimental groups could be compared regarding two indices, namely, their mean ratings of math capability of each of the two hair types of stimulus persons presented in the testing phase. As hypothesized, the mean ratings of the person with the hair put back were higher in the group exposed to the stimulus material in which the gifted math student had her hair put back, $t(98) = 2.06, p < .025$. The mean ratings of persons with hair not put back, were, as hypothesized, higher in the other group; the difference was, however, less reliable, $t(98) = 1.60, p < .10$.

The results were consistent with expectations. It might be speculated that the much weaker effect obtained for the testing phase model who did not have her hair put back was caused to some extent by the fact that this type of hair is more common. Subjects thus might have relatively more relevant, preexperimental experiences that interfered with the effect of manipulation. It seems also plausible that a person with her hair put back presented in a context of two others with the more common hair type might constitute a more salient experience than a person with the more common hair type in the context of two others with their hair put back.

Obviously, there is no evidence to support the claim that the memory representation of the single instance encountered by the subjects in the learning phase was stored in memory in any generalized form (e.g., as a relation between some abstract categories). It is apparent, however, that whatever the nature of that specific memory representation was, it influenced subjects' subsequent perceptions as if it were some general rule. Subjects in this experiment behaved as if they had learned that women with put back hair are good in math, and as if they used this rule in their judgments.

Despite the stated observable symptoms of the process, it seems that the effects of this experiment may be well accounted for by the exemplar model (see Chapter 6) that, as compared to the abstraction model, is a more simple (i.e., requiring less additional assumptions) and a more natural way of representing single instances. The mechanism of drawing an analogy could be represented by a very fast and obviously not consciously controlled process of comparing the test item with every possible (i.e., accessible at the moment), relevant, previously encountered item. (The process may be easily described in terms of the spreading activation model, as discussed in Chapter 6.) The comparisons may result in "borrowing" these features from the relevant memory representation (of the exemplar) that are of interest but unavailable directly in the material and incorporating them into the newly developed representation of the given test item. This hypothesis was tested more directly in the next two experiments.

Experiment 7.5

The first phase of this experiment was designed to make the presentation of the single, crucial stimulus (i.e., the single experience) not salient. Subjects were asked to watch a series of 40 low-resolution graphics presented on the computer screen. The graphics were similar to those used in Experiment 6.7 (see Figure 6.4), but they included about 50% more component figures, and additionally each graphic included 20–30 dots unsystematically spread over the screen. In order to keep subjects alert and have them observe the screen, they were instructed to watch the graphics carefully and memorize them because later there would be a recognition test. Each graphic was exposed for 5–13 s. These exposure times were randomly generated (i.e., subjects never could predict when one graphic would disappear and another appear), but their sequence was the same for all subjects. After the fifteenth and thirtieth exposure, subjects were asked about their estimate, in minutes, of the time that the experiment had taken up to that moment. Twenty times, at various moments of presentation of that material, there was a line of 18–32 dots exposed in the middle of the screen for 50 ms. The spaces between the dots were equal, except the space between the two middle dots, which was two times longer, so each line consisted, in fact, of two symmetrical segments. Since the lines were not masked, they were available to subjects' conscious awareness, but they were not salient, and subjects experienced them as a kind of very brief disturbance on the screen.

All of this was designed to make the single presentation of a crucial stimulus less salient. The crucial stimulus was the seventh exposure of the line of dots, which was presented right after exposure of the tenth graphic. That time, the two segments of the line were not equal. One consisted of 12 and the other of 13 dots, but the break point was, as usual, in the middle of the screen.

There were two experimental groups. In one of them the right, and in the other the left segment was longer. After all 40 graphics were presented, subjects were informed that they would be asked questions, and their task was to respond as quickly as possible ('' according to their very first thought or intuition''). There were two buttons ''left'' and ''right'' available to them, and they were told that no other response besides ''the left'' or ''the right'' alternative was available. At this point approximately 5 min have passed since the crucial exposure, and then unexpectedly (i.e., subjects did not know what they would be asked about), they were exposed for 50 ms to a line consisting of two symmetrical segments, 12 dots each (see Figure 7.2). Immediately after the exposure they were asked which segment (left or right) was longer. Postexperimental interviews

Figure 7.2   The crucial stimulus exposed in Experiment 7.5.

revealed that subjects did not suspect that they had been deceived; subjects seemed to attribute the difficulty of the task to the insufficient duration of the exposure rather than to the fact that the segments were in fact equal.

Eighty undergraduates participated in the experiment. In both groups the majority of subjects responded that the right segment was longer, which might be due to some general bias, cultural stereotype, or some accidental, idiosyncratic elements of the procedure (e.g., glare on the screen, location of the window in the lab room, etc.). Consistent with the manipulation, however, this tendency was slightly stronger in the group exposed in the learning phase to the line with the right segment longer (28/12) than in the other group (21/19). However, the difference did not reach the conventional significance level, $V^2(1, N = 80) = 2.55, p < .10$. It could be expected that various distracting factors that might interfere with the influence of the crucial exposure on subjects' responses (like stereotypes) had a better chance to operate in those subjects who responded more slowly. Subjects' response latency was registered in this experiment. It appeared that after excluding the 25% of subjects with the longest reaction times, the effect became stronger (22/8 and 15/15, respectively, $V^2(1, N = 60) = 3.40, p < .05$.

These results supported the expectation that the single and nonsalient experience may specifically bias subsequent perceptions if no stronger relevant evidence is available. The size of the effects obtained should not be considered small, taking into account that despite all the preventive measures that were taken some subjects could simply not carefully watch the screen at the very moment of the exposure of the crucial stimulus. On a more general level, these results demonstrate the enormous sensitivity of the human cognitive system. Even such nonsalient and peripheral (for a perceiver's main task) stimuli as the one manipulated in this experiment are processed and stored in a form that makes them accessible to subsequent perceptual or judgmental processes. This observation is consistent with results of experiments on the influence of a single exposure of a stimulus on later perception of this stimulus (perceptual enhancement) indicating the existence of long-lasting effects based on a single and nonsalient piece of experience. In their study of perceptual learning, Jacoby and Dallas (1981) found that it was

> surprising that a single presentation of an item has such large and long-lasting effects on its later perceptual recognition. Even low-frequency words have been

read thousands of times by most university students, so one additional reading of
the word in the laboratory should add little. (p. 336)

On a general level, the process demonstrated in this experiment may be
conceptualized in terms of the influence of long-term memory on the
process of encoding stimuli in short-term memory. We are able to consciously identify visual objects (and other stimuli) due to the ability to
employ relevant perceptual categories stored in long-term memory and
responsible for assigning meaningful features to what we perceive. A
good example of this process is the perception of nearsighted people.
Often, they initially cannot recognize a certain well-known but physically
distant object (e.g., a photo of a well-known face), but, when they are told
whose face it is, they instantly start to visually "recognize" the object
(i.e., they report that they instantly started to *see* the face). The other
example is parafoveal vision. Sometimes we have the illusion that we
recognize something that we see peripherally, and, after turning the head
in that direction, we realize that the object is different than what we
expected, and, moreover, that the details we thought we saw do not exist
there—they were imposed by the categories we employed in the process
of recognition.

The analogous process might have taken place in the present experiment. Subjects could not see the crucial detail of the stimulus (i.e., which
segment is longer), and they had to recognize it in terms of two possible
categories (i.e., left segment is longer or right segment is longer). It appeared that the category that biased the recognition process was the one
that was generated (or influenced) by the single and nonsalient experience. The next experiment provided one more demonstration of the process. This time social stimulus material was used.

Experiment 7.6

Participants in a study that was unrelated to the present problem served
as subjects. In this unrelated study each subject took part in a 10 min long
session in which he or she rated on scales the personalities of stimulus
persons presented on slides. The experimenter was an undergraduate
female; she behaved in a very warm and friendly manner, and she tried to
make the testing situation as comfortable for subjects as possible. The
screen was located in front of the subject, and the experimenter sat either
on the right or left side of the apparatus. This constituted the only difference between the two experimental groups in the present study.

At the end of the session subjects moved to a different table with a computer monitor, and they were asked to choose the one of two schematic faces, exposed for a brief moment, that appeared to be more friendly. The faces were exactly the same (see Figure 7.3) and they were exposed for only 1 s. Subjects were told that the two faces would differ only slightly, and that their task was not to try to locate the specific differences between the faces but instead to try to follow the "global impression" the faces produce. They were also asked not to think about their responses and to respond as soon as possible "following their first intuition." In case of "lack of any intuitions" subjects were asked to guess, and they were informed that only "fast responses" were of interest to the experimenter. Since objectively, the only difference between the faces was their location, it was expected that the specific experience of subjects that could be considered relevant to the judgment would be the location of the recently met friendly person (the experimenter).

Seventy-two undergraduates (men and women) participated in the study. Subjects showed a clear tendency to pick the face on the right as more friendly, which might be due to some cultural stereotype associating good things with right (and not left) location (e.g., Christian religions). Consistent with the manipulation, however, this tendency was somewhat stronger ($V^2(1, N = 72) = 2.46, p < .10$) among subjects who had interacted with the experimenter sitting on their right side (29/7) than among those who had interacted with the experimenter sitting on their left (23/ 13). Most subjects claimed that they guessed because the exposure was too brief to allow for a comparison of the faces. They did not seem, however, to suspect that the faces were the same.

The effect obtained is not strong;[9] together with the consistent results of Experiment 7.5, however, it provides support for the notion that a single and nonsalient experience (i.e., the location of the experimenter, which did not contain any explicit, interpretable message for a subject)

Figure 7.3 Two schematic faces exposed in Experiment 7.6.

may constitute an "interpretive" category used in encoding new stimuli that might be considered relevant to the single experience.

This general phenomenon was tested in the next two experiments, which used a very different methodology than all the experiments reported so far. Subjects were tested in quasi-natural conditions.

Experiment 7.7[10]

Assume that a person has to determine which one of two persons is more kind or friendly, when he or she has no other information about those two persons than their appearance. This seems to be a very common real-life situation, for example, when one has to choose one of several bystanders to ask for help. Various social stereotypes and prejudices exist that could guide such a choice. They are not always, however, relevant to the situation, or one might consciously decide not to follow them. What determines a person's choice, then?

It might be hypothesized that a memory search for an answer in such a situation involves the process of loosening the relevance criteria. Namely, if the preliminary memory search fails to reveal any relevant information helpful in making the choice, additional attempts are made, and these employ looser critera for relevance than that used originally. The criterion is made looser and looser in subsequent attempts, up to the point at which the relevant information is found.[11] According to this reasoning, memory representations of persons memorized by the decision maker would be scanned in order to find at least one containing information about friendliness and information about appearance somehow relevant to the appearance of one of the two persons. Finally, a relevant representation will probably always be found, although the criterion of relevance employed may be so loose that in no way would one consciously recognize it as a sufficient rationale for the choice.

Based on this reasoning, the hypothesis for the next two experiments was that a subject's single experience (relevant to friendliness) with a person only remotely similar (physically) to one of two "choice persons" might affect which of them the subject would choose as more friendly, if no stronger support for his or her choice existed. For example, if a choice maker had at some time had a single, nice experience with a person who resembled in some respect one of the two persons he or she had to choose between, this person would have a higher chance to be chosen. This might be the case even if the experience could not provide "objectively" sufficient support for any choice in this new situation and when the subject thought that his or her choice was completely random.

Method

Overview

This experiment was initially designed only as a pilot study aimed at testing the choice of models for Experiment 7.8. It has provided, however, significant evidence and therefore will be presented in detail.

Participants in a study unrelated to the present problem served as subjects. In this unrelated study each subject took part in a 30 min long session in which his or her response times to various questions pertaining to relations between traits were measured (the study involved no experimental manipulation and subjects' activities were almost exactly like those described in the experiment by Ebbesen & Allen, 1979). The experimenter (an undergraduate female) was very warm and friendly, and her behavior toward the subjects during the 30 min long session was hypothesized to provide them with an experience of meeting a person who had a particular appearance, and who was kind. Thus it was expected that if, after having such an experience, subjects had to choose one of two unknown persons as more kind (based only on their appearance), they would be more likely to choose a person who was (even slightly) similar to the experimenter than the one that was less similar.

Subjects were shown two photos of young women and asked to choose the one who, according to their "feelings," was more kind and friendly. The young women displayed in the photos differed in their similarity to the experimenter. Subjects were randomly assigned to two conditions. Half of them were shown the photos and asked for their choice prior to their 30 min long contact with the experimenter, and the other half were shown the photos and asked for their choice at the end of the session. It was expected that the latter condition would favor choosing the stimulus person more similar to the experimenter.

Subjects

Eighty undergraduates (equal numbers of men and women) agreed to participate in the study. None of the subjects were psychology majors. Less than 3% of the people being asked to participate refused for any of a variety of reasons.

Stimulus Persons

The three stimulus persons (i.e., the experimenter and the two models displayed in the photos) were selected from a pool of 20 participants in a seminar in experimental social psychology. Two of them (the experimenter and one of the models) wore glasses, had short hair, and in the opinion of the group had "a similar type of appearance," as compared to the remaining model, who wore no glasses, had long hair, and in the opinion of the group had "a different type of appearance" (see Figure 7.4). An additional pilot study with 20 subjects (undergraduates), who did not know the 3 stimulus persons, confirmed these opinions. In this study participants were presented with the three photos of the stimulus persons (see Figure 7.4) and asked to point to the one who "seemed to you to be different from the remaining two." All 20 subjects pointed out the stimulus person with long hair and without glasses (Figure 7.4, Panel C).

Procedure

Half of the subjects were presented with the photos (9 × 12 cm, see Figure 7.4, Panels B and C) and asked to make their choice, just after entering the lab room. It was explained that collecting these opinions was aimed at choosing one of two candidates to be hired as an experimenter in a large research program that required an especially kind and friendly looking experimenter. Subjects made their choices anonymously (i.e., the experimenter did not see them) by means of a small sheet of paper: They either tore it slightly or not,[12] and they put it into a "secret ballot box" (there was a separate box for each condition). These conditions for making the choice were expected to free the subjects from the influence of social desirability and similar phenomena (otherwise some subjects could choose the model similar to the experimenter in order to please her). The rationale presented to the subjects for asking them for their choice seemed to make real sense to the subjects and to be believable. Thus it was expected to lead them to think that asking for their choice was not a psychological test and, moreover, that it provided a means to help one of the candidates. It seemed reasonable to expect that subjects would want to help the one they liked more, that is, the one they actually thought to be more kind and friendly.

The remaining half of the subjects were asked for their choice in the same way, but at the end of the 30 min long session.

The interaction with the experimenter involved in the session was not very long, since a subject spent most of the time reading stimulus questions from a screen and responding by means of pressing buttons on a control box. The session did involve, however, the presentation of verbal instructions by the experimenter, which took approximately 3 min at the beginning and 2 min in the middle of the session, and answering any possible questions that subjects had (average 2.8 questions per subject). Subjects could observe the experimenter during the presentation of the instructions, while asking questions, and during six breaks in their re-

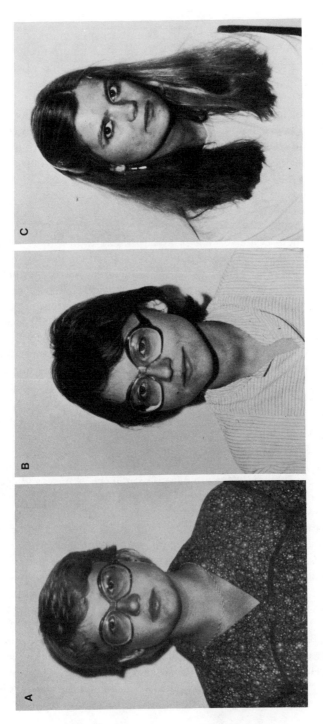

Figure 7.4 Stimulus persons (Experiment 7.7).

sponding of approximately 30 s each. The experimenter tried to be very kind and friendly, and to make each subject as comfortable with the testing situation as possible.

Results and Discussion

Of the 40 subjects who were presented with the photos and asked for their choice before the session, 24 chose the stimulus person similar to the experimenter, as compared to 34 subjects in the other group of 40, V^2 (1, N = 80) = 6.19, p < .02. This indicated that the experience with a single person who was kind and friendly affected the tendency to consider the other who looked roughly similar to also be kind and friendly.

No data concerning subjects' conscious motivations while making their choices could be collected in the present experiment. Thus, consciously controlled reliance on the experience with the single kind and friendly experimenter cannot be totally ruled out. It is apparent though, that consciously supporting such a choice on the basis of a single experience was not very probable because it seems "objectively" irrational.

The question arises at this point as to what extent the "mere exposure" effect (Harrison, 1977) could contribute to the results observed. Subjects chose a photo of a person that was similar to the one they had had a good experience with. It might be argued, however, that what they actually did was simply to choose a person they found more familiar, regardless of the specific experience they had had with the similar experimenter. The *mere exposure* effect pertains to preference for the very stimulus that the subject is familiar with, and not to a similar stimulus (and Model B was not that similar to the experimenter to make the subject think that it was her photo). However, it was shown in recent experiments by Gordon and Holyoak (1983) that the mere exposure effect may generalize to similar, new stimuli.

Another possible alternative explanation of these results is the priming or category accessibility effect (Higgins & King, 1981; Srull & Wyer, 1979, 1980). This explanation seems to be more relevant to the results of Experiments 7.1 and 7.2 since, in those studies, the manipulated categories were quite simple, It might be argued, however, that also in this experiment the interaction with the experimenter had activated some complex category that was still accessible at the point of gathering the choice data.

In order to check for these possibilities, the single experience should be negative, and as such it should produce results opposite to the ones predicted by priming effects or the mere exposure effect. This reasoning suggested the design of the next experiment, in which the subjects had to make a real-life decision of choosing (i.e., approaching) one of two persons as likely to be more kind and friendly, based on dissimilarity of that person to the one they had met previously.

Experiment 7.8

Method

Overview

In the present experiment subjects were asked to enter a lab room and to approach whichever of the two experimenters conducting the experiment there was currently free. The two experimenters were the two stimulus persons displayed in the photos employed in Experiment 7.7 (see Figure 7.4, Panels B and C). They sat at two tables equally distant from the door, and both of them were free. Thus, a subject faced a real-life situation of choosing which one out of two persons to approach. It was expected, based on common intuition, that subjects would approach the one who looked more kind and friendly to them. Prior to this situation of choice the subjects had a brief interaction with the third experimenter who was roughly similar in appearance to one of the models (it was the same person who served as experimenter in Experiment 7.7, see Figure 7.4, Panel A). The interaction had either contained a single unpleasant behavior on the part of this first experimenter or it had not. It was hypothesized that subjects in the condition involving the unpleasant detail of the first experimenter's behavior would subsequently be more likely to approach the experimenter who was less similar to the first one.

Subjects

Forty high school students participated in this study; they were between 18 and 19 years old, and there was an equal number of men and women. They were recruited in a way designed to minimize the probability that subjects knew each other, since it was very important for the present study that subjects did not know the procedure before entering the lab room. Subjects were randomly assigned to two experimental conditions, separately by sex.

After completing this study with 40 students from a regular high school, the experiment was exactly replicated with 30 students (men, 18–19 years old) from a high school specializing in teaching mechanical engineering.

Procedure

The experiment was conducted in two separate rooms which were not adjacent but were located on the same floor. In one of those rooms a subject met the first experimenter (Figure 1, Panel A) and was briefly interviewed. The interview included three questions: their name, the number of the classroom in which the subject was recruited, and the question involving the manipulation: "What is your birth order?" Birth order is not a common word, so, as expected, none of the subjects felt he or she understood it completely—all of them asked "Pardon me?," "What do you mean?," "What does 'my birth order' mean?," or the like. Then, in one condition (which will be referred to as the "negative" condition) the experimenter replied in a slightly irritated way: "You really don't know what 'birth order' means?" The subject responded that he or she did not know, or was not sure, and then the experimenter explained the meaning of birth order and received the subject's response to the question about birth order. In the neutral condition the experimenter explained the meaning of birth order just after the subject's first question. The experimenter's response (either neutral or unkind) to the subject's question was the only difference between the two conditions.[13]

After this short interview, each subject received from the experimenter a small piece of paper with a printed number and was instructed as to the location of the other room in which "the main part of the experiment will take place." The subject was asked to go to this room and to "turn in the number to whichever of the two experimenters conducting the experiment there is currently free." The numbers were introduced for two purposes. First, subjects could have suspected that the data collected in the interview had no purpose, since it could not be identified with the subject's performance in "the main experiment." The second and more important reason was to prevent a situation in which the subject enters the room and waits to be approached by one of the experimenters; with the numbers, the first move (i.e., turning in the number) belonged clearly to the subject. Thus, after entering the room the subject understood that he or she had to make an immediate choice.

The second room was approximately 4 × 5 m, and the entrance was located in the middle of the shorter side, opposite to a window (in this sense the room was symmetrical). The two experimenters (Figure 7.4, Panels B and C) sat at small tables 3.5 m distant from the entrance and facing the entrance. Each of them was located in half of the cases at the left table and in the other half at the right one. The experimenters never looked at the subject at the moment of his or her entering the room but were pretending to be busy writing something in their files. To avoid any possible nonverbal influence from the two experimenters concerning which one of them would be chosen, they were blind to the sequence of conditions. That is, they never knew the condition to which a given subject belonged.

After making their choices subjects were asked to complete the ostensible "main test" (choosing the "most interesting" out of a series of sets of irregular polygons), which took 3–4 min. At the end, each subject was asked to fill out a completely anonymous questionnaire concerning his or her "feelings during the experiment." The experimenter explained "that it is not an integral part of the present experiment, but it helps us to better understand our subjects in general and to make them comfortable during experiments." The questionnaire contained 24 very detailed questions requiring rank ordering numerous possibilities pertaining to all possible phases and details of the experiment and designed to make the question about the motivation of the subjects' crucial choice less salient. This particular question was located close to the end of the questionnaire and it read as follows:

"If your answer to the above (i.e., to the question as to whether any of the experimenters were busy) was "no," on what did you base your choice of which of them to approach?

A. One of them looked slightly more friendly.
B. One of them was slightly similar to a certain person I know, and I like.
C. One of them was slightly similar to a certain person I know, and I dislike.
D. I usually choose left (or right) in cases like that.
E. My choice was completely random.
F. One of them was slightly similar to the first experimenter, whom I liked.
G. One of them was slightly similar to the first experimenter, whom I disliked.
H. One of the experimenters looked at me when I entered the room.
I. Other."

One more question was of interest here. Namely, subjects rated on a 6-point scale how well they liked the first experimenter (Not friendly *1 2 3 4 5 6* Friendly). Subjects then put the completed questionnaires into a secret ballot box.

Results

Frequencies obtained in the first study (with 40 male and female participants) were consistent with predictions. Namely, 9 subjects out of 20 in the neutral condition, and 16 subjects out of 20 in the negative condition, approached the experimenter who was dissimilar to the first experimenter (see Figure 7.4, Panel C), $V^2(1, N = 40) = 5.09, p < .05$. This result was replicated with the 30 male students from a different high school. In this study 6 subjects out of 15 in the neutral condition, and 12 subjects out of 15 in the negative condition, approached the experimenter who was dissimilar to the first experimenter, $V^2(1, N = 30) = 4.83, p < .05$. The aggregated proportions of subjects choosing the dissimilar experimenter in the two studies are 15/35 (42.9%) in the neutral condition, and 28/35 (80.0%) in the negative condition, $V^2(1, N = 70) = 10.55, p < .001$.

Mean ranks assigned by the subjects in the questionnaire to each of the listed items associated with the crucial question (i.e., pertaining to the perceived rationale for choosing one of the two experimenters) were computed separately in each of the two conditions and in each of the four subgroups (i.e., 2 conditions × 2 possible choices made). T-tests revealed no reliable differences. Almost all subjects assigned first rank to the item "My choice was completely random." Surprisingly, however, no systematic difference was revealed between the neutral and negative conditions as far as the rated friendliness of the first experimenter was concerned ($M = 5.15$ and 5.19 respectively), $t(58) < 1$.

Discussion

The behavior observed in this experiment indicates that a single instance as one detail of an interaction is capable of influencing one's subsequent behavior. One unfriendly gesture on the part of the first experimenter was capable of producing a tendency to avoid people even roughly similar to her physically. These results cannot be attributed to priming or mere exposure effects.

The somewhat surprising lack of difference in subjects' ratings of friendliness of the first experimenter does not necessarily reflect a lack of differences in subjects' true feelings, since the scale might not have been sensitive enough to capture the effect. It suggests, however, that even if such a difference in fact existed, consciously considering the first experimenter as not friendly was neither strong nor well-remembered at the time when subjects completed their ratings, since due to anonymity of the questionnaire, subjects had no clear reason to hide their feelings.

Subjects reported that they did not recognize what actually determined their choice (i.e., they thought their choice was completely random). It seems probable that this was in fact the case. The dependent measure employed in this experiment was "natural" in that it seemed highly improbable that subjects thought, at the brief moment of deciding which experimenter they should approach, that their choice was of any importance to the entire study. It was probably not considered by subjects as a decision of much importance, and they probably did not pay much attention to their choice. It is more likely that they focused on the nature of the expected tests, which they knew nothing about, than on the appearance of the experimenter.

The line of experiments presented in this chapter provides consistent evidence indicating that in cases in which reasonable support for a judgment is lacking, the memory representation of even a single and nonsalient instance relevant in some respect to the present situation is capable of nonconsciously influencing the final decision. The results clearly supported the notion that a memory representation of a single instance provides or biases interpretive categories used to encode new stimuli. In the case of ambiguity of certain aspects of these stimuli, the process of encoding and interpreting their meaning is nonconsciously biased in the direction of encoding them as consistent with the memorized single instance.

The data reported in this chapter indicate that even an experience of single instance initiates development of memory representation capable of nonconsciously influencing subsequent behavior. Thus, even a single instance initiates the development of an IPA. If stronger support for a judgment is lacking, the IPA based on a single instance may influence judgments.

On a more general level the data presented in this chapter suggest that knowledge about concrete facts may function (i.e., may influence cognitive processes) like general knowledge and that the commonly used distinction between episodic and semantic memory (Tulving, 1972) does not reflect any real differences in how these two types of information are represented in memory and how they function.[14]

Another general conclusion of this research is that there may be less randomness in human behavior than has been implicitly assumed both in psychology and in common stereotypes and that many instances of human everyday behavior, usually considered to be random, might have their straightforward justification in some theoretically predictable, although "hidden" cognitive processes.

The evidence presented in this chapter demonstrates a highly sensitive and general mechanism of human information processing, which presumably is involved in various stages of both generating concrete judgments and acquiring categorical information. The importance of this phenomenon and its role in acquiring categorical information is due mostly to its self-perpetuating properties. The IPA that, as was demonstrated, may be initiated by even a single and nonsalient experience, specifically influences subsequent encoding processes and, thus, it increases the probability of "encountering" evidence consistent with the IPA.

Notes

1. The term "functionally generalized" does not assume that the knowledge is *represented* in memory in any generalized (i.e., abstract) form, but only that it *functions* as if it had the form of some abstract knowledge. That is, it does not necessarily imply that the cognitive representation based on the limited evidence has some form of relation between abstract categories or abstract trait dimensions. It seems that it might well have the form of an exemplar, but the status of the exemplar-based cognitive representation makes it capable of influencing subsequent relevant cognitive processes in the same way in which semantic or conceptual knowledge does. Thus, even if it has the form of an exemplar it works as if it were some kind of generalization.

2. S. Glucksberg, personal communication, Warsaw, Poland, June 8, 1984.

3. Obviously, there are cases in which single instances are highly relevant: namely, questions about a single, concrete fact (e.g., "Did you see Jim last night?"). Our reasoning, however, pertains to categorical decisions and for such decisions a single instance is minimally relevant.

4. There is one more series of studies on analogical reasoning reported recently (Gilovich, 1981) that is less open to demand characteristics. As Read (1983, 1984) pointed out, however, it seems that in these experiments subjects were relying on some kind of preexisting, stereotypic knowledge rather than on analogy to a concrete instance.

5. Cooperation of Beata Golebiowska, Boguslawa Gatarek, Dariusz Florczak, and Andrzej Majcherczyk in the preparation of stimulus materials and in conducting this study is gratefully acknowledged.

6. Manufactured by Ravensburger, part number 601-5-506-2.

7. It seems that subjects learned relatively more easily or faster about colors than about shapes of figures in this experiment (although they learned about shapes too). In the second guessing, they could not follow color and shape simultaneously, since each combination of color and shape in the matrix was unique. Their responses were influenced by the color of their first choices, so they could not be influenced by the shape.

8. Stimulus materials (photos) for this experiment were selected and tested in this pilot study by Agata Kozanecka, Iwona Langer, and Joanna Pommersbach.

9. In this experiment, excluding the subjects who responded more slowly (cf. Experiment 7.5) did not increase the size of the effect.

10. I am grateful to Jola Falkowska, Kasia Rokicka, and Emilka Matusiak, who contributed to the preparation of Experiments 7.7 and 7.8 and served as the stimulus persons.

11. In the previously stated example the criterion of relevance would pertain to being kind and to being physically similar to one of two persons that one may choose between.

12. For half of the subjects from each experimental group tearing the ballot meant choosing Photo B; for the remaining half it meant choosing Photo C (see Figure 7.4).

13. Actually there was one more difference. Namely, in the negative condition the entire interaction was longer than in the neutral condition by the length of the experimenter's unpleasant question and the subject's response. As noted earlier, however, if the "mere exposure" effect was involved in the present situation, it should produce results opposite to those hypothesized.

14. See Anderson and Ross (1980), McCloskey and Santee (1981) for a discussion of the similar view on the episodic–semantic distinction.

CHAPTER 8

Processes of Activation of Specific Categories in Memory

Introduction

I argued in Chapter 2 that IPAs are capable of initiating specific reactions (e.g., changes in mood, becoming alert) in response to given, nonconsciously encoded stimuli. There is research evidence (see Chapter 1) indicating the existence of a process of nonconscious analysis of stimuli in terms of their subjective relevance (or importance) for a subject (Bargh, 1982; Bargh & Pietromonaco, 1982; Nielsen & Sarason, 1981; Oswaldt, Taylor, & Treisman, 1960; see also Experiment 4.9). In the case of identifying the importance of information, this process may result in nonconsciously directing some of the perceiver's consciously controlled processing capabilities to the processing of the important stimulus. This in turn may result in interference with simultaneous, controlled processing of other information (see Chapter 2).[1]

This interference was observed in a number of experiments employing a dichotic task in which subjects' performance in shadowing deteriorated when self-relevant or threatening information was exposed to the ignored channel (Bargh, 1982; Nielsen & Sarason, 1981; see also Experiment 4.9). However, only one recent experiment was relevant to the hypothesized (see Chapter 2) process of nonconscious selection of a specific program for responding to important encoded information. Bargh and Pietromonaco (1982) asked male subjects to respond to flashes exposed briefly on the monitor by pressing either the left or the right button depending on the location of the flashes. The flashes were in fact subliminally exposed words that were either neutral or hostile (in different groups). Although the authors did not find any effects of the type of words on response latency, they still found, some support for the interference effect, in that subjects exposed to flashes containing the hostile words made more errors (i.e., they pressed wrong buttons more often) than subjects exposed to the neutral words. After this manipulation, subjects rated a fictitious stimulus person on a number of dimensions. It appeared that, consistent with the predictions, subjects for whom the category of hostility had been nonconsciously activated (i.e., became more accessible) rated the stimulus person more negatively on dimensions related to hostility. Since it appeared that these subjects rated the stimulus person more negatively, not only on dimensions related to hostility but also on unrelated dimensions ("a negative halo effect"), the authors also proposed an alternative explanation involving a decrease in subjects' mood due to the exposure to the hostile words.

An additional factor that makes the previously stated effects difficult to interpret is the nature of the hostile words that subjects were subliminally exposed to. The words belonged to a very broad category defined by the authors as "hostile words," including both strong words involving clear threat (e.g., "beat," "whip," "stab") and adjectives denoting some undesirable (but by no means threatening) human traits (e.g., "thoughtless," "inconsiderate"). Thus, what the subjects in the study by Bargh and Pietromonaco were exposed to was a nonhomogenous mixture of words pertaining to various generally undesirable events and features. It is unclear, therefore, what in particular caused the observed effect of a general decrease in subjects' ratings: temporarily increased accessibility of various undesirable adjectives (i.e., personality traits), feeling insecure or threatened (due to encoding some clearly threatening words), a general decrease of subjects' mood, or maybe all of these factors.

The experiment to be reported was designed to replicate and extend findings of Bargh and Pietromonaco (1982). The stimulus materials (i.e., subliminally exposed words) were designed to meet the criterion of homogenity and all of them were nouns referring to physical threat. Thus, the present experiment investigated the effects of nonconscious encoding of stimuli pertaining to physical threat on subsequent person perception. In order to understand better the nature of the phenomenon, I looked for variables that might influence the size of the effect. If the phenomenon observed in Bargh and Pietromonaco's experiment reflected the hypothesized process of nonconscious selection of response, then subjects' reactions to the manipulation should depend on subjects' dispositions relevant to their sensitivity to threat (e.g., permanent high accessibility of the category of threat). This reasoning is indirectly supported by the findings of Experiment 4.9 in which permanent accessibility of the category of threat was found to influence subjects' nonconscious processing of covariation involving this category.

In the present experiment subjects' permanent accessibility of the category of threat was measured. Additionally, as opposed to the Bargh and Pietromonaco experiment in which only male subjects were tested, both male and female subjects participated in this experiment, since gender was expected to be a potential determinant of the hypothesized process of nonconscious selection of response to physical threat.

Experiment 8.1[2]

Method

Overview

The procedure was similar to the one employed by Bargh and Pietromonaco (1982). In the first phase of the experiment subjects were asked to respond to brief flashes that appeared on the screen by pressing either left or right buttons depending on the locations of the flashes. Subjects' accuracy and response latency were registered. The flashes were in fact words. Half of the subjects were subliminally exposed to words related to threat (negative condition), the other half of the subjects were subliminally exposed to neutral words (neutral condition).

In the second phase of the experiment, all subjects were presented with a short and ambiguous description of a stimulus person, and they were asked to rate this person on 10 dimensions. All dimensions were evaluative (i.e., they had a desirable and an undesirable endpoint). Five of these dimensions referred to being threatened, susceptible to threat, or not self-confident, and they allowed for the estimation of how nonconscious encoding of stimuli implying threat influences perception of threat in others.

Additionally, subjects' permanent accessibility of categories related to threat or chronic expectation of threat was measured using the Manifest Anxiety Scale (Taylor, 1953). Subjects filled out the MAS about 1 week before the experimental session.

Subjects

One hundred undergraduates (men and women) participated voluntarily in the study. Five percent of the people who were asked to participate refused for various reasons. Subjects were randomly assigned to two experimental conditions (separately by sex).

Subliminal Exposures.   Both negative and neutral versions of the stimulus material subliminally exposed in the first phase of the experiment consisted of four words (different in each condition). These words were exposed five times (in different orders), so each subject responded to 20 flashes. The threatening words were: "harm," "rape," "attack," and "pain." Each of the four neutral words was chosen to preserve maximum visual similarity to one of the threatening words[3] ("chair," "tree," "button," and "shoe"). Thus, four pairs of visually similar words (one negative–one neutral) were created, and the matching words from the two sets were exposed in the same sequence in the two experimental conditions. In other words, each exposure in one experimental condition had its visually similar counterpart exposed in the same place of the sequence in the other experimental condition.

Description of Stimulus Person.   In the second phase of the experiment subjects were presented with a short (80 words) essay that presented an undergraduate student named Jane. The description was very ambiguous, and it allowed for different interpretations (e.g., "It seems that Jane is friendly and kind, but she has no close friends").

Rating form.   Subjects rated the stimulus person on 10 bipolar, 6-point dimensions (e.g., Self-centered *1 2 3 4 5 6* Helpful). Five of them pertained to dispositions related to not being threatened and being resistant to situations involving threat: (4) "Self-confident," (5) "Even tempered," (7) "Relaxed," (8) "Resistant to threat," and (9) "Not fearful." Five other dimensions pertained to various personality features unrelated to threat and resistance to threat: (1) "Friendly," (2) "Sensible," (3) "Concerned about others," (6) "Helpful," and (10) "Likeable." Half of the dimensions on the rating form had high ratings for the desirable endpoint and half for the undesirable endpoint.

The two phases of the study were introduced to subjects as two unrelated experiments, and they were conducted in two different rooms by two different experimenters (undergraduate females). This was said only to prevent subjects' confusion, since the two phases looked in fact very different. (It was not necessary in the present study to prevent subjects' relating the two phases because the manipulation was totally nonconscious.)

Subjects participated individually. The first phase was introduced to subjects as an experiment on reflexes, and it was explained to them that their only task was to respond as quickly as possible to brief flashes that would appear on the screen in front of them by pressing either the left or the right button on a control box, depending on the location of the flash. Subjects were told that the flashes would be strings of Xs exposed for less than 1 s each. These strings of Xs were all that subjects could see, but they were in fact only masks that followed subliminal exposures of the words, and the Xs were exposed long enough to be noticed. The stimuli were exposed by a programmed rear projection tachistoscope that consisted of two synchronized projectors equipped with electronic shutters (one of them projected the words; the other projected the masks). The sequence and duration of exposures were controlled by a microprocessor timer that also registered subjects' responses and response times. Subjects were instructed to maintain their gaze on the fixation point (middle of the screen) and to press the buttons on the control box with the index fingers of their two hands.

The stimuli were projected onto a rear projection screen (50 cm × 50 cm) in front of the subjects. When subjects sat straight, the screen was about 100 cm distant from their eyes. All words were in upper case letters, 20 mm high, and they appeared as black on white. Each word was exposed in a different part of the screen, but these locations were always clearly either on subjects' left or right side (so there was never any doubt as to which response was correct). The words were exposed for 30 ms and they were precisely masked by strings of Xs of the same lengths as the masked words. The mask remained on the screen for 800 ms. There were 4 s long intervals between presentations, during which the display was blank.

It was demonstrated in a number of pilot studies reported in this book that a masked 30 ms long exposure of a word makes it totally inaccessible to subjects' conscious awareness. This was additionally confirmed in an extensive pilot study (using this particular apparatus) in which subjects were told that the strings of Xs covered briefly exposed words, that the words were recognizable if one tried hard, and that their task was to recognize the words. Subjects were asked to guess if they were unable to see the words. Additionally, in one version of the pilot study subjects were informed before each exposure as to what would be its particular location on the screen. Both versions of the stimulus material (i.e., negative and neutral) were used. Subjects were completely unable to recognize the words.

It is worthwhile noting that the conditions for exposure of subliminal stimuli were much more rigorous in this experiment than in the study by Bargh and Pietromonaco who exposed their stimuli for as long as 100 ms.

After presentation of the instructions, subjects were exposed to a short training series of four flashes. Then, the experimenter ensured that subjects understood their task, and the main series of exposures began. After completing the task subjects were thanked for their participation and were asked "to take part in one more short experiment." They were brought to a different lab in which a new experimenter introduced them to the impression-formation task. Subjects were asked to listen carefully to "description of a person." They were asked to try to imagine the personality of this person but not to relate it to any real person they know. Subjects were also asked not to memorize the description, and they were promised that they would not be asked about any facts included in the description. The experimenter (blind to the conditions that subjects had been assigned to) read the essay. Subjects were then asked to rate the described person on ten 6-point dimensions. After the ratings were completed, each subject was questioned about his or her feelings during the experiment and thanked for the participation.

Results

Latency and Accuracy of Responses

Response latencies to the subliminally exposed words were analyzed by means of a 2(condition: negative vs. neutral) × 2(gender: male vs. female) × 2(MAS score: above vs. below the median) × 4(specific word[4]) × 4(number of exposure, i.e., position in the series of four exposures of a given word) ANOVA with repeated measures on the last two factors. The means indicated no main effect for condition ($F < 1$). There was, however, a clear interaction of experimental condition and gender, $F(1, 92) = 5.24$, $p < .022$. The means suggested (see Figure 8.1) that the predicted effect of an increase in response latency in the negative condition only occurred in women; among men there was an opposite tendency. Planned comparisons (contrasts) revealed that this interaction was entirely due to the longer response latency among women in the negative condition (as compared to women in the neutral condition), $F(1, 92) = 7.09$, $p < .009$. No reliable effect was found for men ($F < 1$).

In order to estimate the separate contributions of each of the four threatening words to these effects, a series of planned comparisons involving each of the words separately was performed in the negative condition. No effects approaching statistical significance were found for men[5]. For women, however, the comparisons revealed that each of the four words contributed to the overall effect: $F(1, 92) = 3.19$, $p < .07$ (attack), $F(1, 92) = 3.31$, $p < .06$ (pain), $F(1, 92) = p < .09$ (harm), but the most

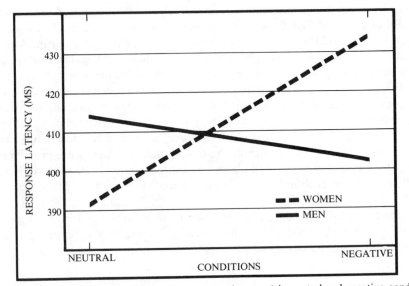

Figure 8.1 Mean response latency (in men and women) in neutral and negative conditions of Experiment 8.1.

pronounced was the contribution of the word "rape," $F(1, 92) = 8.43$, $p < .004$.

Planned comparisons involving the factor of MAS score did not reveal any reliable effects for men either; they suggested, however, that the effect of an increase for response latency was stronger among women with a more accessible category of threat, $F(1, 92) = 5.08$, $p < .024$, than among women having this category less accessible, $F(1, 92) = 2.61$, $p < .10$.

The analogous analysis performed on the accuracy of scores did not reveal any significant effects. Subjects' responses in both conditions were almost perfectly accurate, and this measure showed almost no variation.

Ratings of Stimulus Person

The ratings[6] were analyzed by means of a 2(condition: negative vs. neutral) × 2(gender: male vs. female) × 2(MAS score: above vs. below the median) × 10(rating scales) ANOVA with repeated measure on the last factor. The mean ratings in each experimental condition (separately in men and women) are displayed in Figure 8.2. No main effect for condition was found ($F < 1$). Moreover, no effects consistent across all of the 10 rating scales were found. However, a very consistent pattern of results was found for each of the five scales involving susceptibility to threat (see Figure 8.2, rating scales numbers: 4, 5, 7, 8, and 9). Men in the negative

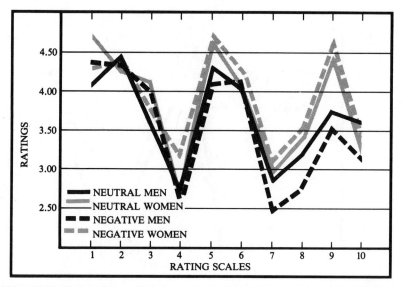

Figure 8.2 Mean ratings on 10 rating scales (in men and women) in neutral and negative condition of Experiment 8.1. The rating scales relevant to threat are 4, 5, 7, 8, and 9.

condition rated the stimulus person (on each of the five scales) lower than men in the neutral condition, while women in the negative condition rated the stimulus person (on each of the five scales) higher than did women in the neutral condition. In other words, men reacted to the nonconsciously exposed threatening words by perceiving the stimulus person as more threatened or susceptible to threat (than in the neutral conditions), while women reacted to the manipulation in just the opposite way—after nonconscious processing of threatening words, they perceived the stimulus person as less threatened or susceptible to threat (than in the neutral conditions). This effect is reliable, as shown by a planned comparison involving only the five crucial rating scales: There was an interaction of experimental condition and gender, $F(1, 92) = 5.08$, $p < .025$. There was no reliable difference between men and women found in the neutral conditions, $F(1, 92) = 1.19$, $p < .29$; in the negative conditions, however, ratings in women were reliably higher than in men, $F(1, 92) = 4.10$, $p < .04$.

Further planned comparisons involving the Manifest Anxiety Scale factor revealed that the consistent effect of the manipulation was strongly mediated by subjects' permanent accessibility of the category of threat. The difference between the ratings of men and women in the negative conditions was almost entirely due to subjects with a more accessible category of threat (see Figure 8.3), $F(1, 92) = 10.86$, $p < .002$, and it was

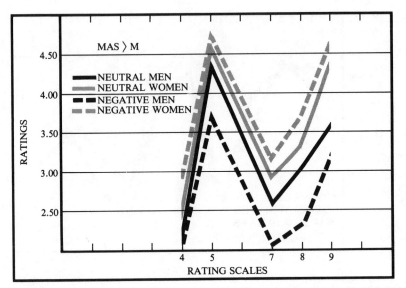

Figure 8.3 Mean ratings on crucial rating scales in men and women with high MAS scores (Experiment 8.1).

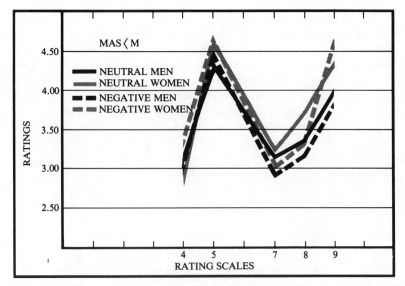

Figure 8.4 Mean ratings on crucial rating scales in men and women with low MAS scores (Experiment 8.1).

virtually absent in subjects with lower accessibility of this category ($F <$ 1), see Figure 8.4.

Prior to discussing these data, I will present briefly a follow-up study designed to replicate the results of Experiment 8.1.

Experiment 8.2

Completing the analysis of Experiment 8.1 coincided with designing the procedure of Experiment 3.3 (see Chapter 3) that employed the matrix scanning paradigm and was devoted to problems completely unrelated to the issue of nonconscious activation of the category of threat. The specific problem of Experiment 3.3, however, required designing 2–3 min long breaks during which subjects had to be engaged in a different and attention-consuming activity (distractor tasks separating the segments of the search task), and I realized that these breaks provided a perfect occasion to make an attempt to replicate the response latency data from Experiment 8.1.

As mentioned in the description of Experiment 3.3, there were four segments of the search task (60 trials each). The breaks in the middle of the segments (i.e., after every first 30 trials of a segment) were 10 s long. During these breaks, subjects were encouraged to "take a deep breath and to relax." Every other break (i.e., between the segments), lasted 10 s (the same as before), and then a new, 2 min long task was introduced to the subjects as "a test of reflexes." The flashes appeared either in the left or the right part of the CRT, and a subject was asked to react to them as fast as possible by pressing either the left or the right button on a control box, depending on the position of the flash.

The flashes were in fact subliminally exposed and immediately masked words. There were two experimental conditions negative and neutral, and the same stimulus words were used in both conditions as in the two conditions of Experiment 8.1. Each of three series of 20 flashes consisted of five subliminal exposures of each of four words. The sequence of these exposures and timing for both words and masks were the same as in Experiment 8.1.

A 2(condition: negative vs. neutral) $\times$ 2(gender: male vs. female) $\times$ 3(segment) ANOVA with repeated measures on the last factor was performed on response latencies. The pattern of results was consistent with the one obtained in Experiment 8.1 (see Figure 8.5). Women reacted to the threatening words by increasing response latency, while no such reaction to these words was observed in men. This effect was reliable, as

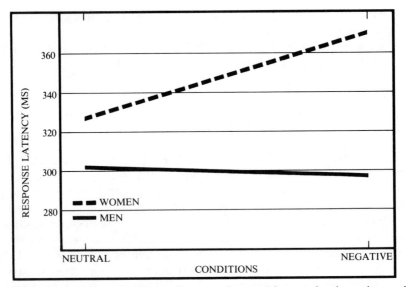

Figure 8.5 Mean response latency (in men and women) in neutral and negative conditions of Experiment 8.2.

shown by the interaction of experimental condition and gender, $F(1, 85) =$
6.96, $p < .01$.

Discussion

The results obtained suggest that subjects encoded and processed the
subliminally exposed stimuli, and that, nonconsciously, subjects reacted
to those stimuli by activating specific categories in their memory. The
inclusion of both men and women in the study turned out to be very
fortunate. It appeared that the same subliminally exposed words produced very different reactions depending on gender. The category of
physical threat (the crucial words referred clearly to physical and not to
psychological threat), that was induced by the four crucial words used in
the stimulus material ("harm," "pain," "attack," and "rape"), appeared
to involve different connotations for men than for women. Activation of
this category in women caused perception of another person as not threatened and as resistant to threat. On the other hand, in men, it involved
perception of another person as threatened and not resistant to threat. It
may be stated that nonconscious activation of the category of physical
threat in men produces a tendency to perceive other people as potential
victims, while in women it produces a tendency to perceive other people

as less likely to be victimized. It may be speculated that the latter effect is due to the fact that activation of the category of physical threat in women involves considering themselves as potential victims, which, in turn, produces a tendency to perceive others as less threatened (or even as a potential source of the threat).

This explanation has some specific support in the data obtained. The longer response latency to the threatening words in women (as compared to men) strongly suggests that in women the crucial words were encoded as a more "important" message, since they interfered more (than in men) with performance in the vigilance task.

Two mechanisms may be responsible for this interference effect. One of them is based on the limited processing capability hypothesis and assumes that in women (as compared to men) more processing resources were allocated to processing the crucial words, and this produced the observed deficit in controlled processing of the information (Kahneman, 1973; Norman & Bobrow, 1976). Thus, according to this hypothesis, the deficit observed in women on the level of controlled processing was a byproduct of extensive nonconscious processing of the crucial information. According to an alternative (but not necessarily contradictory) hypothesis, in women, as opposed to men, the level of controlled processing became purposefully "alerted" or somehow influenced as a result of the nonconscious processing of the crucial words, which were found to carry important information. This influence could involve a shift in mood, becoming tense or alerted at the expense of consciously controlled performance in the vigilance task. Both of these possibilities imply that the crucial words were encoded as containing more important information in women as compared to men.

Another supportive argument can be derived from the fact that the strongest response latency effect was obtained for the word "rape," which in our culture clearly implies more threat for women than for men. For men, this word rather implies that somebody else is threatened or became a victim.

These results are also generally consistent with the cultural stereotype, according to which men are supposed to underestimate the importance of threat (cf. the response latency data) and perceive it as something that pertains rather to others than to themselves (cf. the rating data). Such dispositions are consistently reinforced in men by common socialization procedures (Block, 1973).

The strong and consistent (across sexes) mediating effects of the permanent accessibility of the category of threat, found in both the response latencies and in the rating data, indicate that the two patterns of reactions to the manipulation observed in men and women in this experiment constitute two distinct ways of reacting to stimuli involving physical threat. The more permanently accessible this category was, the greater was the sensitivity to the crucial stimuli, and eventually the stronger was the response.

Because both men and women were included in the present study, it could be demonstrated that reactions to the nonconscious activation of a certain category in subjects' memory cannot be accounted for by simple "category accessibility" effects, as proposed by Bargh and Pietromonaco (1982). If only men had been tested in the present experiment, the effects of the manipulation on ratings of the stimulus person (and response latency results, see Note 5) would be almost exactly the same as found by Bargh and Pietromonaco. In their study, after nonconscious activation of the category of hostility, subjects perceived the stimulus person as more hostile, which was, according to the authors, due to the fact that this category became more accessible. In the present experiment, after nonconscious activation of the category of threat, male subjects perceived the stimulus person as more threatened, which might lead to the misleading conclusion that all that happened in this experiment was that this category simply became more accessible (as Bargh and Pietromonaco proposed). However, including not only men but also women allowed us to observe just the opposite phenomenon. The nonconscious activation of the category of threat in women influenced their perception of the stimulus person in a way that, in terms of Bargh and Pietromonaco's reasoning, would suggest rather a decrease than an increase in the accessibility of the category.

These results indicate that nonconscious activation of certain categories in subjects' memory produces far more complex cognitive consequences than those that could be accounted for in terms of simple category accessibility effects. The difference between men and women in the patterns of their reaction to the manipulation and the mediating role of the permanent accessibility of the manipulated category observed in this experiment suggest that the nonconscious activation of the crucial category *did not* simply produce an increase in the cognitive availability of that category. Rather it triggered an algorithm of "cognitively getting prepared" for some possible situation—specific to subjects' previous experiences—that could have been implied by the activated category. The consequences of this algorithm were specific biases in person perception, which were very different depending on previous experiences (i.e., gender).

These results are consistent with the reasoning presented in Chapter 2, according to which nonconscious encoding of new information not only serves the purpose of nonconscious learning and durable retention of the acquired knowledge for use in some future relevant circumstances, but also it helps the cognitive system to get prepared for some possible events that might follow the nonconsciously encoded information. This "getting prepared" (or specifically alerted) may result in increased sensitivity to certain stimuli or even in specific biases in encoding new stimuli.

Notes

1.   This phenomenon of interference between nonconscious and controlled processing of information was usually explained in terms of so-called limited processing capability (Bargh, 1982; Bragh & Pietromonaco, 1982; Nielsen & Sarason, 1981), which does not seem to be the only possible explanation (see below).

2.   I am grateful to Ala Rogaska who contributed to the preparation of the stimulus materials and to Jola Falkowska and Emilka Matusiak who ran the subjects in this experiment.

3.   The stimulus materials were in Polish; the visually matching pairs of words were: bol or but (pain or shoe), krzywda or krzeslo (harm of chair), gwalt or guzik (rape or button), przemoc or drzewo (attack or tree).

4.   This factor pertained to four visually matching pairs of words (see also Note 3).

5.   It is worthwhile noting that these results are consistent with those obtained by Bargh and Pietromonaco (1982), who also did not obtain any response latency effects in men. However, in the present experiment, unlike in their study, women were tested too, and all response latency effects were found for women only.

6.   Although half of the rating scales had high ratings for the desirable endpoint and half for the undesirable endpoint, the ratings were transformed so that high numbers always indicated desirable ratings. For the dimensions related to threat, high numbers indicated feeling no threat or not being susceptible to threat.

CHAPTER **9**

Conclusions

The evidence presented in this book supports the theory of internal processing algorithms as outlined in Chapter 2. The results demonstrate that people acquire more information than they are aware of, that this nonconsciously acquired information is stored in long-term memory in a form not available at the level of conscious awareness, and that this information nonconsciously influences subsequent relevant cognitive processes. The data support the hypothesis of self-perpetuation of internal processing algorithms and suggest that if there is a lack of salient contradictory evidence (i.e., evidence that is inconsistent with an IPA), then once initiated, the IPA may develop (become stronger) even in the absence of any supporting evidence. This mechanism seems to play an important role in the development of stable dispositions (e.g., various personality dispositions or psychological disorders).

The results demonstrate the enormous sensitivity of the human cognitive system. Even the nonsalient stimuli—which due to a limited, controlled processing capability cannot be processed in a consciously controlled manner—are still nonconsciously registered and stored in a form capable of influencing subsequent, relevant cognitive processes.

The research supports a number of specific hypotheses pertaining to the development of internal processing algorithms and reveals that surprisingly little consistent evidence is required to initiate such processes. The results indicate that nonconsciously acquired information about features of even a single, concrete instance may influence subsequent cognitive processes as if it was providing general information about the relation between features. Nonconsciously acquired information (even if it pertains to a single, concrete instance) can bias the process of encoding subsequently encountered stimuli, thereby promoting the self-perpetuation of internal cognitive algorithms.

The line of experimentation reported in this book demonstrates a powerful and ubiquitous phenomenon (or set of phenomena) that has been almost ignored in previous research, even though it seems to involve basic aspects of the acquisition of cognitive dispositions as well as human information processing in general.

Considering the amount of consistent evidence obtained (using a variety of experimental paradigms, types of stimulus materials, and types of indices), it seems justified to conclude that the research reported confirms the existence of nonconscious acquisition of cognitive algorithms and their important role in human adjustment.

Some of the research reported in this book provides data relevant to the problem of the structure of memory representations of internal cognitive algorithms; yet, still very little is known about the structural properties of these phenomena and the development of structural models of internal-processing algorithms should be a major goal for future research. However, despite the need for knowledge about the memory structures of internal processing algorithms, research on the functional properties of their acquisition and development, and their subsequent influence on perception, seems to be possible and important. Such research may well focus on the development of models addressing specific problems in personality, social, clinical, and developmental psychology. The results from the experiments using social or quasi-natural stimulus materials suggest that such research is promising.

References

Abelson, R. P. (1976). Script processing in attitude formation and decision-making. In J. S. Carroll & J. W. Payne (Eds.), *Cognition and social behavior* (pp. 33–45). Hillsdale, NJ: Erlbaum.

Alba, J. W., Chromiak, W., Hasher, L., & Attig, M. S. (1980). Automatic encoding of category size information. *Journal of Experimental Psychology: Human Learning and Memory, 6*, 370–378.

Alloy, L. B., & Tabachnik, N. (1984). Assessment of covariation by humans and animals: Joint influence of prior expectations and current situational information. *Psychological Review, 91*, 112–149.

Allport, A. (1977). On knowing the meaning of words we are unable to report: The effects of visual masking. In S. Dornic (Ed.), *Attention and performance VI*. Hillsdale, NJ: Erlbaum.

Allport, D. A., Antonis, B., & Reynolds, P. (1972). On the division of attention: A disproof of the single channel hypothesis. *Quarterly Journal of Experimental Psychology, 24*, 225–235.

Anderson, J. R. (1976). *Language, memory, and thought*. Hillsdale, NJ: Erlbaum.

Anderson, J. R. (1983). Retrieval of information from long-term memory. *Science, 220*, 25–30.

Anderson, J. R., & Bower, G. (1972). Configural properties in sentence memory. *Journal of Verbal Learning and Verbal Behavior, 11*, 595–605.

Anderson, J. R., & Ross, B. H. (1980). Evidence against a semantic–episodic distinction. *Journal of Experimental Psychology: Human Learning and Memory, 6*, 441–446.

Atkinson, R. C., & Shiffrin, R. M. (1968). Human memory: A proposed system and its control processes. In K. W. Spence & J. T. Spence (Eds.), *The psychology of learning and motivation: Advances in research and theory* (Vol. 2). New York: Academic Press.

Bargh, J. A. (1982). Attention and automaticity in the processing of self-relevant information. *Journal of Personality and Social Psychology, 43*, 425–436.

Bargh, J. A. (1984). Automatic and conscious processing of social information. In R. S. Wyer and T. K. Srull (Eds.), *Handbook of social cognition* (Vol. 3, pp. 1–43). Hillsdale, NJ: Erlbaum.

Bargh, J. A., & Pietromonaco, P. (1982). Automatic information processing and social perception: The influence of trait information presented outside of conscious awareness on impression formation. *Journal of Personality and Social Psychology, 43*, 437–449.

Beair, K., Peterson, C., & Whitmire, R. (1984). Unconscious acquisition of cognitive algorithms. Unpublished manuscript. University of Tulsa.

Block, J. (1973). Conceptions of sex-role: Some cross-cultural and longitudinal perspectives. *American Psychologist, 28*, 612–625.

Bowers, K. S., & Meichenbaum, D. (1984). (Eds.). *The unconscious reconsidered*. New York: Wiley.

Brooks, L. (1978). Nonanalytic concept formation and memory for instances. In E. Rosch & B. B. Lloyd (Eds.), *Cognition and categorization*. Hillsdale, NJ: Erlbaum.

Carlson, R. (1971). Sex differences in ego functioning: Exploratory studies of agency and communion. *Journal of Consulting and Clinical Psychology, 37*, 267–277.

Chomsky, N. (1980). Language and unconscious knowledge. In N. Chomsky (Ed.), *Rules and representations*. New York: Columbia University Press.

Collins, A. M., & Loftus, E. F. (1975). A spreading–activation theory of semantic processing. *Psychological Review, 82*, 407–428.

Corteen, R. S., & Dunn, D. (1974). Shock-associated words in a nonattended message: A test for momentary awareness. *Journal of Experimental Psychology, 102*, 1143–1144.

Corteen, R. S., & Wood, B. (1972). Autonomic responses to shock-associated words in unattended channel. *Journal of Experimental Psychology, 94*, 308–313.

Czyzewska, M. (1984). *Unconscious social information processing*. Unpublished doctoral dissertation, University of Warsaw, Poland.

deGroot, A. D. (1965). *Thought and mind in chess*. The Hague: Mouton.

Deutsch, J. A., & Deutsch, D. (1963). Attention: Some theoretical considerations. *Psychological Review, 70*, 80–90.

Dulany, D. E., Carlson, R. A., & Dewey, G. I. (1984). A case of syntactical learning and judgment: How conscious and how abstract? *Journal of Experimental Psychology: General, 113*, 541–555.

Dulany, D. E., Carlson, R. A., & Dewey, G. I. (1985). On consciousness in syntactic learning and judgment: A reply to Reber, Allen, and Regan. *Journal of Experimental Psychology: General, 114*, 25–32.

Dulany, D. E., & Eriksen, C. W. (1959). Accuracy of brightness discrimination as measured by concurrent verbal responses and GSRs. *Journal of Abnormal and Social Psychology, 59*, 418–423.

Ebbesen, E. B., & Allen, R. B. (1979). Cognitive processes in implicit personality trait inferences. *Journal of Personality and Social Psychology, 37*, 471–488.

Elio, R., & Anderson, J. E. (1981). The effects of category generalizations and instance similarity on schema abstraction. *Journal of Experimental Psychology: Human Learning and Memory, 7*, 397–417.

Ellis, A., & Marshall, J. (1978). Semantic errors or statistical flukes: A note on Allport's "On knowing the meaning of words we are unable to report." *Quarterly Journal of Experimental Psychology, 30*, 569–575.

Erdelyi, M. H. (1974). A new look at the new look: Perceptual defense and vigilance. *Psychological Review, 81*, 1–25.

Ericsson, K. A., & Simon, H. A. (1980). Verbal reports as data. *Psychological Review, 87*, 215–251.

Eriksen, C. W. (1956). Subception: Fact or artifact? *Psychological Review, 63*, 74–80.

Eriksen, C. W. (1960). Discrimination and learning without awareness: A methodological survey and evaluation. *Psychological Review, 67*, 279–300.

Eriksen, C. W. (1962). *Behavior and awareness: A symposium of research and interpretation*. Durham, NC: Duke University Press.

Fisk, A. D., & Schneider, W. (1983). Category and word search: Generalizing search principles to complex processing. *Journal of Experimental Psychology: Learning, Memory, and Cognition, 9*, 177–195.

Fisk, A. D., & Schneider, W. (1984). Memory as function of attention, level of processing, and automatization. *Journal of Experimental Psychology: Learning, Memory, and Cognition, 10*, 181–197.

Fowler, C. A., Wolford, G., Slade, R., & Tassinary, L. (1981). Lexical access with and without awareness. *Journal of Experimental Psychology: General, 110,* 341–362.

Gara, M. A., & Rosenberg, S. (1979). The identification of persons as supersets and subsets in free-response personality descriptions. *Journal of Personality and Social Psychology, 37,* 2161–2170.

Gara, M. A., & Rosenberg, S. (1981). Linguistic factors in implicit personality theory. *Journal of Personality and Social Psychology, 41,* 450–457.

Garner, W. R. (1970). The stimulus in information processing. *American Psychologist, 25,* 350–358.

Gilovich, T. (1981). Seeing the past in the present: The effect of associations to familiar events on judgments and decisions. *Journal of Personality and Social Psychology, 40,* 797–808.

Glucksberg, S., & Cowen, G. N. (1970). Memory for nonattended auditory material. *Cognitive Psychology, 1,* 149–156.

Glucksberg, S., & McCloskey, M. (1981). Decisions about ignorance: Knowing that you don't know. *Journal of Experimental Psychology: Human Learning and Memory, 7,* 311–325.

Gordon, P. C., & Holyoak, K. J. (1983). Implicit learning and generalization of the "mere exposure" effect. *Journal of Personality and Social Psychology, 45,* 492–500.

Harrison, A. A. (1977). Mere exposure. In L. Berkowitz (Ed.), *Advances in experimental social psychology* (Vol. 10). New York: Academic Press.

Hasher, L., & Zacks, R. T. (1979). Automatic and effortful processes in memory. *Journal of Experimental Psychology: General, 108,* 356–388.

Hasher, L., & Zacks, R. T. (1984). Automatic processing of fundamental information: The case of frequency of occurrence. *American Psychologist, 39,* 1372–1388.

Higgins, E. T., & King, G. A. (1981). Accessibility of social constructs: Information processing consequences of individual and contextual variability. In N. Cantor & J. Kihlstrom (Eds.). *Personality, cognition, and social interaction.* Hillsdale, NJ: Erlbaum.

Holyoak, K. J., & Glass, A. L. (1975). The role of contradictions and counterexamples in the rejection of false sentences. *Journal of Verbal Learning and Verbal Behavior, 14,* 215–239.

Hochberg, J. (1978). *Perception.* Englewood Cliffs, NJ: Prentice Hall.

Howell, W. C. (1973). Storage of events and event frequencies: A comparison of two paradigms in memory. *Journal of Experimental Psychology, 98,* 260–263.

Jacoby, L. L. (1983). Perceptual enhancement: Persistent effects of an experience. *Journal of Experimental Psychology: Learning, Memory, and Cognition, 9,* 21–38.

Jacoby, L. L., & Dallas, M. (1981). On the relationship between autobiographical memory and perceptual learning. *Journal of Experimental Psychology: General, 110,* 306–340.

Kahneman, D. (1973). *Attention and effort.* Englewood Cliffs, NJ: Prentice-Hall.

Kahneman, D., & Tversky, A. (1973). On the psychology of prediction. *Psychological Review, 80,* 237–251.

Kaufman, L. (1974). *Sight and mind: An introduction to visual perception.* New York: Oxford University Press.

Kellogg, R. T. (1980). Is conscious attention necessary for long-term storage? *Journal of Experimental Psychology: Human Learning and Memory, 6,* 379–390.

Kendall, M., & Stuart, A. (1979). *The advanced theory of statistics* (Vol. 2). New York: Hafner.

Kihlstrom, J. (1984). Conscious, subconscious, unconscious: A cognitive perspective. In K. S. Bowers and D. Meichenbaum (Eds.), *The unconscious reconsidered* (pp. 149–211). New York: Wiley.

King, D. R. W., & Anderson, J. R. (1976). Long-term memory search: An intersecting activation process. *Journal of Verbal Learning and Verbal Behavior, 15,* 587–605.

Kunst–Wilson, W. R., & Zajonc, R. B. (1980). Affective discrimination of stimuli that cannot be recognized. *Science, 207,* 557–558.

Lachman, R., Lachman, J. L., & Butterfield, E. C. (1979). *Cognitive psychology and information processing: An introduction.* Hillsdale, NJ: Erlbaum.

Lazarus, R. S. & McCleary, R. M. (1951). Autonomic discrimination without awareness: A study of subception. *Psychological Review, 58,* 113–122.

Lazarus, R. S. (1956). Subception: Fact or artifact? A reply to Eriksen. *Psychological Review, 63,* 343–347.

Lewicki, P. (1981). Trait relationships and experience. Technical Report. Institute for Social Research (RCGD), University of Michigan.

Lewicki, P. (1982a). Social psychology as viewed by its practitioners. *Personality and Social Psychology Bulletin, 8,* 409–416.

Lewicki, P. (1982b). Trait relationships: The nonconscious generalization of social experience. *Personality and Social Psychology Bulletin, 8,* 439–445.

Lewicki, P. (1983). Self-image bias in person perception. *Journal of Personality and Social Psychology, 45,* 384–393.

Lewicki, P. (1984a). Self-schema and social information processing. *Journal of Personality and Social Psychology, 47,* 1177–1190.

Lewicki, P. (1984b). Birth order and person perception dispositions. *European Journal of Social Psychology, 14,* 183–190.

Lewicki, P. (1985). Nonconscious biasing effects of single instances on subsequent judgments. *Journal of Personality and Social Psychology, 48,* 563–574.

Lewicki, P. (1986). Processing information about covariations that cannot be articulated. *Journal of Experimental Psychology: Learning, Memory, and Cognition, 12,* 133–144.

Lewicki, P. (in press). Processing information about covariation between unattended stimuli: The acquisition of stable dispositions. *Journal of Personality and Social Psychology.*

Lewis, J. L. (1970). Semantic processing of unattended messages using dichotic listening. *Journal of Experimental Psychology, 85,* 225–228.

Logan, G. D. (1980). Attention and automaticity in Stroop and priming tasks: Theory and data. *Cognitive Psychology, 12,* 523–553.

Mandler, G. (1975). *Mind and emotion.* New York: Wiley.

Marcel, A. J. (1980). Conscious and preconscious recognition of polysemous words: Locating the selective effects of prior verbal context. In R. S. Nickerson (Ed.), *Attention and performance* (Vol. 8). Hillsdale, NJ: Erlbaum.

Marcel, A. J. (1983a). Conscious and unconscious perception: Experiments on visual masking and word recognition. *Cognitive Psychology, 15,* 197–237.

Marcel, A. J. (1983b). Conscious and unconscious perception: An approach to the relations between phenomenal experience and cognitive processes. *Cognitive Psychology, 15,* 238–300.

McCloskey, M., & Glucksberg, S. (1979). Decision processes in verifying category membership statements: Implications for models of semantic memory. *Cognitive Psychology, 11,* 1–37.

McCloskey, M., & Santee, J. (1981). Are semantic memory and episodic memory distinct systems? *Journal of Experimental Psychology: Human Learning and Memory, 7,* 66–71.

Medin, D. L., & Schaffer, M. M. (1978). A context theory of classification learning. *Psychological Review, 85,* 207–238.

Moray, N. (1959). Attention in dichotic listening: Affective cues and the influence of instructions. *Quarterly Journal of Experimental Psychology, 11,* 56–60.

Neisser, U. (1967). *Cognitive psychology.* New York: Appleton–Century–Crofts.

Nielsen, S. L., & Sarason, I. G. (1981). Emotion, personality, and selective attention. *Journal of Personality and Social Psychology, 41,* 945–960.

Nisbett, R. E., & Ross, L. (1980). *Human inference: Strategies and shortcomings of social judgment.* Englewood Cliffs, NJ: Prentice–Hall.

Nisbett, R. E., & Wilson, T. D. (1977a). Telling more than we can know: Verbal reports on mental processes. *Psychological Review, 84,* 231–259.

Nisbett, R. E., & Wilson, T. D. (1977b). The halo effect: Evidence for unconscious alteration of judgments. *Journal of Personality and Social Psychology, 35,* 250–256.

Norman, D. A. (1969). Memory while shadowing. *Quarterly Journal of Experimental Psychology, 21,* 85–93.

Norman, D. A., & Bobrow, D. G. (1976). On the role of active memory processes in perception and cognition. In C. N. Cofer (Ed.), *The structure of human memory.* San Francisco: Freeman.

Ostrom, T. M., Lingle, J. H., Pryor, J. B., & Geva, N. (1980). Cognitive organization of person impressions. In R. Hastie, T. M. Ostrom, E. B. Ebbesen, R. S. Wyer, D. L. Hamilton, D. E. Carlston (Eds.), *Person Memory: The cognitive basis of social perception.* Hillsdale, NJ: Erlbaum.

Oswaldt, I., Taylor, A., & Treisman, M. (1960). Discrimination responses to stimulation during human sleep. *Brain, 83,* 440–453.

Posner, M. I. (1978). *Chronometric explorations of mind.* Hillsdale, NJ: Erlbaum.

Posner, M. I., & Snyder, C. R. R. (1975). Attention and cognitive control. In R. L. Solso (Ed.), *Information processing and cognition: The Loyola Symposium.* Hillsdale, NJ: Erlbaum.

Read, S. J. (1983). Once is enough: Causal reasoning from a single instance. *Journal of Personality and Social Psychology, 45,* 323–334.

Read, S. J. (1984). Analogical reasoning in social judgment: The importance of causal theories. *Journal of Personality and Social Psychology, 46,* 14–25.

Reber, A. S. (1967). Implicit learning of artificial grammars. *Journal of Verbal Learning and Verbal Behavior, 5,* 855–863.

Reber, A. S. (1976). Implicit learning of synthetic languages: The role of instructional set. *Journal of Experimental Psychology: Human Learning and Memory, 2,* 88–94.

Reber, A. S., & Allen, R. (1978). Analogy and abstraction strategies in synthetic grammar learning: A functional interpretation. *Cognition, 6,* 189–221.

Reber, A. S., Allen, R., & Regan, S. (1985). Syntactic learning and judgments: Still unconscious and still abstract. *Journal of Experimental Psychology: General, 114,* 17–24.

Reber, A. S., Kassin, S. M., Lewis, S., & Cantor, G. W. (1980). On the relationship between implicit and explicit modes in the learning of a complex rule structure. *Journal of Experimental Psychology: Human Learning and Memory, 6,* 492–502.

Reber, A. S., & Lewis, S. (1977). Implicit learning: An analysis of the form and structure of a body of tacit knowledge. *Cognition, 5,* 333–361.

Rhoades, H. M., & Overall, J. E. (1982). A sample size correction for Pearson Chi-square in 2×2 contingency tables. *Psychological Bulletin, 91,* 418–423.

Rips, L. J., Shoben, E. J., & Smith, E. E. (1973). Semantic distance and the verification of semantic relations. *Journal of Verbal Learning and Verbal Behavior, 12,* 1–20.

Rock, I. (1975). *Introduction to perception.* New York: Macmillan.

Rollins, H. A., & Thibadeau, R. (1973). The effects of auditory shadowing on recognition of information received visually. *Memory and Cognition, 1,* 164–168.

Rosenberg, S., & Sedlak, A. (1972). Structural representations of implicit personality theory. In L. Berkowitz (Ed.), *Advances in experimental social psychology* (Vol. VI). New York: Academic Press.

Runeson, S. & Frykholm, G. (1983). Kinematic specification of dynamics as an informational basis for person-and-action perception: Expectation, gender, recognition, and deceptive intention. *Journal of Experimental Psychology: General, 112,* 585–615.

Schank, R., & Abelson, R. P. (1977). *Scripts, plans, goals and understanding.* Hillsdale, NJ: Erlbaum.

Schneider, D. J., Hastorf, A. H., & Ellsworth, P. C. (1979). *Person perception.* Reading, MA: Addison–Wesley.

Schneider, W., & Shiffrin, R. M. (1977). Controlled and automatic human information processing: I. Detection, search, and attention. *Psychological Review, 84,* 1–66.

Seamon, J. G., Brody, N., & Kauff, D. M. (1983a). Affective discrimination of stimuli that are not recognized: Effects of shadowing, masking, and cerebral laterality. *Journal of Experimental Psychology: Learning, Memory, and Cognition, 9,* 544–555.

Seamon, J. G., Brody, N., & Kauff, D. M. (1984b). Affective discrimination of stimuli that are not recognized: Effect of delay between study and test. *Bulletin of the Psychonomic Society, 21,* 187–189.

Seamon, J. G., Marsh, R. L., & Brody, N. (1984). Critical importance of exposure duration for affective discrimination of stimuli that are not recognized. *Journal of Experimental Psychology: Learning, Memory, and Cognition, 10,* 465–469.

Shiffrin, R. M., & Schneider, W. (1977). Controlled and automatic human information processing: II. Perceptual learning, automatic attending, and a general theory. *Psychological Review, 84,* 127–190.

Smith, E. E. (1978). Theories of semantic memory. In W. K. Estes (Ed.), *Handbook of learning and cognitive processes* (Vol. 6). Hillsdale, NJ: Erlbaum.

Smith, E. E., Adams, N., & Schorr, D. (1978). Fact retrieval and the paradox of interference. *Cognitive Psychology, 10,* 438–464.

Smith, E. E., & Medin, D. L. (1981). *Categories and concepts.* Cambridge, MA: Harvard University Press.

Smith, E. E., Shoben, E. J., & Rips, L. J. (1974). Structure and process in semantic memory: A featural model for semantic decisions. *Psychological Review, 81,* 214–241.

Smith, E. R., & Miller, F. D. (1978). Limits on perception of cognitive processes: A reply to Nisbett and Wilson. *Psychological Review, 85,* 355–362.

Srull, T. K., & Wyer, R. S. (1979). The role of category accessibility in the interpretation of information about persons: Some determinants and implications. *Journal of Personality and Social Psychology, 37,* 1660–1672.

Srull, T. K., & Wyer, R. S. (1980). Category accessibility and social perception: Some implications for the study of person memory and interpersonal judgments. *Journal of Personality and Social Psychology, 38,* 841–856.

Stefanski, R. (1984). Unconscious stereotypes and perception of faces. Unpublished manuscript. University of Warsaw.

Taylor, J. A. (1953). A personality scale of manifest anxiety. *Journal of Abnormal and Social Psychology, 48,* 285–290.

Treisman, A. M., Squire, R., & Green, J. (1974). Semantic processing in dichotic listening? A replication. *Memory and Cognition, 2,* 641–646.

Tulving, E. (1972). Episodic and semantic memory. In E. Tulving & W. Donaldson (Eds.), *Organization of memory.* New York: Academic Press.

Tulving, E. (1974). Cue-dependent forgetting. *American Scientist, 62,* 74–82.

von Wright, J. M., Anderson, K., & Stenman, U. (1975). Generalization of conditioned

GSRs in dichotic listening. In P. M. A. Rabitt & S. Dornic (Eds.), *Attention and performance*. New York: Academic Press.

Walker, J. H. (1975). Real-world variability, reasonableness judgments, and memory representations for concepts. *Journal of Verbal Learning and Verbal Behavior, 14,* 241–252.

Wardlaw, K. A., & Kroll, N. E. A. (1976). Automatic responses to shock-associated words in a nonattended message: A failure to replicate. *Journal of Experimental Psychology: Human Perception and Performance, 2,* 357–360.

White, P. (1980). Limitations on verbal reports of internal events: A refutation of Nisbett and Wilson and of Bem. *Psychological Review, 87,* 105–112.

Wilson, W. R. (1979). Feeling more than we can know: Exposure effects without learning. *Journal of Personality and Social Psychology, 37,* 811–821.

Winograd, T. (1975). Computer memories: A metaphor for memory organization. In C. N. Cofer (Ed.), *The structure of human memory*. San Francisco: Freeman.

Wyer, R. S., & Carlston, D. E. (1979). *Social cognition, inference, and attribution*. Hillsdale, NJ: Erlbaum.

Zajonc, R. B. (1980). Feeling and thinking: Preferences need no inferences. *American Psychologist, 35,* 151–175.

Zajonc, R. B. (1984). On the primacy of affect. *American Psychologist, 39,* 117–123.

Author Index

Numbers in italics refer to pages on which complete references are found.

A

Abelson, R. P., 174, *222, 227*
Adams, N., 171, *227*
Alba, J. W., 20, *222*
Allen, R., 20, 22, 23, *226*
Allen, R. B., 196, *223*
Alloy, L. B., 31, *222*
Allport, A., 26, *222*
Allport, D. A., 17, 104, *222*
Anderson, J. E., 26, 115, 131, 132, 170, 171, 174, 205, *222, 223, 225*
Anderson, K., 15, *228*
Antonis, B., 17, 104, *222*
Atkinson, R. C., 15, 18, *222*
Attig, M. S., 20, *222*

B

Bargh, J. A., 15, 16, 26, 35, 103, 104, 206, 207, 208, 219, 220, *222*
Beair, K., 25, *222*
Block, J., 217, *222*
Bobrow, D. G., 217, *226*
Bower, G., 26, *222*
Bowers, K. S., 13, 14, *222*
Brody, N., 19, 183, *227*
Brooks, L., 21, 22, 174, *223*
Butterfield, E. C., 13, *225*

C

Cantor, G. W., 21, *226*
Carlson, R., 98, *223*
Carlson, R. A., 22, *223*
Carlston, D. E., 174, *228*
Chomsky, N., 13, *223*
Chromiak, W., 20, *222*
Collins, A. M., 74, *223*
Corteen, R. S., 15, 26, *223*
Cowen, G. N., 17, *224*
Czyzewska, M., 16, 117, 172, *223*

D

Dallas, M., 168, 179, 192, *224*
deGroot, A. D., 24, *223*
Deutsch, D., 15, *223*
Deutsch, J. A., 15, *223*
Dewey, G. I., 22, *223*
Dulany, D. E., 14, 22, *223*
Dunn, D., 15, *223*

E

Ebbesen, E. B., 196, *223*
Elio, R., 26, 115, 170, 174, *223*
Ellis, A., 26, *223*
Ellsworth, P. C., 117, *227*
Erdelyi, M. H., 18, 144, *223*
Ericsson, K. A., 27, *223*
Eriksen, C. W., 14, 26, *223*

229

Subject Index